MERCHANT FLEETS

MERCHANT FLEETS

First Published 1987
1989 Nov: Updated and reprinted.
British Library Cataloguing Publication Data

Haws, Duncan
Merchant Fleets, vol. 12
Cunard Line
1. Merchant Marine — History
1. Title.

ISBN 0 946378 08 8

TEXT photoset in 8 on 9 pt Times
by C. I. Thomas and Sons (Haverfordwest) Ltd.,
Merlins Bridge, Haverfordwest, Dyfed.
TCL Publications, Travel Creatours Ltd, 1 Meadowbank, Hereford HR1 2ST.

INTRODUCTION

The Cunard Line formed a part of the companies featured in "Merchant Fleets in Profile; Volume 2; Cunard, American, Red Star, Inman, Leyland, Dominion, Atlantic Transport and White Star Lines", published in 1979. As such the amount of detail that could be given about each company was limited by space considerations. Despite being long out of print requests for a Cunard history continue unabated. This is being met by this volume which contains much more detail and each drawing has been re-done. The whole format being reset in the "Merchant Fleets" style and brought up to date at mid-1987.

The work also proudly commemorates the 200th anniversary of the birth of Samuel Cunard on November 21, 1787.

The demand for a new history of the company again reveals the esteem and deep affection shown for this magnificent concern to whom the public at large have given to the English language the name 'Cunarder' as a mark of respect for all that is regarded as excellent, reliable and safe at sea. An accolade unmatched by any save that other great enterprise whose vessels were referred to as 'Blue Funnellers'. No other shipping concern can ever match Cunard for the number of its ships that became and remain household names: *Queen Mary, Queen Elizabeth, Mauretania, Aquitania,* sadly *Lusitania* to name but a few.

As a Liverpudlian ship fanatic I have, since boyhood, collected merchant ships like other people collect stamps. But I must pay tribute to two men whose works I much admire and whose facts I defer to even if they differ from my own — for they are usually right. I refer, of course, to John Isherwood whose contributions to Sea Breezes are widely held to be the best thing they do and to the late Noel Bonsor whose North Atlantic Seaway will stand for all time as a masterpiece in a class all of its own. Without their dedication (for it is not money that is the reward) much about the world's merchant fleets would be lost to all but a few.

Duncan Haws — Burwash, June 1987

CUNARD LINE
Chronological History

1787 Nov 21: Samuel Cunard was born in Halifax, Nova Scotia, the second son of Abraham Cunard, a German emigrant Quaker. Originally resident in Philadelphia he had crossed into Canada after the American War of Independence.

1813 July 2: Abraham Cunard & Son despatched their sailing ship *White Oak* across the Atlantic. It was their first venture to Europe although they had engaged in local trading before this.

1814 The contract to carry the mails between St Johns, Newfoundland-Halifax-Boston-Bermuda was obtained. This was an interest which the family retained for many years even though it was to remain on the periphery of the Cunard Line's activities.

1819 Abraham Cunard retired; the firm was renamed Samuel Cunard & Co. In addition to its fleet of sailing vessels the company also operated as whale fishery and ironworks on Prince Edward Island, Nova Scotia.

1825 The agency in Halifax for the Honourable East India Company was obtained. This brought Samuel Cunard into contact with British shipowners and parliamentarians; a connection that was radically to alter his life.

1827 By now Samuel Cunard was a member of the Council of Twelve who were the *de facto* rulers of the province. He was also a Director of Cogswell's Bank and Nova Scotia's first appointed Commissioner for Lighthouses.

He now became the local agent for the General Mining Association of London.

1831 Cunard and his two brothers, Joseph and Henry, were the leading stockholders in the pioneer Quebec-Halifax summer service operated by *Royal William.*

1833 Aug 5: Leaving Quebec, with a call at Pictou (where Samuel Cunard inspected her), *Royal William* crossed the Atlantic entirely by steam, sail assisted of course, but only in order that she might be sold. She arrived at Gravesend on Sept 12 and was taken on charter by the Portuguese Government within the month.

1838 Some 40 sailing vessels were owned or, mainly, operated by Samuel Cunard but during this year *Sirius, Great Western* and *Great Liverpool* each made successful Atlantic steam crossings. The Admiralty in London, who were responsible for the mails, now recognised the need to organise a regular transatlantic mail service.

Nov: The Admiralty called for tenders for a North Atlantic mail service and a copy of this was sent to Cunard. When he found that support in Halifax was lacking he decided to go to London.

1839 Jan 4: Samuel Cunard left for Falmouth aboard the regular Government packet ship. The Admiralty had by now rejected the tenders put in by the St George Steam Packet Co, owners of the *Sirius,* and the Great Western Steamship Co. The former offered sailings from Cork with a Liverpool feeder and the latter offered Halifax only, without the required Boston call; also they would start in two years time with newly built vessels.

Feb 11: Cunard offered twice monthly sailings to Halifax, using 300 HP ships, coupled with two feeder services; one to Boston and the other from Pictou to Quebec in the summer when the St Lawrence was not frozen. For this he asked £55,000 annually, payable in advance and for a period of ten years.

If accepted the service would commence on May 1, 1840. After due consideration the Admiralty awarded the contract to Samuel Cunard.

Next James Melvill, Secretary to the East India Company, for whom Cunard acted as agent in Halifax, introduced him to Robert Napier who had built the engines for their first paddler *Berenice.* Napier quoted £40 per ton or £32,000 for each 800 ton vessel. Cunard's counter offer of £30,000 for three identical ships was accepted.

On March 18 the contract was signed but by now was for paddlers of 960 tons, 375 HP and the price £32,000 each.

May 4: The formal contract for seven years was signed between the Lords of the Admiralty and Cunard and was subject to 12 months notice by either side. The rules stipulated that the ships should have wooden hulls, be paddle driven and that the mails should be in the charge of an appointed Naval officer. For a missed sailing a reduction of £15,000 would be made (thus four missed voyages would erase the subsidy) and where a sailing was delayed by more than 12 hours a fine of £500 would be imposed. Within days Napier advised Cunard that his tests with a vessel just completed for the City of Glasgow Steam Packet Co. revealed that the proposed ships were too small to maintain the envisaged schedule. He said that he would honour the contract but strongly advised against it. The revised enlarged ships were beyond the means of Samuel Cunard, who accepted Napier's word. Napier offered all his resources but this only assisted partially. The London market was disinterested in offering finance. Robert Napier now introduced Cunard to James Donaldson, a Liverpool merchant connected with the City of Glasgow S.P. Co. who had recently merged his firm with that of George and James Burns. The suggestion was that if Cunard offered the Glasgow agency to the Burns brothers and the Liverpool agency to David and Charles MacIver, also of Glasgow but in competition with Burns, then between them all the necessary extra money would be forthcoming. After initial reluctance this idea gained acceptance. Because of the historical importance of these events they are set down below:

May 4: The contract was signed for a £55,000 per annum subsidy payable to Samuel Cunard. May 14: George Burns and David MacIver paid £25,000 for half the mail contract plus the three ships involved. They were to have the right to introduce others into their share of the partnership.

July 4: The Admiralty signed an amended contract to cover the larger ships. The annual subvention was raised to £60,000.

July 23: Burns and MacIver with 19 others formed a co-partnership with the long winded title of '*The Glasgow Proprietory in the British and North American Royal Mail Steam Packets, established for the purpose of carrying mails, passengers, specie and merchandise between Britain and certain north American ports*'. The sum thus pledged was £82,500.

1840 Feb 5: *Britannia* was launched by Robert Napier's daughter Isabella. Samuel Cunard was present; he now had experience of the North Atlantic in winter. He also realised that the winter business would not warrant twice monthly sailings. Furthermore storm damage could cause £15,000 missed voyage penalties. Although not pleased the Admiralty saw his point and permitted the withdrawal of four winter voyages at a cost of £1,000 each.

April: Despite overtime it became clear that the contracted June 4 sailing date would not be met. Equally important *Acadia* (3) was a month behind *Britannia* (2) and the fortnightly sailings could not commence.

A still forbearing Admiralty agreed to a month's grace and the *Caledonia* (4) should inaugurate the fortnightly sailings when she entered service in September.

In preparation for the Pictou-Quebec service (the mail travelling overland from Halifax to Pictou on the St Lawrence) the British & North American Steam Packet Co. purchased G. & J. Burns' Liverpool-Glasgow packet *Unicorn* (1). Her commander was to be Capt. Walter Douglas who, in *Culinaire,* had surveyed the St Lawrence for the Canadian Government.

May 15: *Unicorn* sailed from Liverpool with 27 passengers including Samuel Cunard Jr.

May 28: Samuel Cunard brought his half share into the co-partnership in order that the capital could be restructured to enable additional expansion capital to be raised when needed. The capital was £270,000 of which Cunard had 135 £500 shares equivalent to £67,500. When the shares were later, December, reduced to £100 units his shares were adjusted to 550 representing £55,000. Out of 33 subscribers he was the largest shareholder with James Donaldson next; with 160 shares. A condition of shareholding was that they could not be sold outside the partnership without first being offered to the other members.

July 4: *Britannia* left Liverpool for Halifax to inaugurate the first transatlantic mail service to America. She carried 63 passengers including Samual Cunard and his daughter.

Aug 4: *Acadia* entered service, Sept 19; *Caledonia* followed.

1841 Jan 5: A fourth ship had been ordered and as *Columbia* (5) she completed the quartet.

The winter experience was worse than had been anticipated and it became clear that further negotiations were necessary. The Government was again approached and with the strong support of the Canadians the terms were finally revised. The new subvention was to be £81,000 but, in consideration a fifth reserve ship would be constructed.

1843 Apr 19: *Hibernia* (6), the fifth ship, entered service. This turned out to be timely because on July 2 *Columbia,* with 85 passengers, grounded enroute Halifax-Boston and was lost even though the mail and all aboard were saved.

1844 Jan 4: *Cambria* (7) replaced the lost ship.

1845 David MacIver died. His brother Charles took over David MacIver & Co. The close working relationship which had grown up between the Burns brothers and the MacIvers now bore fruit. The

Burns and MacIver shipping interests were merged 60% Burns and 40% MacIver with Burns in control. Burns ran Glasgow and MacIver Liverpool.

In the autumn of the year the Pictou-Quebec service was discontinued but those linking Newfoundland via Halifax-Boston-New York to Bermuda were improved.

1846 The United States Postmaster General backed the establishment of the Ocean Steam Navigation Company by means of a mail contract on the route New York-Southampton-Bremen. To counteract this Cunard renegotiated their contract so as to provide a weekly service for eight months of the year with twice monthly in winter. New York was to become the new terminus port. The annual mail subsidy was increased to £156,000 and four new ships were to be built.

1847 Dec 6: *Hibernia* inaugurated the New York service.

1848 Apr 15: The first of the four new ships *America* entered service. By the year end the company had eight paddle steamers.

1850 The Collins Line (The New York & Liverpool United States Mail Steamship Co) took over the U.S. mail contract.

On the strength of this backing four paddle ships were introduced: *Atlantic, Arctic, Baltic* and *Pacific*. Their sailings were from New York to Liverpool direct. To counter this *Asia* (13), *Africa* (14), *Andes* (16) and *Alps* (17) omitted Boston and Halifax. Sailings became weekly.

1851 The Navigation Acts had been repealed in 1849 thereby enabling goods from Europe to be transhipped via Britain either to North America or to the Mediterranean. Charles MacIver took advantage of this by chartering the steamer *British Queen*. Now, April 26, he sent her, as owner, to Constantinople and the Levant there by commencing the Mediterranean trade which was to become for Cunard an important element of their business. Samuel Cunard and George Burns joined the enterprise which operated as Burns & MacIver.

1852 The new Collins Line carried more passengers than British & North American. Furthermore the Cunard ships were too small and, at 9 knots, slow. To counter this the company ordered two ships from Robert Steele & Son which were designed to be faster and more comfortable than the competition; they had only slightly greater passenger berths but on a larger hull design. Collins was, however, experiencing difficulties. When Royal Mail lost their *Amazon* by fire Cunard sold *Arabia* (18), on the stocks, to them for a profitable £120,000 and immediately ordered an identical replacement.

As an interim passenger numbers measure second class was introduced on the 'A' vessels.

1853 Charles MacIver invested, with his colleagues, in new building for the Mediterranean. Five ships, commencing with *Balbec* (21), came from Denny.

1854 The Crimean War commenced in March but had, in reality, been the result of the Battle of Sinope in November 1853 when the Russians had destroyed a cornered Turkish fleet. A French and a British Army had been shipped to Varna, Bulgaria, to protect the Turks. Now it was decided to destroy the Russian naval base at Sevastopol. The two armies had therefore to be taken by sea to the Crimea and this required a veritable armada of ships. Eleven Cunard vessels were taken over and their North Atlantic sailings almost ceased.

1855 Oct 1: The Cunard investors formed the British & Foreign Steam Navigation Co. into which they consolidated all their Mediterranean activities. The 1,000 shares were owned by James Burns, George Burns, John Burns, Charles MacIver and Samuel Cunard. The eight ships which passed into the ownership of the new concern were *Alps* (17), *Andes* (16), *British Queen* (73), *Damascus* (36), *Lebanon* (28) *Karnak* (24), *Teneriffe* (23) and *Taurus* (22).

1856 Apr 16 saw the ending of the Crimean War by the Treaty of Paris but it was October before the final Cunard ships were released from homewards trooping.

This was also the year when the Burns brothers ran into financial problems and were obliged to withdraw from the British & Foreign S.N.Co. and within the year from the British & North Atlantic R.M.S.P.Co. *Persia* (19) became the company's first iron hulled ship. She went straight into North Atlantic service and in July took the record with 9 days 4 hours 45 minutes at an average of 13½ kts.

1861 On Jan 9 South Carolina passed a resolution of secession from the United States and thereby triggered off the American Civil War. Initially Cunard was not greatly affected because virtually all their trade had been with the Union states, Liverpool had the dubious distinction of trading abundantly with both sides and supplied a considerable number of the Confederate blockade runners.

1862 Robert Napier delivered *China (46),* the Company's first screw propelled North Atlantic liner, for which Admiralty permission had to be obtained because the mail contract stipulated paddle propulsion. From the same yard came *Scotia* (45), the largest and fastest paddler afloat, except for the *Great Eastern.*

1863 In his annual report Sir Samuel Cunard commented that the Civil war was interfering with the company's trade; mainly that passenger carryings, especially emigrants, were down.

1865 Apr 9: The American Civil War ended with the Appomattox surrender of General Lee. On the 28th of the month Sir Samuel Cunard died in London aged 78. The effect of his death was to cause much reconstruction of the company and a redistribution of the shares.

A surge of emigration recommenced and during the period no fewer than 25 new liners entered service including Cunard's *Java* (50).

1867 The service to Canada ceased and was not resumed until 1911 when the Thomson Line was purchased. This arose from the decision of the Postmaster General not to renew the mail contract when it expired on Dec 31 1867. A new one was, in fact, concluded but on a poundage basis with a reduced subsidy. *Russia* (56) had been built with the mail contract in mind and lesser sized vessels followed the change in the contract.

1869 Sir Edward Cunard, the eldest son died. His brother William took over his share in the company.

1871 Cunard's supremacy was challenged by the advent of Thomas Ismay's White Star Line ships *Atlantic, Baltic, Oceanic* and *Republic.* These ships outshone all other North Atlantic vessels. The Company was faced with the need to match this new competition.

1874 The two Cunarders commissioned in the year, *Bothnia* (69) and *Scythia* (70), were still behind the standards set by White Star.

1878 May 21: The Cunard Steam Ship Company was formed. The main partners undertook for five years to continue their services as managing agents, Burns & MacIver at Liverpool, W. & W. S Cunard at London and G & J Burns at Glasgow. They were also barred from competitive shipowning for 14 years. It was noted at the time that the title did not now include the words 'Royal Mail'.

1881 *Servia* (79) entered service, steel hulled and engined for 17 knots she was the first express passenger liner built to rely solely on passenger revenue derived from fast passages. She was Cunard's leap ahead.

1882 *Aurania* (80) joined *Servia.* She consolidated the new look by having suites of accommodation. To her fell the role of catering for the wealthy and the aristocracy. But neither ship ever held an Atlantic record; mainly because Cunard seldom went in for advanced ideas and were noted for their conservatism which was said to derive from the Scottish and Quaker influence of the founders.

1883 The Guion Line ran into difficulties in making payments for their new liner *Oregon* (78) which had been built to outpace all competition. Cunard took her over and with her regained the 'Blue Riband'.

1884 Cunard had initially been slow to respond to the White Star challenge due to their involvement with the mail contracts. Now came *Umbria* (81) and *Etruria* (82) which outclassed allcomers with their size and passenger capacity but with compound engines that virtually made them out of date at the time of commissioning.

1885 Charles MacIver died.

1887 The new Cunard ships were sharply challenged by Inman's beautiful *City of New York* and *City of Paris* as well as by White Star's magnificent *Teutonic* and *Majestic.* Cunard reacted by ordering what were to be the largest and fastest ships afloat.

1890 George Burns died.

1893 On April 22 *Campania* (84) was delivered to be followed by *Lucania* (85) in the September. They were designed to be record breakers from the start. Initially *Campania* vibrated so badly at speed that it was even contemplated returning her to the builders but in the event only the final payment was withheld until the fault was cured. The interactive effects of twin propellers was little known at this time and it was some months of pondering before it was realised that the vibration was related to propeller speed. The cure was found by altering the pitch of the blades and pointing instead of blunting the blade tips. Cavitation entered into the language of the designers. Even so it was a whole twelve months before the matter was finally resolved.

1897 The two Cunard record breakers were challenged by Norddeutscher Lloyd's *Kaiser Wilhelm der Grosse,* the first four funneller.

1898 Satisfied with their New York quartet the Company strengthened their Boston service. Here speed was of less importance and cargo space played a substantial part in the planning. *Ultonia* (91) was purchased on the stocks as a cattle carrier but she was almost at once converted to play a passenger role to Boston.

1900 To add to the Boston route two purpose built ships were constructed. *Ivernia* (94) came first to be followed by the very similar *Saxonia* (95). Both were able to carry 2,300 passengers as well as 14,000 tons of cargo. Their main claim to fame lies in an extraordinarily tall funnel which dominated their somewhat ungainly profile.
In October the Boer War started with the need to rush reinforcements to Cape Town. Six Cunarders were pressed into service including *Servia, Aurania* and *Umbria.* Unfortunately *Carinthia* (87) was wrecked during her war service.

1902 J. Pierpoint Morgan formed the International Mercantile Marine and purchased several transatlantic companies in order to do so.
The British firms acquired included White Star, Dominion and Leyland. The situation gave rise to national concern. Cunard, which had remained outside of the new combine changed its Articles of Association to preclude control by any foreigner.

1903 The Government now also concluded a twenty year agreement with the company. Two new record breakers of troopship capability were to be built and £2,600,000 at 2¾% interest was to be loaned to finance them; repayable over the period of the agreement. A 20-year subsidy of £150,000 per annum was to be paid to cover the Admiralty specifications that had to be built into the construction of the two ships. The plans that emerged produced *Lusitania* (101) and *Mauretania* (102).
Nov: After having been appointed the official agent of the Hungarian Government for emigration to America *Aurania* (80) opened the new service Fiume-Trieste-Venice-Palermo-New York, *Pannonia* (97) and *Slavonia* (98) were purchased for the route and were joined by *Carpathia* (96).

1904 For only the third time in its history the company made a loss; of £78,000 (1894 and 1895 were the others).

1905 In February *Caronia* (99) was commissioned followed in December by her sister *Carmania* (100). They were known as the 'pretty sisters'. They also had the distinction of being powered differently. *Carmania* had the 'newfangled' turbines while *Caronia* was quadruple expansion driven. In service *Carmania* was one and a half knots faster and turbines became standard for all Cunard passenger liners until *Queen Elizabeth 2* (188) was converted to diesel in spring 1987.

1907 *Lusitania* (101) was delivered. On her second voyage she took the Atlantic record with an average speed of 24 knots. In Nov *Mauretania* left Liverpool on her maiden voyage and on her homeward run she beat *Lusitania's* record by 21 minutes in 4 days, 22 hours and 29 minutes.

1911-12 *Franconia* (106) and *Laconia* (107) entered service to strengthen the Boston route. They were designed with the capability to undertake winter cruises out of New York to the Mediterranean.

At this time both the Hamburg America Line and White Star began to introduce their giants of over 40,000 tons, *Bismarck, Imperator, Vaterland, Olympic* and *Titanic.* Cunard replied by laying down one of the most lovely ships of them all, the *Aquitania* (116).

To re-enter the Canadian service Cunard purchased the Thomson Line from Cairns, Noble. It was not so much the ships as the trading base which was the objective. From this could be built up a business for which a new range of ships could be built. The Canadian vessels were given names commencing with 'A'.

In November 1911 the whole of the share capital of Anchor Line (Henderson Brothers) Ltd was acquired. Beyond the Boardroom no change in Anchor line took place but certain interchanges of ships later occurred.

1914 May 31: The maiden voyage of *Aquitania* (116) was overshadowed by the tragic loss two days earlier of Canadian Pacific's *Empress of Ireland* which sank after being hit in the St Lawrence river with the loss of 1,023 lives.

Aug 4: The First World War started, *Aquitania (116)*, *Caronia (99)* and *Carmania (100)* were called up for conversion into Armed Merchant Cruisers. *Carmania* fought the first action when she engaged and sank, Sept 9, the German *Cap Trafalgar,* Hamburg-Sud Amerika Linie.

Lusitania (101) was earmarked for Government use but she was returned to the company in order that a passenger service to New York could be provided. On Oct 3 32 transports escorted by 5 warships left Gaspé with the First Canadian Army bound for France. The Cunarders in this convoy were *Alaunia* (113), *Andania* (112), *Franconia* (105), *Ivernia* (94), *Laconia* (107) and *Saxonia* (95). Approaching the U.K. the convoy separated into three divisions and went to different ports of disembarkation.

1915 May 7: Off the Old Head of Kinsale *U-20* torpedoed *Lusitania* (101) which went down in under 20 minutes with the loss of 1,198 lives. Ever since her sinking has been the subject of controversy, Germany claimed that she was carrying weapons and was a war target. The United States was outraged at the loss of 124 American lives by unrestricted submarine warfare while in Britain there was angry debate about the way the ship had been handled in an area where a submarine had been active. From time to time the press resurrects this story.

1916 The fleet and goodwill of the Canadian Northern Steamship Co., together with its subsidiary the Uranium Steamship Co., was purchased. Anchor also acquired Donaldson's four passenger ships to give the group entry into the Glasgow-Canada market. To trade with Australia the Commonwealth & Dominion Line (the Port Line) was purchased and given Cunard funnel colours atop their grey hulls.

1917 Cunard Building, the new headquarters at Liverpool's Pier Head was completed.

1918 Nov 11: The fighting ceased with the 11.00 hrs armistice. Cunard had lost 22 ships during the four years. They were: *Alaunia* (113), *Andania* (112), *Ascania* (109) wrecked, *Aurania* (115), *Ausonia* (110), *Caria* (108), *Carpathia* (96), *Feltria* (122),*Flavia* (122), *Folia* (124), *Franconia* (106), *Ivernia* (94), *Laconia* (107), *Lusitania* (101), *Lycia* (105), *Thracia* (104), *Ultonia* (91), *Valeria* (119) burnt out, *Vandalia* (118), *Veria* (92), *Vinovia* (117) and *Volodia* (120). Many of the ships were almost brand new.

To replace these Cunard ordered 13 ships to be built as soon as conditions allowed. It was, at the time, the largest order, in terms of tonnage, ever placed. (Royal Mail had ordered 14 with which to open their services).

1921 *Albania* (137) was the Company's first post-war ship and she was a hybrid having been completed for cargo rather than passengers. Her career with Cunard was not to last long. She was to be followed by five 20,000 tonners, six 'A's of 14,000 tons for the Canadian services and one odd man out, *Tyrrhenia* (147).

1921 *Scythia* (138) and *Samaria* (139) were commissioned.

1922 *Andania* (141), *Antonia* (142), *Ausonia* (143), *Tyrrhenia/Lancastria* (147) and *Laconia* (140) entered service.

With the allocation of Hapag's *Imperator,* renamed *Berengaria (136),* the momentous decision was taken to place the refurbished *Mauretania* (102) and *Aquitania (115)* with her on a service from Southampton to New York in place of the traditional Liverpool route. It marked the end of Liverpool as Great Britain's major North Atlantic gateway. One aspect was that the giants of the thirties never visited their home port.

1923 *Franconia* (148) was delivered.

1924 *Aurania* (144) The fourth of the Canadian 'A' class took up station.

1925 The final three ships of the post war programme were delivered: *Alaunia* (146), *Ascania* (145) and *Carinthia* (149), a ship which bore one of the public's favourite names. Cunard noticed that some ships were more popular than others when it came to advanced bookings.

Passengers frequently booked ships by name.

1929 Norddeutscher Lloyd's *Bremen* entered service and took both Atlantic records from *Mauretania* (102) which she had held since 1907, Cunard were, however, designing two massive ships to replace their ageing Southampton trio.

1930 Dec: The keel of the then un-named No 534 was laid at John Brown's Clydebank Yard. She was to become the *Queen Mary* (156).

Anchor Line had not declared a dividend for seven years and Chairman Sir Percy Bates wrote down the investment by 50%. The sum written off was £750,000.

1931 The economic depression which struck America and cascaded over into Europe caused work on '534' to cease.

1933 The Government advanced £3,000,000 to complete '534' with £1,500,000 up front as working capital. There was to be a further loan of £5,000,000 if a sister ship was built. The assistance was also conditional upon the merging of White Star with Cunard in order that a cohesive British North Atlantic service could be operated. Cannily the authorities foresaw the need to repeat the same exercise with White Star in order that they could effectively compete. Dec 30 saw the agreement signed.

1934 Feb: The merger came into being and with it the name Cunard-White Star Ltd. White Star contributed: *Majestic, Olympic, Homeric, Britannic, Georgic, Laurentic, Doric, Calgaric, Albertic* (laid up) and the old *Adriatic* which was scheduled for breaking up; she went in November. The Mediterranean ships of Cunard were not involved and remained separate. Work on '534' restarted and she was launched in September by Queen Mary.

1935 Anchor Line was placed into liquidation and Anchor Line (1935) was formed with Cunard having no participation. In May the French line's *Normandie* entered service and took the records from Norddeutscher Lloyd.

1936 Almost a year to the day after *Normandie* the *Queen Mary* (156) sailed on her maiden voyage and at the year end the keel of her consort was laid down on the same berth at John Brown's.

1938 July: A new *Mauretania* (157) was launched at Birkenhead by Queen Elizabeth (now the Queen Mother) in the presence of her husband King George VI to become the largest liner ever to have been built in England. She demonstrated the size of ship that Cunard-White Star could afford to build without Government aid. *Mauretania* was designed with the ability to work with the *Queens* on the express New York route or with the 20,000 tonners on the secondary sailings. London was also in mind and her dimensions took the river Thames into consideration.

1939 Sept 3: World War II began. Two days later *Bosnia* (154) became the second ship to be sunk, after *Athenia,* out of the 4,786 British and Commonwealth losses. Initially *Queen Mary* was laid up in New York and the hurriedly completed *Queen Elizabeth* (158) joined her.

1940 In March both the *Queens* were taken over for trooping; they were the core of the six giant liners whose speed enabled them to sail out of convoy (except in coastal waters). The others were *Aquitania, Mauretania* with Canadian Pacific's *Empress of Britain* and Shaw, Savill & Albion's *Dominion Monarch.* Other Cunard-White Star ships called up were *Georgic, Britannic, Franconia* (148), *Scythia* (138), *Samaria* (139), *Laconia* (140) and *Lancastria* (147) all of which served as troopships.

Carinthia (149), *Laurentic* and all six 'A' class were converted into Armed Merchant Cruisers.

1942 Oct: *Queen Mary* (156) collided with her escorting cruiser *Curacao* and cut her in two with the loss of over 300 of her crew. The post war court case found in favour of the *Queen Mary.* On appeal a ⅓:⅔ blame was apportioned.

1945 Sept: The war ended. The company had lost: *Andania* (141), *Bosnia* (154), *Carinthia* (149), *Laconia* (140), *Lancastria* (147) and *Laurentic, Antonia* (142) had become *HMS Wayland, Aurania* (144) was *HMS Artifax* and *Alaunia (146)* and *Ausonia* (143) kept their names as *HMS Alaunia* and *HMS Ausonia.* All four were heavy repair ships to the navy. In all ten ships failed to return to the Company's service.

1946-1948 was the period during which the fleet slowly returned to its normal duties as one by one they were released from national service. Rebuilding began. The four large liners had survived but *Aquitania* (116) needed replacement. The Canadian 'A's were reduced to *Ascania* (145) and the five 20,000 tonners were down to three ageing veterans. The replacement programme that now began lasted for twelve years. Cargo tonnage was added to replace wartime standard ships and two intermediate liners with first class only were built; they were *Media* (167) and *Parthia* (168). The combination of vast cargo capacity coupled with passenger space was again shown not to be a happy combination.

1947 During 1947 the Cunard S. S. Co., as opposed to Cunard-White Star, brought into service *Brescia* (162) their first addition since the merger of the Atlantic vessels.
July 30: The 38% minority holding in Cunard-White Star held by White Star, in the form of Ocean S. N. Realisation Co., was acquired at a cost of £7,600,000 of which Cunard borrowed almost £5,000,000.

1949 In January *Caronia* (168) sailed on her maiden voyage. In size and speed she was a consort to *Mauretania* (157) but was a dual purpose Atlantic-cum-cruising ship. Her new green livery earned her the name 'Green Goddess'. By the year end *Aquitania* (115) was up for disposal after 580 crossings and 1,500,000 passengers safely carried.
Dec 31: In order to streamline the organisation Cunard S. S. Co., took over their wholly owned subsidiary Cunard-White Star. It saved, for example double accounting and separate staffing. It also arose partly because of the devaluation of sterling against the dollar which led to fare increases as well as an upward surge in operating costs. Where once the word 'profit' had been used the accounts now showed the word 'surplus' because future cash requirements were not easy to forecast. The only sign of White Star which remained was the buff funnels that *Britannic* and *Georgic* still wore.

1955-57 Replacements for the ageing *Ascania* (145), *Franconia* (146), *Samaria* (139) and *Scythia* (138) were commissioned. They were *Saxonia* (175), *Ivernia* (176), *Carinthia* (177) and *Sylvania* (178) and were the largest Cunarders to be built for the Canadian trade.

1959 Cunard commenced services to Chicago with four chartered ships.

1960 Cunard now operated ten splendid passenger ships: The two *Queens, Mauretania, Caronia,* the four Canadian ships plus *Media* and *Parthia*. But jet passenger aircraft were biting into sea traffic and the operating costs were rising dangerously. The period was also one of penal taxation coupled with bad labour relations which led to prolonged disputes in many ports world wide. *Media* (167) and *Parthia* (168) were sold for further trading. They were replaced by two Swedish cargo ships which operated from Liverpool in Cunard colours as *Nordia* and *Maronia.* When the St Lawrence Seaway was opened Cunard chartered German tonnage to extend their service. *Auguste Schulte* was renamed *Veria* and *Wiedenborstel* became *Caria.*

1963 Passenger services to Canada were now uneconomic but the four ships were not dual purpose and could not be used for cruising; a growing area of profitable usage, *Saxonia* and *Ivernia* were rebuilt for cruising and renamed *Carmania* (174) and *Franconia* (175). The passenger fleet was now down to six. On the cargo side seven 'A' class vessels served the Atlantic with three engaged in trade to the Mediterranean.

1964 H. H. Moss & Co., Tankers Ltd., was purchased to aid diversification. With this came three modern tankers: *Lucellum, Lucigen* and *Luxor.*

1965 The decline in passenger profitability continued and *Mauretania* (157) was sold for breaking up at the end of the summer season.

Since 1962 Cunard had been involved with air travel, firstly with Cunard Eagle and then by means of a 30% stake in BOAC-Cunard. The contribution to Cunard during this year peaked at £504,000 but the era of the Jumbo Jet had arrived and Concorde lay ahead.

At sea passenger ships lost £1.5 million while cargo made £1.4 profit. The three Mediterranean ships were sold and their place taken by chartered tonnage.

1966 Chairman Sir Basil Smallpiece faced a draining of cash; the seaman's strike had cost £4 million in revenue and the passenger operations had lost £14.1 million in five years. The one thing that was certain was that the Company could not afford its 30% share of the cost of re-equipping BOAC-Cunard. In September this share was sold to BOAC for £11,500,000, furthermore the survival of the Company depended upon selling off the unprofitable passenger ships. An added worry was that Port Line made a loss for the first time. Nov 24: On this sad day *Sylvania* (178) made the final Liverpool-New York sailing.

1967 Jan: Cunard acquired a 20% holding, and the UK representation, in the Atlantic Container Line Ltd.; the other partners were the French Line, Holland America, Swedish America, Transatlantic A/B and Wallenius. Cunard were to build two ships which would be chartered to the company to make ten in all.

The head office of Cunard moved to London and Cunard Building at Liverpool was sold. Other offices were closed, except for New York. *Queen Mary* (156) was retired and sold to the City of Long Beach.

1968 Cunard-Brocklebank Ltd., was formed and an order worth $20 million was placed with Astilleros Españoles, Madrid, for 8 bulk carriers.

1969 By now only three passenger liners remained *Queen Elizabeth 2* (188), *Carmania* (175) and *Franconia* (176) but 58 cargo vessels were still owned by the Group. The return on their investment was however only about 5%, a sum insufficient to replace them.

Clearly yet a further fleet rationalisation had to be undertaken and the move into container ships accelerated. In 1966 Cunard were founder members of Associated Container Transportation Ltd.

through their subsidiary Port Line. The other members being Blue Star, Ben Line, Ellerman and T. & J. Harrison. They now took steps to concentrate Port Line, with Crusader Shipping, into this trade and to reduce the conventional cargo fleets. Brocklebank was amalgamated into Cunard-Brocklebank with bulk cargo priorities and they too were stripped of their India trading conventionals. Brocklebank had managed the H. E. Moss concern and this was set down for expansion under their guidance. Offshore Marine, another Cunard subsidiary, which serviced oil rigs was also to be developed.

1971 Aug: A successful bid of £26 million for the Cunard shares was made by Trafalgar House Investments Ltd. They took over assets worth £43 million. In all they controlled some 260 subsidiary companies. Initial fears that the assets, written down by valuation to £39 million, would be sold for cash were unfounded and the Main Board established a Shipping Division.

During the year *Cunard Adventurer* (189) (and *Cunard Ambassador* (190) in 1972), the last two ships ordered by the Cunard Company, were brought into service for cruising. Only their non 'ia' names indicated the new ownership.

1972 *Cunard Campaigner* (191), the first of the eight bulkers built in Spain for Cunard-Brocklebank Bulkers Ltd. was delivered. They were only to last for some five years before disposal.

1974 saw the arrival of two new cruise liners *Cunard Countess* (199) and *Cunard Conquest/Cunard Princess* (200) but the year was marred by the fire which gutted *Cunard Ambassador.* Although not destroyed the company decided against rebuilding and she was sold for conversion into a live cattle carrier.

Across the whole spectrum of shipowning the fleet now stood at 64 ships, owned and part owned.

1976 Sept 3: The fleet of the ailing Maritime Fruit Carriers Co., was broken up and Cunard purchased ten with which to enter into the fruit and dairy products field. To the delight of the shipping world they were given traditional Cunard names.

Cunard and Group Chairman Nigel Broakes (1984 Knighted) announced that the deal was for twelve ships at a cost of $122 million with the proviso that two ships (*London Clipper* and *Maranga*) be at once taken over by Willy Bruns & Co., Hamburg, for $16,450,000.

Nov 30: The Trafalgar House fleet was recorded as being:

Cunard	Passenger services	3 ships	98,498 grt	
	A.C.L.	2 ships	29,892 grt	
	A.C.T. (Australia)	6 ships	67,267 grt	(part owned)
	Brocklebank	7 ships	65,157 grt	
	Port Line	6 ships	81,929 grt	
Cunard	Fruit carriers	10 ships	107,268 grt	
	H. E. Moss	7 ships	202,474 grt	
	Cunard-Brocklebank	6 ships	159,972 grt	
	Offshore Marine	27 ships	19,864 grt	
	Total	74 ships	671,924 grt	

There were four ships under construction at this date.

Like so much of the recent sad history of the Royal Merchant Service the number of vessels was to decline dramatically over the next decade.

1982 On April 2, 10,000 Argentine troops took over the Falkland Islands. A Task Force was sent and retook the islands. Among the fleet were *Queen Elizabeth 2* (188), *Saxonia* (209), *Cunard Countess* (199), *Atlantic Conveyor* (A.C.L.) which was destroyed by Exocet missile, and *Luminetta,* (H. E. Moss). In order to service the Falklands from both South Africa and Ascension during the construction of the necessary sized airport *England* (211) was acquired from D.F.D.S.

1983 Trafalgar House acquired 4.9% of the shares of P. & O. and a take over struggle ensued. The net worth of the two was, at the time, estimated at Trafalgar House £403 million and P. & O. £461 million. The value of the Trafalgar House offer was £290 million and was not successful.

1984 Norwegian American Cruise Lines had been formed in 1980 with Norske Amerikalinje holding 90% and Leif Hoegh 10% which by 1981 became 100%. They owned two ships acquired from the Norske Amerikalinje the *Sagafjord* (212) and *Vistafjord* (213). This concern was now taken over retaining its title, mainly Norwegian crews and ships names. The only change was the introduction of Cunard funnels.

1986 Jan 15: Lord Matthews, Deputy Chairman to Sir Nigel Broakes, retired.
Aug 14: The two vessels of Norske Cruises A/S, *Sea Goddess I* and *Sea Goddess II,* built for luxury cruising, were taken over. These yacht like ships relied upon an American clientele and after the American bombing raid on Libya plus the atomic disaster at Chernobyl were left without sufficient passengers. Their builders, Wartsila, were still owed $50 million and sought to repossess them. Midland Bank took over the debt and Cunard took both ships on a twelve year charter with an option to purchase.

In June the famous shipbuilding name of John Brown was acquired but as engineers and constructors not shipbuilders. In fact their last ship was *Queen Elizabeth 2.* During the winter she went to Bremerhaven to be converted to diesel-electric drive with the intention of having her life extended by a further twenty years by the end of which she will be approaching forty.

1987 Cunard's passenger fleet continue to maintain the Company's historical pre-eminence in this field. Cargo has moved across entirely to the Group's Atlantic Container Line (ACL) with five ships due for re-engining and the latest even being lengthened. The three H. E. Moss product tankers *Lucerna, Lumiere* and *Luminetta* remain and trade on charter.

The long traditional Mediterranean cargo trade, now extended to the Red Sea, is maintained by Cunard-C.A.M.E.L. (Cunard Arabian Middle East Line) using chartered ships bearing Brocklebank funnels. Trafalgar House plc purchased the Ellerman shipping interests for £24.1 million, by the issue of £22.5 million in new shares plus loan stock held by finance houses. Ellerman Holdings retained 3,750,000 shares and 5,480,000 were placed on the market at £3.83 per share. The acquisition was renamed Cunard-Ellerman and Cunard's cargo activities were transferred to it.

Perhaps most comforting of all is that Cunard's seven passenger ships remain 'probably the most highly rated in the world'.

November 21 sees the 200th anniverary of the birth of Sir Samuel Cunard. He would be proud of the history of the seagoing ships which still yet bear his name.
1990 July 4: 150th anniversary of the first sailing.

LIVERY

Funnels Cunard: Bright red containing a tinge of orange, Black top, One to three pin-stripe black bands on the red.
White Star: Buff, black top.

Hull Cunard: Black red water-line with, from 1880, thin dividing white stripe.
Cruise ships: white except for green livery which was mid green hull, thin dark green band and pale green uppers,
Sagafjord, Vistafjord and *England:* Grey no white divider.
Reefers: white, later grey.
White Star: Black, thin gold band, red water-line.
During fitting out some Cunarders had grey undercoat hulls which were painted black after trials (e.g.: *Mauretania* (I)).

Uppers White. The earliest ships had varnished wood deck houses.

Masts Cunard: Golden brown.
White Star: Funnel buff.

Lifeboats White, *Berengaria* had black 1921-1935.

Vents Black or white with some mast colour on cargo vessels.
Inside of cowls red.

Deck Fittings Cunard originally used a lot of black, even house tops, with modern times more white was introduced with grey winches.
White Star: Similar usage with a change about 1900 to funnel buff or white.
Steel decks varied. The reefers were dark green, the Cunard-Brocklebank bulkers were painted dark chocolate or dark grey.
In the earlier ships the deck rails were brown.

House flags Cunard-White Star. The houseflag of the pre-merger owner was flown above that of the other.

ROUTES

1840-1847	Liverpool-Halifax-Boston with feeder services Halifax-rail to Pictou-Quebec. New York-Bermuda feeder.
1845	The Pictou-Quebec service ended.
1847-1966	Liverpool-Boston (terminus) -New York. (1931 Belfast/Galway).
1847-1966	Liverpool-New York direct (except for Crimean war).
1850	New York-Nassau-Havana.
1853-1969	Liverpool-Gibraltar-Mediterranean ports also Liverpool-Cherbourg.
1856	Le Havre-New York. Replaced by Liverpool-Le Havre feeder.
1857-1859	Marseilles-Malta-Alexandria (European & Australian).
1858-1870	Connecting services New York-Nassau-Havana-Jamaica.
1859-1968	Calls at Queenstown (Cobh) were introduced.
1867	Canadian calls terminated. Liverpool-Boston direct.
1872-1874	Glasgow-West Indies.
1880	Liverpool-Suez-Bombay. (One Cunard test voyage).
1909-1914	Fishguard disembarkation call.
1903-1914	New York-Palermo-Venice-Trieste-Fiume (Rijeka).
1911	New York-Mediterranean cruises introduced.
1911-1967	Southampton-Quebec-Montreal (Thomson Line). Winter: Portland.
1913-1967	Liverpool-Quebec-Montreal (Thomson Line). Winter: Halifax.
1916-1922	Avonmouth-Canada.
1920	Rotterdam and Antwerp were advertised cargo ports of call.
1922-1951	London-Southampton-Quebec-Montreal (except for cargo).
1922-1940	(Hamburg)-London-Southampton-Cherbourg-New York.
1922-1987	Southampton-Cherbourg (1931 Le Havre instead) -New York. The accent on cruising, including 'Round the World', increased enormously.
1948-1950	Cuxhaven-Le Havre-Halifax/Quebec.
1960-1970	Liverpool-Gulf of Mexico (New Orleans, Galveston, Houston, Mobile, Tampa, Corpus Christie, Pensacola and Brownsville). London-Le Havre-Gulf of Mexico (same range of ports).
1971-1989	Caribbean and Florida based cruising.
1972-1987	Worldwide bulk and perishable trades. 1987: To Cunard Ellerman.
1984-1989	Pacific cruising out of Los Angeles.

FLEET INDEX

ILLUSTRATED FLEET LIST

SCALES: Ships 1-93 1:1200, 94-215 1:1360 except where shown beneath the name

CUNARD LINE

UNICORN

1 **UNICORN**
B 1838 Robert Steele & Son, Greenock. **T** 648g, 390n.
D 185/56,39 oa x 23.5/7.16 x 17.3/5.28. Width over sponsons 45.2/13.77.
E Pad 2 cyl simple side lever, 570 IHP, 18 rpm. 18psi. 9½ kts. By Caird & Co., Greenock. Coal 453 tons at 18 per day. Pad diameter 22.9/8.21 floats. 10½ rpm. **H** Wood, carvel built. 2 dks + poop. Square stern. Unicorn figurehead. **P** 40 Crew 35.
1836 May: Launched for George & John Burns for their Glasgow-Liverpool service.
1840 The first ship to sail for Samuel Cunard. The new contract called for a feeder service Halifax-Pictou-Quebec. *Unicorn* was chartered for six years for this duty. May 16: First voyage Liverpool-Halifax-Boston commanded by Captain Walter Douglas. 27 passengers. She reached Halifax on May 30 and Boston on June 3rd.
1843 Nov: Rescued the passengers and crew of the sailing ship *Premier* wrecked at the mouth of the St. Lawrence.
1845 The feeder service was discontinued.
1846 Became a corvette in the Portuguese navy.
1848 Reboilered. Sold for service Panama-San Francisco.
1853 Moved to Australian waters and then Manila-China coast service.
1858 Hulked. Trace lost.
Note: Her two sisters *Eagle* and *City of Glasgow* (II) remained with G. & J. Burns.

BRITANNIA, ACADIA, CALEDONIA, COLUMBIA, HIBERNIA, CAMBRIA

2 **BRITANNIA**
B 1840 Robert Duncan & Co., Greenock. **T** 1,156g, 619n.
D 230/70.1 oa, figurehead to taffrail, 207/63.1 x 34.5/10.51 x 22.5/6.86. 56/17.06 over paddle boxes.
E Pad, 2 cyl side lever. 440 NHP, 8.5 kts at 16 rpm. 9 psi with 4 blrs. By Robert Napier & Sons, Vulcan Foundry, Glasgow. Pad diam: 28/8.53, floats 8.8/2.64 wide. **H** Wood. 2 dks. Coal 640 tons at 37 per day.
P 115 Cabin. Crew 89. Cargo 225 tons.

1840 Feb 5: Launched by Miss Isabella Napier, the first ship for the British & North America Royal Mail Steam Packet Company.
July 4: M/v Liverpool-Halifax-Boston with the mails. Commander Capt. Henry Woodruff R.N. The date was chosen because of American Independence day. Her departure was from midstream because she was too large to berth alongside at Liverpool. The sailing was the first regular mail service across the Atlantic but it caused no excitement at Liverpool. Her arrival from the Clyde on June 12, docking at Coburg Dock, merited two lines only in the press. The reason was that her size was nothing special even in those days. On Friday, July 3 *Britannia* anchored in the Mersey off Laird's yard at what was to become known as Cunard's buoy. At noon on Saturday the full complement of 63 embarked from the Egremont slip. Samuel Cunard and his daughter were passengers. By 2 p.m. she was away. *Britannia* reached Halifax in 11 days 4 hours (and Boston in 14 days 8 hours). Her best daily distance was 280 miles.
She docked at Halifax in the early hours of Thursday, July 17, to a gun salute from *HMS Winchester*. After 8 hours she sailed. At Boston the reception was tumultuous. She was escorted in by the USN cutter *Hamilton* and the shore batteries saluted her. The following Monday, July 21, 2,000 people marched to Cunard Wharf where a tremendous banquet was held.
1844 When Boston harbour froze the ship was freed by the cutting of a seven mile channel to the open sea.
1849 After 40 crossings the vessel was sold to the North German Federation navy for conversion into a frigate. R/n *Barbarossa*.
1852 The North German Federation navy became the Prussian navy. *Barbarossa* was later converted into a hulk at Kiel.
1880 Demolished at Kiel. Some records say sunk by gunfire.

3 **ACADIA**
Details as 2 except: **B** John Wood & Co., Port Glasgow. **T** 1,154g, 616n.
E By Robert Napier.
1840 Her owners were given as the North American Ocean Steam Navigation Co., Aug 4: M/v Capt. E. C. Miller RN. Each ship in the class differed fractionally according to the hull builder's style.
1852 Nov 4: Completed her 33rd voyage and laid up at Liverpool pending disposal. *Andes* (16) took her place.
1849 March 9: Followed her sister into the North German navy. Became *Erzherzog Johann;* commanded by Admiral Brommy. March 12: During her delivery voyage to Bremen she grounded at Terschelling but came off unscathed.
1852 Sold to W. A. Fritze & Co., R/n *Germania.*
1853 Aug 3: Now owned by Karl Lehmkuhl she opened the Bremen-New York service.
1855 Chartered to the British Government as a Crimean War transport to Varna.
1856 Resumed Baltic trading for her owners.
1858 Broken up on the Thames.

4 **CALEDONIA**
Sister of 2 except: **B** Robert Wood & Co., Greenock. **T** 1,156g, 619n.
E By Robert Napier.
1840 Sept 19: M/v under Capt. Richard Cleland.
1850 Outmoded by the second generation of ships she was sold, with *Hibernia* (7), to the Spanish navy and converted into a frigate. The price for the two was £35,000. Replaced by *Africa* (14).
1851 Wrecked at Havana, Cuba, when she ran onto a rock shelf at the harbour mouth. She had to be abandoned as she lay.

5 **COLUMBIA**
Details as 2 but **B** 1841 Robert Steele & Son, Greenock. **T** 1,175g, 625n. **E** By Robert Napier.
1840 Sept: Launched. Cost £49,877.
1841 Jan 5: M/v under Capt. Ewing.
1843 July 2: Wrecked inbound in dense fog on Seal Island, Halifax with 85 passengers. No lives were lost and both the cargo and the mails were saved but the vessel herself could not be got off. 90% (£45,000) of the value was met by the underwriters, Bennett, Browne. The remainder was carried by the shareholders, mainly Charles MacIver.

6 **HIBERNIA**
Details as 2 except: **B** 1843 Robert Steele. **T** 1,422g, 791n.
D 240/73.15 oa, figurehead to taffrail. x 37.8/11.48. Width over paddle sponsons 58/17.68. **E** Fitted with jet condensers, coal 740 tons. **H** Cargo 300 tons. **P** 125 Cabin.
1842 Sept 8: Launched. This ship and *Cambria* (7) were slightly enlarged versions principally to carry 100 tons more coal which had been found to be advisable during winter westbound crossings.

1843 Apr 19: M/v under Capt. Ryrie.
1847 Dec: Inaugurated the Liverpool-Queenstown-New York direct service.
1849 Aug 31:Grounded near to Halifax. Salvaged and repaired in New York.
1850 Aug 24: Final sailing then sold with *Caledonia* (4) to become the Spanish frigate *Habanois*. Based at Cuba.
1868 Lost.

7 **CAMBRIA**
Sister to *Hibernia*. **B** 1845. **T** 1,423g, 792n.
1844 Aug 1: Launched.
1845 Jan 4: M/v to Boston. Nicknamed 'the Flying Cambria'.
1848 Jan 1: Her terminus was switched to New York.
1852 Mizzen mast removed. Brig rigged, square sails on each mast.
1854 March: Chartered for use as a Crimean war transport initially to Varna then to the Crimea.
1856 March 29: Reverted to the North Atlantic after a refit. Nov: Placed in service Marseilles-Malta for the European & Australian Royal Mail line which had sub-contracted this service and Southampton-Alexandria to the British & American R.M.S.P. Co. (A mouthful that was already being referred to as the Cunard Line — particularly in Canada and America).
1860 Sold at Malta to Agostino Bertani of Palermo, Siciliy. June: Sold to Giuseppe Garibaldi as a troopship. Nov 17: To Sardinian navy.
1875 March 31: Broken up.

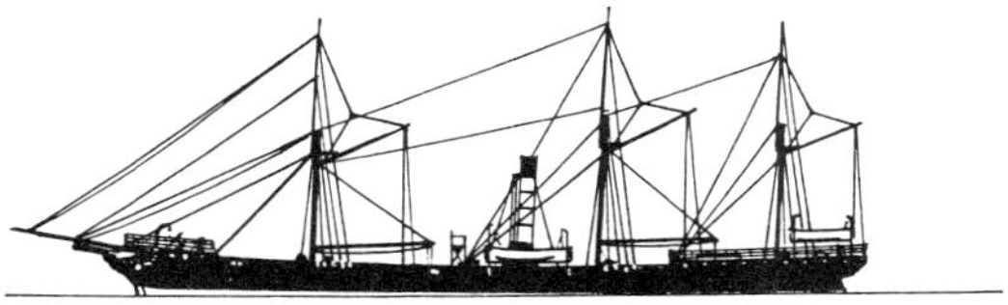

MARGARET

8 **MARGARET**
B 1839 Caird & Co., Greenock. **T** 700g, 387n.
D 185/56.4 x 26.1/7.98 x 17/5.18. **E** Pad, 2 cyl side lever. 200 IHP, 8 psi. 9 kts. By builder. **H** Wood. 1 dk. Cargo 1,200 tons.
1839 Built for G. & J. Burns, Glasgow-Belfast-Dublin.
1847 Used on Mediterranean routes for Burns but under Cunard contracts.
1850 Used on the Cunard services to Constantinople and the Levant.
1855 Not included, because of age, in the vessels which formed the British and Foreign Steam Navigation Co.
1856 Sold and converted into a coal hulk.

AMERICA, NIAGARA, EUROPA, CANADA

9 **AMERICA**
B 1848 Robert Steele & Son, Glasgow. **T** 1,826g, 984n.
D 249.4/79.1 x 35.2/10.72 x 25/7.62.
E Pad. 2 cyl side lever jet condensing. 670 NHP; 18 psi, 4 flue blrs, 16 furnaces using 60 tons coal per day. 10 kts. By Robert Napier.
H Wood. 2 dks. Coal 840 tons. Cargo 450 tons. **P** 140 Cabin. Crew 90.
1847 May 13: Launched. Introduced navigation lights at night; Port red, Starboard green and foremasthead white. Again slightly larger than either *Britannia* or *Hibernia* and one knot faster in all weathers.
1848 Apr 15: M/v to New York but then either there or Boston. By now the average Liverpool-New York steaming time was down to 12 days 22 hours including ports of call.

1856 Dec 12: Suffered severe storm damage off Cape Clear. Lifeboats lost and funnel unseated, returned to Liverpool.
1863 July 23 Chartered to the Allan Line for 4 voyages Liverpool-Quebec-Montreal.
1866 Reduced to cargo only; Liverpool-Le Havre. Later in the year became the sailing ship *Coalgaconder*.
1877 broken up.

10 **NIAGARA**
As 9 except: **T** 1,842g, 984n. Length 251/76.5.
1847 July 28: Launched.
1848 May 20: M/v to Boston. Then served either Boston or New York.
1854 Crimean War transport.
1855 March: Formed part of the flotilla which carried the Sardinian Army Corps from Genoa to Balaklava.
1855-1862 North Atlantic services.
1866 Nov: Sold to the shipbuilders J. & G. Thomson, Glasgow who converted her to sail. Sold to Duncan Dunbar; same name.
1875 June 6: Wrecked near to South Stack, Anglesey, North Wales.

11 **EUROPA**
As *America* except: **B** John Wood & Co., Port Glasgow. **T** 1,834g, 992n. **D** 251/76.5.
1847 Sept 29: Launched.
1848 July 15: M/v with 113 passengers Liverpool-Halifax-Boston. Captain Lott. Then onto the New York berth.
1849 June 27: Collided with and sank the American barque *Charles Bartlett* in dense fog. 135 aboard the barque were lost when the two drifted apart and the *Charles Bartlett* sank some hours later.
1853 Reduced to brig rig by the removal of the mizzen mast.
1854 Chartered by the Government for Crimea work.
1858 Aug 14: Collided off Cape Race in fog with the company's *Arabia* (19)
1866 Feb 3: Made her final sailing to Boston.
1867 Sold for conversion into a barque; lengthened in the process.

12 **CANADA**
Sister to *America* except: **T** 1,831g, 990n.
1848 June 2: Launched. Nov 25: M/v to the new terminus of New York; she then traded also to Boston as required.
1850 Oct 27: Grounded at Halifax without damage.
1854 April 18: Ran down and sank the sailing vessel *Belle*. Nov 25: Collided off Boston with the American steamer *Ocean*.
1866 Feb 3: Final Cunard sailing.
1867 Became the sailing ship *Mississippi,* Portugal.
1883 Broken up. However it is reported that after this date she was seen at Bombay loading for Mauritius and bearing the name *Canada.*

ASIA, AFRICA

13 **ASIA**
B 1850 Robert Steele & Son, Greenock. **T** 2,226g, 1,214n.
D 280/85.34 oa x 40.5/12.34 x 27.6/8.41 (58/17.68 over sponsons).
E Pad. 2 side lever jet condensing, 2 cyl simple, 814 NHP, 2,400 IHP, 18psi, 12½kts. Paddle diam. 37.6/11.46 with 28 floats each 9.2ft/2.8m wide and 3.2/.97m deep and held by three arms off the axle. At her 19ft/5.78m draught 8 floats were in the water. She had 4 flue blrs and 28 furnaces burning 76 tons of coal per day. Engine by Robert Napier & Sons.
H Oak, double planked with the gap filled with rock salt. 2 dks. The saloon was on the main deck aft and was 60/18.29 x 20/6.1. Fitted to carry cannon. Cargo: 600 tons. Coal: 890 tons.

P 130 Cabin (1st), 30 2nd. Crew 112 of which the engine room staff comprised 6 engineers and 32 stokers working 4 six hour shifts at 2 men per boiler. A shift moved 18 tons of coal.
1850 Jan 31: Launched. The first of the 'Second generation' paddlers and the longest steamer afloat, May 18: M/v to Boston; Captain C. H. Judkins. The mails officer being Lt. Ellis, R.N.
In service she and her sister *Africa* were not up to the standard of the Collins Line competition.
1852 Brig rig, mizzen mast out. **P** 40 1st, 30 2nd.
1861 In the build up to the American Civil War tension between the UK and the USA escalated when Royal Mail's *Trent* was stopped and two Confederate passengers taken off. *Asia* was chartered by the Admiralty to take British troops to Canada.
1867 May 11: Made her final round trip to Boston. Then used as a floating barracks at Liverpool during the Fenian riots. Sold in autumn to Robb & Co., Glasgow and converted to sail.
1877 Dec 2: Burnt out at Bombay while loading cotton for the UK.

14 **AFRICA**
As *Asia*.
1850 Oct 26: M/v Liverpool-New York direct.
1851 Oct 25: Went aground in Belfast Lough. Repaired at Liverpool.
1867 Dec 7: Her final sailing to Halifax and Boston was also Cunard's final wooden hulled departure. She then joined her sister at Liverpool during the Fenian riots.
1868 Sold.

SATELLITE (I)

15 **SATELLITE (I)**
B 1848 Robert Napier & Sons, Glasgow. **T** 157g, 82n.
D 108.6/32.46 x 18.7/5.69 x 9.6/2.92.
E Pad. 2 cyl simple, 80 NHP, 11½psi, 8 kts, 1 blr with 4 furnaces. By builder. **H** Iron. 1 dk.
P 600 plus their baggage.
1848 Tender at Liverpool; Capt Parry. At this time all passengers embarked in mid stream from the Egremont ferry slip at Liverpool.
1884 Relieved by *Skirmisher* (83). Remained as a crew servicing tender.
1902 Sept: Sold for £410 to Alexander Gordon, Annalong, County Down, Broken up shortly afterwards.

ANDES, ALPS

16 **ANDES**
B 1852 Wm. Denny & Bros, Dumbarton. **T** 1,852g, 1,440 n.
D 236/71.93 oa x 34/10.36 x 24.2/7.38.
E Sgl scr, 1 cyl beam geared simple exp. 300 NHP, 9 kts, 2 blrs, 12 furnaces. By Tulloch & Denny, the engine building side of Wm. Denny.
H Iron. 2 dks. **P** 62 Cabin. 122 2nd. Cargo: 1,000 tons.
1852 Aug 18: Launched for a New York-Panama service at a cost of £60,700 the pair (with *Alps*). The Company's first iron hulls. Slow ships.
Dec 8: M/v Liverpool-New York. Due to abornally low tides she could not clear the dock and the voyage actually commenced on Dec 25.
1853 After delivery to New York she opened the New York-Chagres (Panama) route on an experimental basis.
1854 Late in the year taken up for Crimean War service as a hospital ship at the rate of £505 per month.
1855 Transferred to the British & Foreign S.N.Co. upon its foundation.
1856 Reverted to the Chagres service.
1858 The New York-Chagres service was discontinued. *Andes* returned to Liverpool and was laid up.
1859 Sold to J. & G. Thomson; overhauled and sold to the Spanish Government for trooping to Cuba. Renamed *Lagos*.

17 **ALPS**
Details as *Andes*.
1852 Sept 28: Launched.
1853 Jan 2: Maiden delivery voyage to New York for the Chagres service.
1854 Joined *Andes* as a hospital ship; same terms.
1855 Transferred to British & Foreign S.N.Co. at its formation.
1859 Went with *Andes* to J. & G. Thomson. Lengthened by 30ft/9.14m at Harland & Wolff, Belfast. Then sold to the West Indies & Pacific S.N.Co. (Leech, Harrison & Forwood, managers), Liverpool.
1871 Broken up.

ARABIA (I), PERSIA (I)/ARABIA (II)

18 **ARABIA (I)**
This ship was laid down by Robert Steele at Greenock and she was well advanced when Royal Mail S.P.Co. purchased her for £125,000 to replace their burnt out *Amazon*. Under their flag she became *La Plata*. An identical sister had been planned by Cunard and she had been allocated the name *Persia*. Work on her continued but she was to emerge as *Arabia*.

19 **PERSIA (I)/ARABIA (II)**
B 1852 Robert Steele & Son, Greenock. **T** 2,402g, 1,474n.
D 309/94.18 oa, 284/86.56 x 41.1/12.53 x 27.5/8.36. 66.5/20.27 over paddle sponsons. Dft: 19/5.79.
E Pad. 2 x sgl cyl side lever, 938 NHP, 3,250 IHP, 18 psi, 13 kts at 15 rpm. 4 tubular bls 24 furnaces, 130 tons coal per day. By Robert Napier.
H Oak. 2 dks. Coal 1,400 tons. Cargo 750 tons. **P** 180 Cabin.
1852 Laid down as *Persia*. June 21: Launched. The last great wooden paddler built to combat the speed advantage of the Collin's Line vessels.
Details: Hull: Flat bottomed with rounded bilges. The oak frames were closely spaced and diagonally tied with crossed iron braces. All the fastenings below the water line were copper. The outer planking was sheathed with hair felt followed by rock elm planking and then covered overall with a copper skin. The figurehead was of an Arab chieftain. *Arabia* was Cunard's first two funneller and was brig rigged not barque or barquentine.
Accommodation: Nominally for 180 all in one class although at peak periods an extra 20 could be accommodated on settees or cot beds. The main saloon was abaft the mainmast and had a glass dome. The ship carried a library, smoking room and nursery. One innovation was that she was steam heated throughout which put her ahead of her rivals.
Engines: At the time these were the largest in any British ship and had to be installed as the ship was being built. Normally an engine consisted of one cylinder, its piston, the connecting rods and the crank which turned the paddles. *Arabia* had two bolted to the bed plate and at full speed the 9ft/2.74m stroke took two seconds to traverse so that a cycle took four seconds which equalled one paddle revolution.
Boilers: *Arabia* had two pairs of box boilers, fitted with tubes, which were also installed as construction continued. There were 6 furnaces to each and since each boiler faced the other the stokers reported them as being hard to work because the men got in each others way. The boilers were paired to each funnel uptake two forward of the engine and two aft.
Paddles: The diameter was 35.5ft/10.82m with 28 blades each 10.5/3.2 wide and 3.2ft/.97 deep. They turned at 15 rpm. Full speed was 17 rpm.
Performance: Because of her fine lines (she was 20ft/6.1m longer than *Asia* on virtually the same beam) there was insufficient buoyancy to lift the bow in a seaway. Consequently *Arabia* was a very wet ship. Worse, she lost headway easily and her average crossing was almost always below her designed speed. Moreover in such conditions her heavy engines shook the hull. This was sometimes so severe that she was forced to slow down.
Fuel consumption: This was far too high. 120 tons per day compared with *Asia's* 76 for only a knot more speed (and 20 more passengers). Her bunkers held 1,400 tons and at the commencement of a voyage her paddle axles were only 2 feet out of the water. By the journey end they stood 5 feet clear. Early paintings show this: English painters have the ships low in the water looking very squat. Their American counterparts depict veritable bulks towering out of the harbour surrounds.

1852 Dec 29: Moved into the Mersey. Captain C. H. Judkins.
1853 Jan 1: M/v Liverpool-New York direct. Adverse winds forced her into Halifax to refuel.
1854 Chartered to the Government for the Crimea at 50 shillings per ton per month. During this service she carried 289 officers, 5,074 men and 803 horses.
1858 Aug 14: Collided with her consort *Europa* off Cape Race.
1864 New building enabled her to be sold after a relatively unsuccessful career. Converted to sail.
1868 Wrecked near Halifax, N.S.

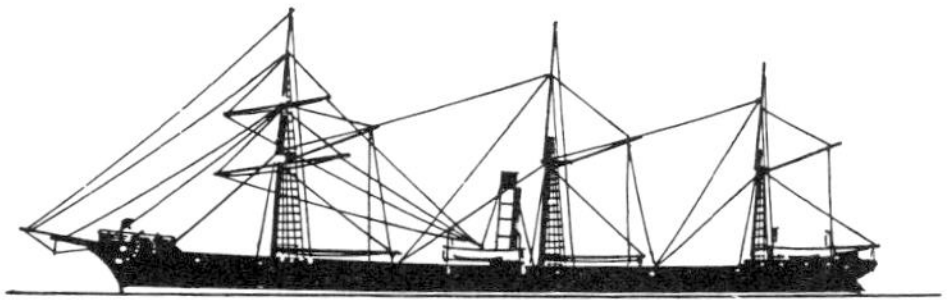

SHAMROCK

20 **SHAMROCK**
B 1847 Caird & Co., Greenock. **T** 714g, 348n.
D 195/59.43 oa x 25/7.62 x 18/5.49.
E Sgl scr, 1 cyl Vertical direct acting, 140 NHP, 1 blr, 18 psi, 9 kts. By builder. **H** Iron. 1 dk and poop.
P 25 Cabin, 100 3rd.
1847 Built for Charles MacIver & Co. for their Levant, Constantinople trade out of Liverpool. His first iron hull. From her early days she operated in conjunction with Cunard sailings and wore their funnel.
1851 On Cunard's Mediterranean routes in conjunction with George Burns.
1854 Sold as being too small prior to the formation of the British & Foreign S.N.Co. Operated Dublin-Bristol-London.
1875 Broken up.

BALBEC

21 **BALBEC**
B 1853 Wm. Denny & Bros., Dumbarton. **T** 774g, 468n.
D 209.2/63.75 oa, 210/61.26 x 30/9.19 x 17/5.18.
E Sgl scr, 1 cyl beam geared. 137 NHP, 9 kts. By Tulloch & Denny.
H Iron, 1 dk + poop. Brig rig. **P** 29 Cabin, 157 3rd.
1852 Ordered by Gee & Co., Hull as *Czarina.* June 9: Offered to George Burns for £16,000 on behalf of Cunard. Nov 9: Launched for Cunard with her name recorded as *Baalbek.* She was completed as *Balbec.*
1853 Jan: Entered the Mediterranean services.
1859 Sept 10: Made the first of two relief voyages Liverpool-New York.
1863 Placed on the Liverpool-Le Havre route.
1873 Compounded by J. Jack Rollo, Liverpool.
1884 March 28: Holed off the Longships, Cornwall by a submerged object and beached at Plymouth. At 21 years old she was written off as a constructive total loss.

TAURUS, TENERIFFE, KARNAK

22 **TAURUS**
B 1853 Wm. Denny. **T** 1, 126g, 986n.
D 210/64 oa, 202/61.56 x 30/9.25 x 18/5.49.
E Sgl scr, 1, cyl beam geared, 220 NHP, 2 blrs, 9 kts. By Tulloch & Denny.
H Iron. 1 dk. P 40 1st, 100 2nd.

1853 Feb 21: Launched. A slightly enlarged version of *Balbec* having one foot greater moulded depth but no poop. She was ordered as a pair with *Teneriffe* for £32,000. Initially ordered by Charles MacIver but then transferred to the new British & Foreign S.N. Co., upon its formation in 1855. Apr 20: M/v to Constantinople, July 6: The first of two voyages to New York from Liverpool.
1854-55 Crimean War transport, mainly horses.
1859 Sold to the Spanish Government for transport duties; based Ceuta.

23 **TENERIFFE**
As *Taurus*
1853 Levant trade. At this time the cost of a passage to Constantinople was £40; relatively expensive but the journey was longer than a transatlantic crossing.
1854 Served with her sister to the Crimean theatre.
1855 Transferred to the British & Foreign S.N. Co., at its formation.
1859 Sold with her sister to Spain as a troop transport.

24 **KARNAK**
As *Taurus* except **T** 1,116g.
1853 Originally conceived as a sister to *Balbec* and allocated the name *Karnac*. Cost £18,000. Apr 19: A spar deck was added for the carriage of boxed fruit and she was completed as a sister to *Taurus*. The final price became £22,340. Sept 22: Launched as *Karnak* for the Mediterranean routes. However she was then switched to the New York-Nassau-Havana mail service which connected with the Liverpool-New York mail steamers.
1855 Became a part of the British & Foreign fleet but still on the New York berth.
1862 Wrecked off Bermuda.

DELTA

25 **DELTA**
B 1853 Barclay Curle & Co., Glasgow. **T** 645g, 432n.
D 205/62.48 x 29.1/8.89 x 15.8/4.8.
E Sgl scr, 2 cyl beam geared, 120 NHP, 2 blrs, 6 furnaces. 9 kts. By builder. **H** Iron 2 dks. Had 1 18 pounder pivot gun aft.
1853 Owned by Samuel Cunard not the British & North American R.M.S.P. Co. At this time many of the ships were registered in the names of various individuals although they were a part of the fleet proper. Operated Halifax-New York-Bermuda.
1860 Passed into Halifax ownership.

MELITA

26 **MELITA**
B 1853 Alexander Denny & Co., Dumbarton. **T** 1,254g, 1025n.
D 233/71.52 x 29.3/8.94 x 18.2/5.54.
E Sgl scr, 2 cyl beam geared, 9 kts. By Macnab & Clark, Greenock.
H Iron. 1 dk + fcsle. **P** Steerage only.
1852 Aug 3: William Denny & Bros., took over a half share in the building of this ship.
1853 March 27: Launched for the Mediterranean route. The ship was a larger sister to the *Taurus* class except for the fcsle. Cost £19,100. Aug 11: Chartered to John Burns for Cunard's Mediterranean service.
1855 Joined the British & Foreign fleet at its formation.
1860 June 13: Chartered to the Allan Line. Sept 5: Her first Cunard sailing Liverpool-Halifax-New York.

1861 Taken by Peter Denny in part payment for *Sidon* (43) and *Morocco* (44).
1862 Sold to S. & S. Isaac; same name. Price £23,500. Ran Enfield rifles to the confederate states.
1866 June 6: Chartered to the Warren line; her first sailing for them. Liverpool-Queenstown-Boston-Philadelphia.
1868 Sept 5: Burnt at sea. All were taken off by the sailing ships *Jacob A Stamler* and *Monequash*.

EMEU

27 **EMEU**
B 1854 Robert Napier & Sons, Glasgow. **T** 1,538g, 1,252n.
D 268.8/81.91 x 34.5/10.49 x 27.5/8.38.
E Sgl scr, 2 cyl beam geared eng, 276 NHP, 20 psi, 10 kts (Service speed 8). By builder. **H** Iron. 2 dks + fcsle. **P** 80 1st, 130 2nd.
1853 Aug 22: Launched for the Australasian Pacific Mail Steam Packet Co. Her sisters were *Black Swan, Dinornis, Kangaroo* and *Minura.*
1854 Feb 21: The first advertised sailing date. March 30: Was the new date given for the intended monthly sailing Southampton-Panama (with transhipment)-Tahiti-Wellington-Sydney. A journey time of 59 days including the Panama transfer. PSNC were appointed managers with Royal Mail doing Southampton-Aspinwall (Colon). March 27: The scheme was abandoned. *Emeu* (with *Kangaroo*) was chartered to the Admiralty for six months at £50 per diem each.
1855 Because of their Crimean commitments *Emeu* was purchased by Cunard for the Mediterranean services.
1856 Placed on the New York service.
1857 June: Chartered to the European & Australian R.M.S.P. Co., to replace their wrecked *Oneida.* Sept: Ashore in the Red Sea bound for Suez.
1858 Oct 9: Sold to P. & O. for delivery at Sydney at the end of her current voyage (Feb 1859).
1859 Placed on P. & O's Sydney-Mauritius-Suez service.
1873 Nov 5: Sold for £6,508; became the sailing ship *Winchester* owned by W. MacArthur, London.
1880 July 14: Grounded in the Straits of Magellan, salvaged.
1898 Recorded as a hulk in Chile. Some records give her as being wrecked on the coast of Borneo in 1880.

LEBANON

28 **LEBANON**
B 1855 J. & G. Thomson & Co., Glasgow. **T** 1,383g.**D** 252.5/76.96 x 30.5/9.27 x 25.3/7.7.
E Sgl scr, 2 cyl oscillating geared. 220 NHP, 2 blrs with 8 furnaces, 30 psi, 10 kts. By builder. **H** Iron 2 dks. Fcsle and poop. **P** 80 Cabin (1st) only.
1854 Nov 22. Launched as *Aerolith,* Robert Sloman, Hamburg, for Mediterranean work.
1855 Acquired. Not included in the fleet of the British & Foreign Line. Acted as a relief or extra vessel on the North Atlantic. July 31: First such sailing.
1856 June 28: Placed on the Le Havre-New York route.
1857 Chartered by the Government as an Indian Mutiny troopship.
1859 Off charter but did not resume Atlantic work. Laid up at Liverpool. Sold to the Spanish Government and converted into an armed troop carrier. Renamed *Cadiz.*

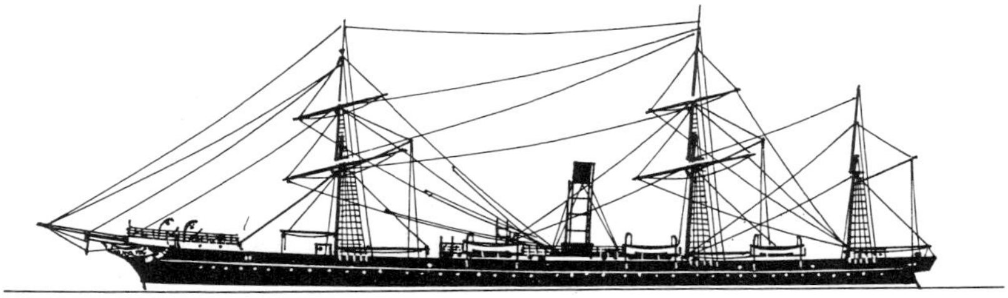

JURA, ETNA

29 **JURA**
B 1854 J. & G. Thomson & Co., Glasgow. **T** 2,241g, 1,789n.
D 316/96.32 x 36/10.97 x 22/6.7.
E Sgl scr, 2 cyl beam geared, 440 NHP, 2 blrs, 8 furnaces; 11 kts. By builder. **H** Iron 2 dks. Fcsle.
P 120 1st, 400 3rd.
1854 June 27: Launched for the Liverpool-West Indies service. Sept 24: On her arrival at Liverpool she was at once requisitioned for Crimean war service. She was at the time the longest steamer yet built.
1855 Jan: King Victor Emanuel II of Sardinia declared war on Russia, March: 18,500 troops were assembled at Genoa and a fleet of transports embarked them for Balaklava. Among the ships were the Cunarders *Jura, Etna, Andes* and *Niagara.*
1856 Returned to Cunard service to the Mediterranean.
1857 March 12: Chartered to the European & Australian R.M.Co., for four months to cover their Southampton-Malta-Alexandria route. Sept 16: Placed on the Liverpool-New York service.
1861 Feb 2: Final sailing for the Company, Aug: Chartered to the Allan line for two round trips on their Liverpool-Montreal route and then purchased by them. Oct 24: First sailing under their ownership.
1864 Nov 3: Ran aground on the Crosby shore of the Mersey at a spot which has claimed more than one victim. Broke her back and became a total loss.

30 **ETNA**
Details as *Jura* except: **B** 1855 Caird & Co., Greenock. **T** 2,115g, 1,794n.
D 305/92.96 x 36.3/11.05. E By builder.
1854 Aug 26: Launched for the West Indies service.
1855 Jan 21: Taken over at Liverpool for Crimean War service. Maiden voyage to Varna and then to Genoa for the Sardinian Army uplift. March: Left for Balaklava.
1856 Feb 5: First sailing Le Havre-New York then on the Liverpool-New York berth until she took up her service with *Andres* (16) on the New York-Chagres feeder route.
1857 Chartered, with her sister, by the European & Australian R.M.Co. Southampton-Alexandria via Malta.
1859 Jan 15: On the Liverpool-New York service.
1860 Oct: Sold to the Inman Line; same name. Dec 5: First Inman sailing.
1871 Spring: Rebuilt by Laird Bros, Birkenhead. Lengthened to 349.4/106.49. T 2,655g. Compounded. 12 kts. Renamed *City of Bristol.* Aug 8: Resumed sailings to New York.
1975 Sept: Chartered to the American Line for one voyage to Philadelphia.
1876-79 Operated by Inman with charters to American Line.
1880 Dec 13: Final Atlantic crossing then sold to J. P. Davies, Liverpool.
1881 Became *Messico.*
1883 Renamed *Sempione,* Raffaele Rubbatino, Genoa.
1884 Became *Adria,* Navigazione Generale Italiana, Genoa.
1896 Broken up in Italy.

31 **STROMBOLI**
B 1856 J. & G. Thomson, Glasgow. **T** 734g.
D 198.3/60.45 x 28.8/8.76 x 17.5/5.33.
E Sgl scr, 1 cyl vertical direct acting, 105 NHP, 2 blrs, 4 furnaces, 9 kts. By builder. **H** Iron 1 dk.
1856 Built for the Liverpool-Levant service but also served for some years on the Liverpool-Le Havre route.
1866 Reboilered.
1877 New compound inverted engines installed; the vertical type not being capable of alteration by the addition of the second cylinder.
1878 Lost off the Lizard, Cornwall enroute to Le Havre.

PERSIA (II)

32 **PERSIA (II)**
B 1856 Robert Napier & Sons, Glasgow. **T** 3,700g, 2,079n, 5,850 disp.
D 390/228.7 oa 376/114.6 x 45/13.72 x 31.5/9.6.
E Pad. 2 cyl side lever jet condensing. 4,570 IHP, 8 tubular blrs at 20 psi, 13 kts at 17 rpm. By builder. Pad-wheels 38/11.58 diam with 30 floats 10.5ft/3.2m wide.
H Iron 2 dks. Cargo: 1,050 tons Coal: 1,640 tons at 143 tons per day.
P 200 Cabin, 50 2nd, Crew 440.
1853 This ship was ordered from Wm. Denny & Bros. (allocated yard number 45) who shortly afterwards asked to be released from the contract; the price of which was £43,512. No reasons were recorded but a glance at the price from Napiers explains a gross quotation error so enormous that Cunard did not attempt to enforce it.
1855 July 3: Launched. To cost £130,000.
1856 Jan 8: Trials. She was the longest vessel afloat and the first iron-hulled transatlantic liner*. Barque rigged. She was commanded for most of her career by Captain Lott who made over 300 crossings in her.
Jan 26: M/v to New York commanded by Capt Judkins.
During the voyage she scraped the side of an iceberg but arrived safely at her destination. Tragically Collin's *Pacific* left Liverpool on the previous day to *Persia* and was never heard of again. It was the record holding *Pacific* that *Persia* had been designed to beat.
July: Crossed to New York in 9 days, 1 hr and 45 mins at an average of 13.82 kts. She held the Blue Riband until 1862.
1861 trooped to Canada during the tension created between Britain and the USA, Unionist North, over the *Trent* incident.
1868 Feb 10: Sold to J. R. Thomson for £10,000 and had her engines removed. July 11: Re-sold to Wm. McArthur & Matthew Wilson, Glasgow.
1871 Jan 9: Owned by J. Moss & Co.
1872 Feb 9: Sold to S. N. & A. Castle. Broken up in the same year.
*Note: *Andes* (16) was iron hulled but she was not intended for the regular mail service across the Atlantic.

AUSTRALASIAN

CALABRIA

33 **AUSTRALASIAN/CALABRIA**
B 1857 J. & G. Thomson, Glasgow. **T** 2,760g, 1,954n.
D 360/109.73 oa x 42.1/12.83 x 20.8/6.32.

E Sgl scr, 2 cyl vertical director acting, 600 NHP, 6 blrs. 30 furn. 14 kts. By builder.
H Iron, 2 dks + spar deck. Equipped with Cunningham patent reefing sails and Clifford patent lifeboat launchers. Cargo: 1,100 tons. Coal: 1,180 tons. **P** 200 Saloon, 60 2nd.
1857 June 10: Launched as *Australasian* for the European & Australian Royal Mail Co. for their Suez-Australia service. Cost £110,000. Sept 21: Trials. Oct 12: M/v Southampton-Alexandria. Her consorts were *African, Asian, Columbian, European, Oneida, Simla* and *Tasmanian* on the Australian leg with Cunard's *Cambria, Etna & Jura* on the Alexandria sector. Burns & McIver were the agents for the Company.
On her return to Southampton she left for Sydney commaned by Captain Geoffrey Scales. The service was not a financial success.
1859 Arrested at Sydney when £3,000 wages and stores money failed to arrive. Sold to Cunard for £50,000; less than half her price two years earlier: this met the sums due to them at the time of collapse.
1860 Feb 25: First Liverpool-New York sailing.
Apr 4: Chartered for one voyage to the Allan Line.
1869 Re-engined; 2 cyl vertical direct acting with surface condenser. 4 new blrs, 24 furnaces on 86 tons coal per day. 450 NHP. 12½ kts. Her fore funnel and jib were removed. Renamed *Calabria.*
1870 Jan 8: First sailing as *Calabria* to New York.
1877 Sold to the Telegraph Construction & Maintenance Co. Converted into a cable layer with 3 tanks to carry 35,500 cu ft cable. Twin bow and sgl stern sheaves.
1879 Less powerful engines fitted, 2 cyl compound, 220 NHP. 2 blrs. These enabled her to steam economically at slow speed when cable laying.
1898 Broken up at Bolnes, Netherlands.

34 **ITALIAN**
B 1855 J. & G. Thomson & Co., Glasgow. **T** 784g, 533n. **D** 201.3/61.36 x 28.8/8.76.
E Sgl scr, 1 cyl vertical, 1 blr 2 furnaces. 9 kts. By builder.
H Iron 1 dk.
1855 Built for McLean & McLarty & Co., Liverpool. Later Lamont & McLarty. Virtually a sister of *Stromboli* (31) and used on the same services.
1856 Chartered to Cunard for the Mediterranean routes.
1857 Cunard intended to purchase the vessel but found that she was already contracted. They therefore acquired *Damascus* (36), *Italian* was therefore never actually owned by Cunard.
1864 Sold. No further trace.

JACKAL

35 **JACKAL**
B 1853 Glasgow. **T** 185g. **D** 124.3/38.2 x 19.5/5.92 x 9.7/2.95.
E Pad. 2 cyl oscillating, 80 NHP. 1 blr. 2 furnaces. 8 kts.
H Iron. 1 dk. **P** 200 deck with their baggage.
1853 The Cunard tug and tender based at Glasgow. Registered as owned by Burns & MacIver.
1862 Reboilered. **1879** Owned by Cunard. **1888** Based at Liverpool.
189? Hulked. Broken up on the Tranmere shore of the Mersey.

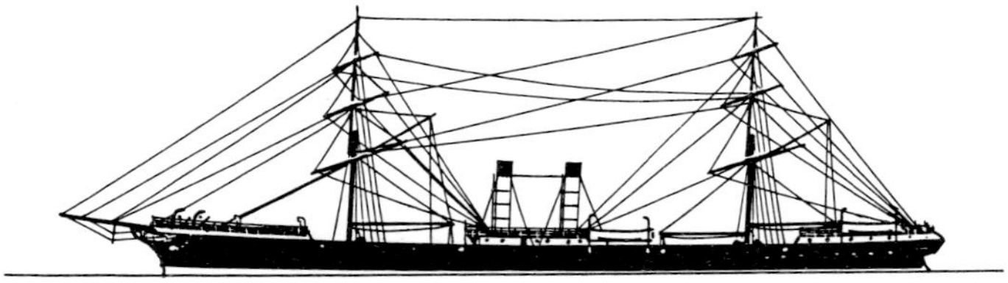

DAMASCUS

36 **DAMASCUS**
B 1856 Wm. Denny & Bros, Dumbarton.**T** 1,214g.
D 253.5/77.27 x 31.2/9.5 x 22.2/6.76.
E Sgl scr, 2 cyl vertical direct acting. 2 blrs, 5 furnaces, 10 kts. Coal 260 tons. By Tulloch & Denny.
H Iron. 2 dks. **P** 30 1st berthed aft. Cargo 670 tons.
1855 Dec 14: Laid down as *St. George* for D. R. MacGregor & Co., Leith. Her sister was *St. Andrew.* Cost £60,000 for the two.

1856 Sept 30: Launched. Acquired during fitting out by Cunard to replace *Italian* (34). Mediterranean services. R/n *Damascus.*
1860 May: Sold to the Italian unification patriot Guiseppe Garibaldi and given his name. Intended to carry his 'Red Shirts' to Sicily. When the scheme fell through the ship reverted to *Damascus.* Oct: Transferred to the Liverpool-New York cargo service but too small for Cunard needs.
1861 Oct 25: Sold to Peter Denny, Chairman of the builders, in part payment for *Morocco* (44).
1862 Apr: Chartered to the Allan Line. April 30 First voyage Glasgow-Quebec-Montreal after the unfreezing of the St. Lawrence.
1865 Acquired by Allan Line; same service with Halifax in the winter.
1870 Rebuilt. Length 288.3/87.87. Compounded by Greenock Foundry Co. 218 NHP, 10 kts. **T** 1,517g. Reduced to one funnel. R/n *Corinthian.* Sept 13: Resumed service to Montreal.
1881 Sold to Italian owners. R/n *Genova.*P. Zenoglio, Genoa.
1883 Became *Giovani Lanza,* Paolo Gaggino, Santa Castagnola.
1885 Renamed *Guiseppe Garibaldi,* Soc. di Assicurazioni 'Italia'. Genoa-S. America.**P** 1512.
1886 Owned by Idarei Massousieh, Constantinople. R/n *Foulazi Osmani.*
1901 R/n *Sakariah* by her owners.
1912 Broken up.
Note Lloyds Register says built as *G. Lanza.* Correct records are as above.

A *PALESTINE,* A *ATLAS*

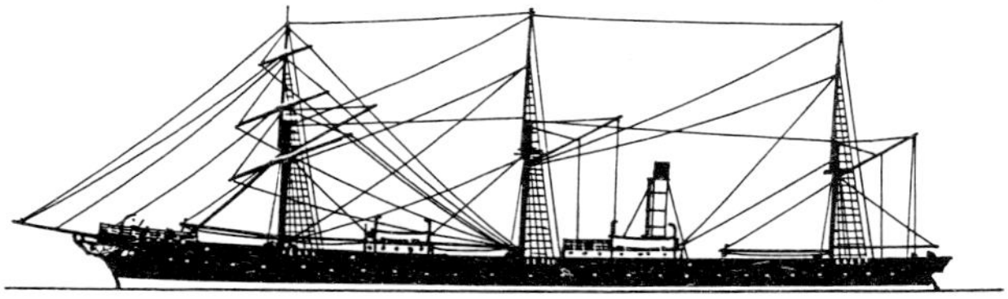

B *PALESTINE*

37 **PALESTINE**
B 1858 Robert Steele & Son, Greenock. **T** 1,800g.
D 276/84.12 oa, 255.2/77.77 x 34.3/10.44 x 24.3/7.39.
E Sgl scr, 2 cyl, oscillating. 232 NHP, 2 blrs, 12 furn, 10 kts. By Napier.
H Iron 2 dks. **P** 32 1st, 280 Steerage. Crew 84.
1858 A class of seven very similar ships were built for the Mediterranean route of the British and Foreign branch of the Cunard concern. *Palestine* was placed on the Boston-Mediterranean route.
1860 London-Boston-New York service. May 16: Chartered for six month tos Allan Line for Liverpool-St. Lawrence route. At the end of the season she served Portland (Maine). Dec: Reverted to Cunard.
1870 Sold to Langlands & Co., Glasgow, for coastal services.
1872 Owned by W. H. Jones, Liverpool. Modernised. Length 352/107.29. Compounded by J. & G. Thomson. 300 NHP, 60 psi, 12 kts. Given three masts, schooner rig. Drawing 37 B.
1873 Chartered to the Dominion Line. Mar 26: Initial sailing Liverpool-Portland.
1876 Chartered to the Warren Line. June 24: Placed on Liverpool-Boston run.
1881 Reboilered. Her owners were now styled as E. S. Jones & Co. Reduced to brig rig.
1896 Broken up.

38 **ATLAS** (Drawing page 34)
As 37 except: **B** 1860 J. & G. Thomson. **T** 1,794g. **E** By builder. Coal: 30 tons per day.
P 69 Cabin (1st), 833 3rd.
1860 Mar 8: Launched. Mediterranean services.
1873 Modernised by builder. **T** 2,393g. Length: 339/103.33. Compounded, 2 cyl direct acting. 300 NHP. 10½ kts. Three masts, barquentine rig. Drawing 38B. May 1: Placed on the Boston route and remained there.
1896 Broken up.

38B *ATLAS*
OLYMPUS

39 **OLYMPUS**
B 1860 J. & G. Thomson, Glasgow. **T** 1,794g.
D 328/99.8 x 36.3/11.05 x 25.7/7.82.
E Sgl scr, 2 cyl oscillating. 350 NHP, 10 kts. By builder.
H Iron. 2dks. **P** 70 Cabin, 900 3rd.
1860 As completed she was very similar to *Palestine* (37) but with two masts.
1863 From the Mediterranean to Liverpool-New York route.
1872 Modernised by builder. **T** 2,415g. Length 340/103.63. Compounded; same speed but, of course, 40% more economic. Given three masts as drawn.
1979 Used as a transport for the first Zulu War.
1881 July 13: Sold to J. & G. Thomson for £2,700 in part payment for *Pavonia.* Resold to A. Galbraith, Glasgow.
1891 Broken up at Manchester.

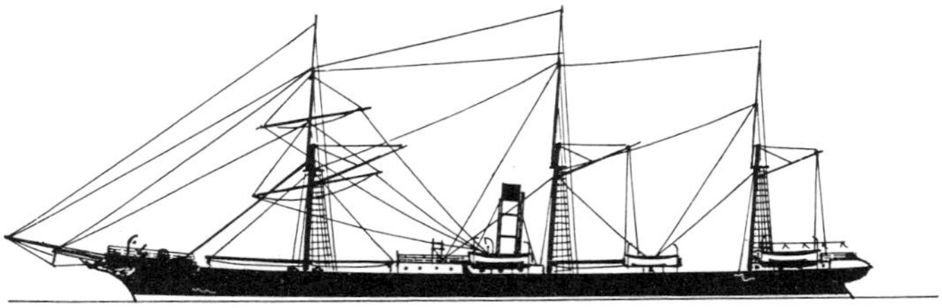

(A) *MARATHON,* (A) *HECLA*

(B) *MARATHON,* (B) *HECLA, KEDAR, SIDON, MOROCCO*

40 **MARATHON**
B 1862 Robert Napier & Sons, Glasgow. **T** 1,784g.
D 274/83.52 x 36.3/11.07 x 25.7/7.82.
E Sgl scr, 2 cyl osc, sgl reduction geared. 650 NHP. 2 blrs 22 psi, 25 rpm. 10 kts. Coal 30 tons per day. By builder.
H Iron 2 dks. **P** 69 Cabin, 850 3rd.
1860 Built for the Mediterranean service. Drawing 40 A.
1866 Jan 8: After one voyage to New York transferred to the Boston service.
1873 Modernised by J. & G. Thomson. Length 336/102.41. Drawing 40 B.
1882 Chartered to the Admiralty for £1.50 per ton for use in the Egyptian Expedition. Thereafter on Mediterranean routes.
1884 Reverted to the North Atlantic.
1892 Sept 8: Final Atlantic voyage. Sold for £2,615 to Workman, Clark, Belfast. Became *Cypria.* Broken up in Italy later in the year.

41 **HECLA**
As *Marathon* except: **T** 1,790g.
1860 Entered service to the Mediterranean but also to be used as an extra seasonal vessel on the Atlantic routes.

1863 June 16: Transferred to the North Atlantic services making 28 sailings.
1871 Modernised by J. & G. Thomson. Length 339/103.33. **T** 2,421g. Compounded.
1872 May 23: Resumed service to Boston. Drawing 41 B.
1881 Taken over by Laird Bros. in part payment for *Cephalonia* (77). Overhauled and sold to Conde de Vilana, Spain. R/n *Conde de Vilana.*
1882 Sold to Gartland y Cia, Buenos Aires. Became *P. A. Gartland* although she is also listed by them as *Claris.*
1892 Renamed *Pedro Tercero;* same owner.
1895 Traded as *Tiempo;* same owner.
1897 Transferred to the Ministry of Marine, Buenos Aires as *Tiempo* then renamed *Rio Negro.* Operated Buenos Aires-Volmaia with passengers and convicts.
1924 In collision with *Highland Loch,* Nelson line, in fog off Buenos Aires.
1954 Broken up after serving some years as a pontoon in the River Plate.

42 **KEDAR**
Marathon class except: **B** 1861 Wm. Denny & Bros. **T** 1,763g, 1,215n.
D 275.5/83.97. **E** By Tulloch & Denny.
1860 Feb 11: Keel laid. Aug. 17: Launched. Oct. 25: Delivered. Cost: Hull £29,985; Machinery £10,801. John Burns wrote to Denny Bros complaining of problems on the delivery voyage. The engine was difficult to start. Twice it jumped out of gear when at sea. And in the Mersey it took an hour to engage astern. Samuel Cunard also disliked the knots in the deck planking; he required 'virgin wood'. However it all seemed to be sorted out. Nov 27: M/v Liverpool-New York. The ship was, in fact, owned by the British and Foreign Line.
1865 Placed on the Mediterranean routes.
1869 Reverted to the New York service.
1873 Compounded by J. Jack Rollo & Co., Liverpool. 212 NHP, 60 psi. 12 kts. At this time her masts were reduced to two as drawn.
1897 Sold for £2,105 to Workman, Clark, Belfast. Broken up in Genoa.

43 **SIDON**
As *Kedar* except: **B** 1861. **T** 1,872g, 799n.
Ordered with *Morocco* (44) as duplicates of *Sidon* for £41,000 each. Burns was to sell Cunard's *Melita* and his own *Leopard* for £21,000 of the amount, Cunard's *Damascus* was to be exchanged for *Morocco* for a sum equivalent to about £11,000.
1861 Aug 20: Launched. Owned by John Burns, John Clelland Burns, Charles MacIver and Sir Samuel Cunard. Described as being 'infinitely superior to *Kedar*'. Placed on her assigned Mediterranean route.
1863 May 19: First sailing on the Liverpool-New York service.
1873 Compounded by J. Jack Rollo, Liverpool. 212 NHP. 12 kts.
1874 Basically a Mediterranean vessel with relief Atlantic work.
1885 Oct 27: Wrecked near Malpica, Spain.

44 **MOROCCO**
Details as *Kedar* except: **B** 1861, **T** 1,855g, 1,193n.
1861 Registered to the same owners as *Sidon.* Spent the whole of her career on the Mediterranean routes.
1874 Compounded by J. Jack Rollo, Liverpool. Masts reduced to two as drawn.
1896 Sold for £2,150 to Workman, Clark, Belfast. Broken up on Merseyside.

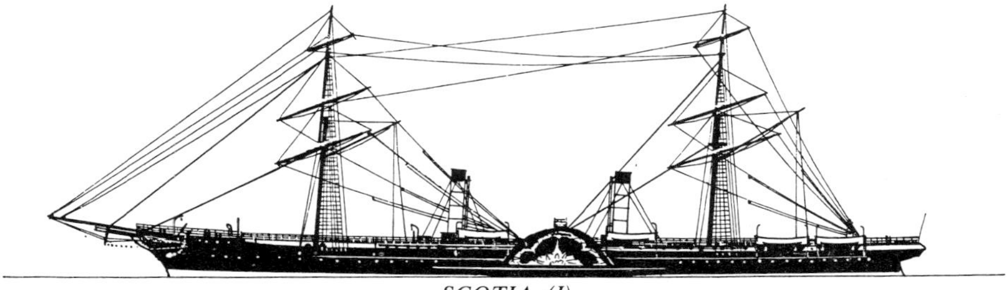

SCOTIA (I)

45 **SCOTIA (I)**
B 1862 Robert Napier & Sons, Glasgow **T** 3,871g, 2,125n, 8,755disp.
D 397/121 oa, bowsprit to taffrail, 379.4/115.62 x 47.8/14.53 x 30.5/9.3.
E Pad. 2 x 2cyl side lever jet condensing; 4,570 IHP, 8 tubular blrs, (4 to each funnel), 40 furnaces; 20

psi, 13½ kts on 140 tons coal per day. Coal: 1,800 tons. By builder Pad diam: 40/12.2 with 25 floats.
H Iron, 2 dks. Cargo 1,050 tons. **P** 275 Cabin, 300 2nd, Crew 440.
1861 June 25: Launched. A near sister to *Persia* (32) but with more beam. The ship was built with three masts but these were reduced to two during fitting out. Except for the *Great Eastern* she was the longest ship afloat; she was also Cunard's last paddle steamer. The company had continued with paddle solely because the Admiralty mail contract so stipulated. On her trials she reached 13½ kts.
1862 May 19: M/v Liverpool-New York; Captain Judkins.
1863-1869 During her career she held the eastbound Blue Riband for five years with a time of 8 days and 3 hours at an average speed of 14.0 kts
1867 Inman's *City of Paris* took the westbound record from her.
1875 Laid up at Liverpool.
1878 Sold to the Telegraph Construction & Maintenance Co. Converted into a cable layer by Laird Bros, Birkenhead. She was re-engined and converted to twin screw. 3 cable tanks fitted. Her career was mainly Atlantic viz: Lizard-Bilbao; Portcurno-Gibraltar but also Aden-Bombay.
1896 Sixty miles off Eddystone an explosion in her cable anti-fouling paint store blew out her bow.
1903 Sold to the Commercial Cable Co. for use as a repair ship in the Pacific. Her main base was Guam.
1904 March 11: Grounded on Spanish Rock, Catalan Bank, Guam enroute for Honolulu and broke her back before salvage could commence.

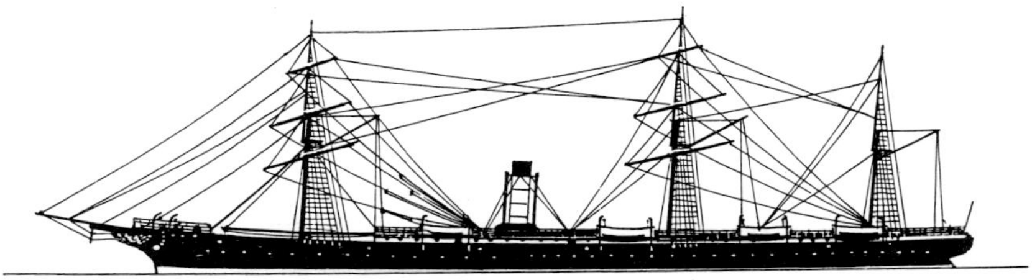

CHINA

46 **CHINA**
B 1862 Robert Napier & Sons, Glasgow. **T** 2,638g.
D 326.2/99.42 x 40.6/12.34 x 27.5/8.38.
E Sgl scr, 2 cyl oscillating, sgl reduction geared: 480 NHP; 4 blrs 24 furnaces using 82 tons coal per day. By builder.
H Iron, 3 dks. F 50/15.24. Cargo 1,050 tons. Coal 1,200 tons.
P 150 1st, 753 3rd.
1861 Oct 10: Launched.
1862 Mar 15: M/v to New York where she connected with the *British Queen* (73) for Nassau.
1872 Sept 21: Outbound from Queenstown her cylinder block and bedplate cracked. Put back into Liverpool and sent for compounding.
1873 Jan: The work was carried out by Barclay, Curle & Co, Glasgow.
1874 Apr 7: Resumed on her New York route.
1879 Used as a Zulu War troop transport.
1880 Sold to Spain. R/n *Magallanes;* owned by the Marques de Campo, Cartagena. Spanish ports to South America.
1889 Sold to Norway; converted into a 4-masted barque. R/n *Theodore.*
1906 March 2: Left Tampa, Florida, for Japan and went missing.

47 **ALPHA**
B 1863 Barclay, Curle & Co, Glasgow. **T** 653g.
D 221.8/67.6 x 27.6/8.41 x 14.9/4.54.
E Sgl scr, 2 cyl oscillating direct drive. By builder. **H** Iron. 1 dk + Poop. **P** 25 1st 150 3rd.
1863 Registered in the name of William Cunard, 68 Cromwell Rd, London (he was the younger of Samuel's two sons) and used on the Halifax-New York-Bermuda feeder service. These services were not a success and were gradually phased out.
1869 Sold to R. Pickford & W.A. Black, Glasgow; operated by the Halifax & West India SS.Co.
1880 Re-engined by J. & G. Thomson.
1894 Owned by S. Barber, Vancouver for Vancouver Island trading.
1900 Wrecked British Columbia.

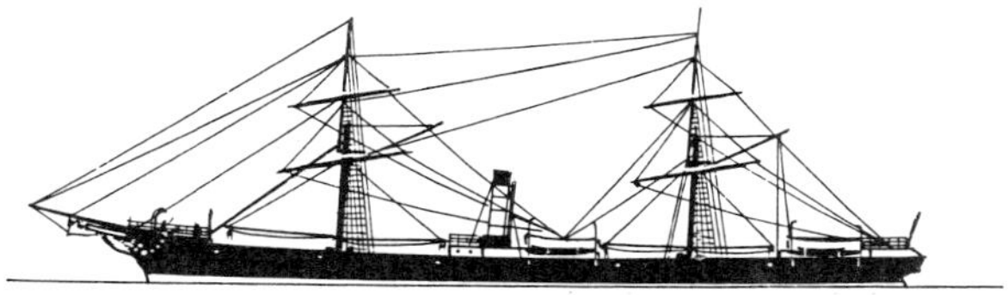

CORSICA

48 **CORSICA**
B 1863 J. & G. Thomson & Co, Glasgow. **T** 1,134g, 681n.
D 224/68.28 x 32.1/9.8 x 24/7.32.
E Sgl scr, 2 cyl geared oscillating, 182 NHP, 2 blrs, 8 furn. 10 kts. By builder.
H Iron 1 dk. **P** 1st, berthed aft.
1863 Built for the Mediterranean services to Italy, Sardinia and Corsica.
1868 Found to be too small. Sold to Royal Mail S.P. Co. to replace their *Wye* which had been overwhelmed in the great hurricane at St. Thomas.
1877 Sold to R. Foll, Junior for West Indies trading.
1879 Compounded by Wallsend S.B. & E. Co, Wallsend.
1888 Out of register.

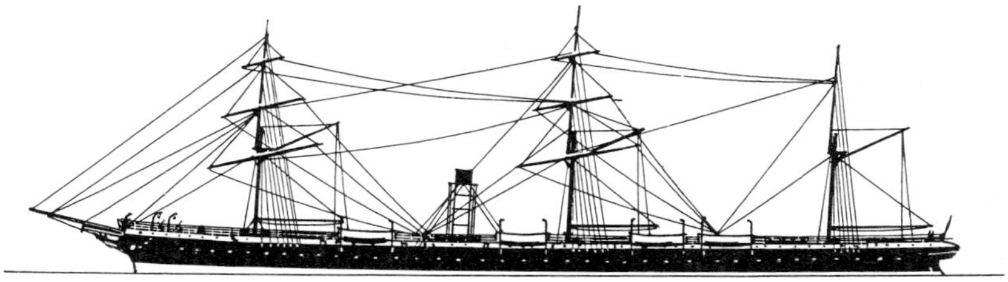

CUBA JAVA

49 **CUBA**
B 1864 Tod & McGregor, Glasgow. **T** 2,832g, 1,534n.
D 338.2/103.1 oa, 325/99.67 x 42.3/12.9 x 27.5/8.38.
E Sgl scr, 2 cyl geared oscillating with surface condensers; 650 NHP; 4 blrs, 24 furn; 12½ kts. By builder.
H Iron. 2 dks. F 60/18.29. Cargo 1,230 tons. Coal 1,100 tons.
P 300 1st (with one meal sitting in the saloon). 1,500 troops.
1864 July 21: Launched. Cost £110,000.
1864 Dec 3: M/v to New York. Captain J. Stone.
1866 Served Boston for two seasons then reverted to New York.
1876 Sold to D. Brown & Sons, London. Converted into the 4-masted sailing ship *Earl of Beaconsfield.*
1887 Nov 6: Wrecked near to Withernsea enroute Calcutta-Hull with jute.

50 **JAVA**
Details as *Cuba* except: **B** 1865 J. & G. Thomson & Co, Glasgow. **T** 2,969g, 1,761n.
D 337.1/102.75 oa. **E** Inverted direct action; 540 NHP.
1865 June 24: Launched; she was the builder's first designed transatlantic liner. Both vessels had Cunningham's patent topsails. Oct 2:1 M/v Liverpool-New York. Acquired the nickname 'The Jumping Java'.
1877 Compounded and reboilered by Fawcett, Preston & Co, Liverpool. Oct 20: Chartered to the Warren Line for their Portland, Maine service.
1878 Apr 30: Sold through Richardson, Spence & Co to the Red Star Line. Made her first sailing for them as *Java* then r/n *Zeeland.* Antwerp-New York run.
1889 March: Sold and converted into a sailing barque. R/n *Electrique,* French flag.
1892 Became *Lord Spencer.*
1895 Apr 9: Left San Francisco for Queenstown via the Horn. Missing at sea.

ALEPPO, TARIFA, MALTA

51 **ALEPPO**
B 1865 J. & G. Thomson & Co, Glasgow. **T** 2,057g, 1,399n.
D 292.5/89.15 x 38.2/11.63 x 26.2/7.98
E Sgl scr, 2 cyl oscillating, 280 NHP, 25 psi, 10 kts on 48 tons coal per day. By builder.
H Iron. 1 dk. Fcsle and bridge. **P** 46 Cabin, 593 3rd.
1864 Nov 1: Launched, for the Mediterranean routes.
1865 Feb: Delivered. Sept 15: Placed on the North Atlantic Liverpool-Halifax-New York. Continued on the route or to Boston for 40 more voyages.
1872 Reverted to the Med. service.
1879 Compounded and rebuilt by J. Jack & Co. Liverpool. Direct acting surface condensing type. 212 NHP; 60 psi. Coal 35 tons per day. Continued on Mediterranean routes.
1890 Tpl exp fitted. 212 NHP and still 60 psi but on 18 tons per day and with Howden's forced draught system. The saving in coal from simple to triple expansion is graphically demonstrated by this ship.
1890 Supplementary North Atlantic sailings.
1909 Sold to Thos W. Ward for £4,000 and scrapped at Preston.

52 **TARIFA**
Sister to *Aleppo* except: **T** 2,058g, 1,400n.
1865 Jan 12: Launched; a Mediterranean vessel. July 22: M/v to New York to cater for the boom conditions on the Atlantic. Cunard (British & Foreign) chartered ships to fill the gaps caused by using these excellent sisters on the Atlantic for which they were satisfactory on secondary sailings.
1872 Placed on the Mediterranean routes where she was to remain for the remainder of her career.
1879 Compounded by J. Jack & Co, Liverpool
1898 Sold for breaking up in Italy.

53 **MALTA**
As *Aleppo* except: **B** 1866. **T** 2,132g, 1,450n. **D** 303.1/92.38 x 39.3/11.96.
1865 Oct 19: Launched.
1866 Feb 20: M/v Liverpool-New York. She then continued on this route or to Boston for seven years taking the Intermediate Service on Tuesdays.
1873 Transferred to the Mediterranean routes from Liverpool.
1879 Compounded by J. Jack & Co, Liverpool.
1881 July 6: Reverted to the New York run.
1883-1889 Mediterranean sailings.
1889 Oct 15: Wrecked off Cape Cornwall, the only cape in England, Cornwall. All saved.

TRIPOLI

54 **TRIPOLI**
B 1864 as the forerunner of the *Aleppo* class with the same details except **T** 2,146g, 1,271n. **P** 46 Cabin, 250 3rd.
1863 Aug 15: Launched for Mediterranean service.
1865 Aug 19: Transferred to the New York route with some sailings to Boston.
1872 May 17: Wrecked on Tuskar Rock, southern coast of Ireland during her 50th voyage.

PALMYRA

55 **PALMYRA**
B 1866 Caird & Co, Greenock. **T** 2,044g, 1,390n.
D 290.7/88.6 x 38/11.58 x 26.1/7.96.
E sgl scr, 2 cyl oscillating. 260 NHP 23 psi: 10 kts. By builder.
H Iron 1 dk. **P** 46 Cabin, 656 3rd (Steerage).
1865 Dec 23: Launched; a sister to *Tripoli* except for the engine room lay out which combined the donkey boiler uptake with the main boiler trunking so that the funnel was forward of the boiler room.
1866 Apr 25: M/v to New York.
1873 Placed on the Constantinople and Levant service.
1878 Compounded and reboilered by J. Jack, Rollo & Co, Liverpool in the year before that company split into two concerns, 212 NHP; 10 kts.
1879 Feb: Resumed her Mediterranean trading.
1880-1881 Employed as a transport to the Zulu war.
1882 Chartered for 22s 6d per ton per month for the Egyptian campaign.
1896 Nov: Sold for £2,600 and broken up in the following year.

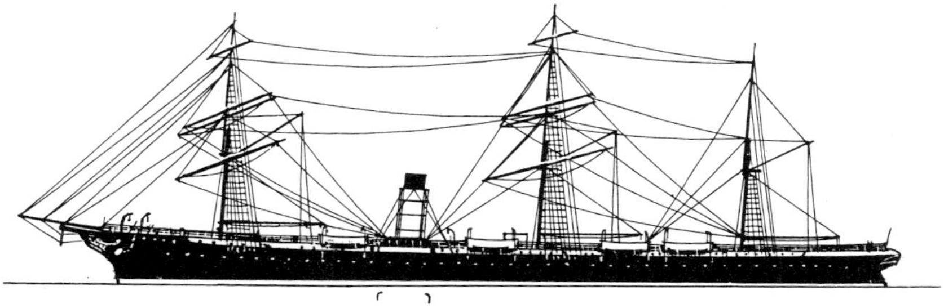

RUSSIA

56 **RUSSIA**
B 1867 J. & G. Thomson & Co, Glasgow. **T** 2,960g, 1,710n.
D 358/109.12 x 43/13.11 x 27.7/8.43.
E Sgl scr, 2 cyl inverted. 600 NHP, 4 blrs, 24 furnaces; 25 psi; 13 kts on 90 tons coal per day. By builder.
H Iron, 2 dks. Cargo 1,260 tons. Coal 1,180 tons.
P Initially 430 Saloon; no steerage. Later 235 Saloon.
1867 March 20: Launched. The last British & American ship with a clipper stem. Ordered to partner *Scotia* (45). Her nickname was the 'Rolling Russia'. June 15: M/v to New York. She remained on the route and held the eastbound record with 8 days 28 minutes averaging 14.2 kts. She never held the westbound Blue Riband.
1878 Nov 2: Left on her final Cunard sailing to New York.
1880 Sold to the Red Star Line who completely rebuilt her. **T** 4,752g, 3,736n. Length 435/132.59. Compounded by builders and given four masts. Emerged as *Waesland.* P 120 1st, 1,500 3rd. Dec 6: Entered Antwerp-New York route.
1889 Back to her builders for triple expansion by the addition of a high pressure cylinder (which needed a longer stroke). New boilers at 160 psi installed. Speed increased to 15 kts. The work took only six weeks. **P** 235 Saloon.
1895 Chartered to the American Line. Sept 11: Philadelphia-Liverpool.
1902 Mar 2: Mar 7: Sunk in fog off Holyhead in collision with Houston's *Harmonides.* 2 lost. Fifty three were taken aboard *Harmonides* and landed at Liverpool.

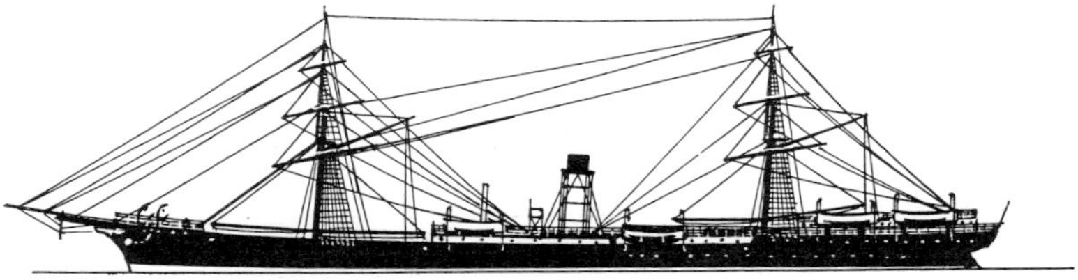

SIBERIA

57 **SIBERIA**
B 1867 J. & G. Thomson & Co. **T** 2,498g, 1,698n.
D 320/97.54 x 39.2/11.94 x 26.2/7.1.
E Sgl scr, 2 cyl inverted direct action; 280 NHP, 2 rectangular tubular blrs, 14 furnaces; 25 psi. 13 kts. By builder. **H** Iron 2 dks. **P** 124 1st, 800 3rd.
1866 Laid down as *Sumatra;* renamed either to prevent confusion with the P. & O. steamer of the same name or because of the 'ia' ending now being company policy for the Atlantic ships. Both reasons are recorded.
1867 July 2: Launched. Sept 24: M/v to New York.
1879 Mar 26: Made her last sailing to Boston having been displaced by *Gallia* (71).
1880 Sold for £15,000 to the Marques de Campo, Cartegena; r/n *Manila* for services to the Spanish colonies.
1881 May 11; Wrecked at San Juan, Puerto Rico.

SAMARIA (I)

58 **SAMARIA (I)**
Details as *Siberia* except: **B** 1868, **T** 2,500g, 1,695n. Length: 320.5/97.69.
1868 July 4: Launched. Sept 29: M/v to New York.
1878 Compounded by J. Jack, Rollo & Co, Liverpool.
1880 Reduced to 40 Saloon. Became the reserve steamer and used on most routes during overhaul or marine damage across the fleet.
1896 Jan 30: Made her final sailing to Boston. Laid up at Liverpool.
1902 Sold for £5,000 and broken up at Genoa.

ABYSSINIA, ALGERIA, PARTHIA (I)

59 **ABYSSINIA**
B 1870 J. & G. Thomson. **T** 3,376g, 2,159n.
D 367.5/112 x 42.2/12.85 x 34.5/10.52.
E Sgl scr, 2 cyl inverted, 500 NHP; 4 blrs, 24 furnaces, 60 psi; 12½ kts on 90 tons coal per day. By builder.
H Iron. 2 dks + spar dk. Cargo 1,600 tons. Coal 1,190 tons.
P 200 1st, 1,050 3rd. Cargo 1,600 tons. Coal 1,190 tons.

1870 March 3: Launched. The first Cunarders with bathrooms; one port, one starboard. Even so they were inferior to the White Star and Inman ships of the day. May 24 M/v Liverpool-New York.
1871 Outmoded by the arrival of White Star's *Oceanic* class.
1880 Jan: Taken by the builder in part payment for *Servia* (79) and *Catalonia* (75). Re-sold to Guion Line to replace their lost *Montana.* Nov 20: First sailing for them Liverpool-New York.
1882 Compounded by J. Jones & Sons, Liverpool.
1885 Owned by Sir William Pearce, the proprietor of the Guion Line.
1887 Feb 11: Employed on the Canadian Pacific Railway Co's route Vancouver-Yokohama-Shanghai-Hong Kong. The three vessels used were not chartered but on an 'all available business' basis *(Batavia* (62) and *Parthia* (61) were the other two). The deal was to last until their own ships were built.
1891 Nov 28: Returned to New York to re-enter service with the Guion Line.
Dec 18: Abandoned on fire five days out from New York en route Liverpool. Her passengers and crew were rescued by Norddeutscher Lloyd's *Spree.*

60 **ALGERIA**
As *Abyssinia* except: **T** 3,428g, 2,193n. Funnel 10/3.04 taller.
1870 Sept 27: M/v to New York.
1881 Oct 22: Final Cunard sailing to New York. Sold there to the Red Star Line. R/n *Pennland.*
1882 Compounded by J. Jack & Co, Liverpool. 432 NHP. 80 psi. 12 kts. May 13: Entered the Antwerp-New York service.
1888 Spar deck fitted. **T** 3,760g. **P** 200 1st, 1050 3rd.
1895 Chartered to the American Line. May 18: First voyage Philadelphia-Liverpool.
1901 May 4: Transferred to the Antwerp-New York route. During her winter overhaul she was reduced to 3rd class only.
1903 Dec: Sold and scrapped in Italy.

61 **PARTHIA (I)**
A smaller sister to *Abyssinia.* **B** 1870 Wm Denny & Bros, Dumbarton.
T 3,167g, 2,035n, 3,140dwt. **D** 360.5/109.89 x 40.3/12.29.
E Compound inverted, 480 NHP, 1,750 IHP. By builder. She steamed on 40 tons per day instead of 90 and required only half the bunker space. **H** 4 dks. Cargo 3,139 tons. Coal 881 tons.
1870 Feb 2: Keel laid. Sept 10: Launched. Registered in the names of John Burns, John Clelland Burns and Charles MacIver. Cost £94,970. During these negotiations Denny offered *Nemisis* for £4,000 of the sum. Note: *Parthia's* funnel was thinner and closer to the mainmast. Dec 17: M/v to New York.
1874 When leaving New York steaming parallel to White Star's *Adriatic* the two came too close to each other and the venturi effect pulled the ships together but without serious damage.
1880 March: Took in tow the waterlogged barque *Mary A. Marshall* but the vessel sank next day. Nov: Rescued the crew of the foundering barque *James Edwards.*
1881 Carried troops to Alexandria for the relief of Khartoum.
1883 Nov: Laid up at Liverpool at the end of her 119th round voyage.
1884 Taken, with *Batavia,* by John Elder & Co in part payment for *Umbria* (81) and *Etruria* (82). Triple expansion fitted.
1887 Sir William Pearce, Elder's owner, allocated her to the Canadian Pacific Railway's Transpacific route.
1891 Aug 20: Final C.P.R. sailing. The ship was modernised; 2 masts.
1892 R/n *Victoria,* Guion Line. Transferred to the Tacoma-Hong Kong service of the Northern Pacific SS. Co. British Flag.
1898 Oct: Entered service with the U.S. flag Northern American Mail S.S. Co. Same route. She also trooped to Manila.
1901 Oct: Reverted to Northern Pacific ownership. British flag.
1904 Owned by the Northwestern S.S. Co; Alaska run.
1908 Feb. Northwestern's fleet of 12 ships was merged with the Alaska S.S. Co. San Francisco-Seattle-Nome, Alaska.
1910 *Victoria* survived a stranding on Hinchinbrook Island.
1924 Overhauled and fitted for oil fuel.
1933 Bottom damage from grounding in fog at St Michael, B.C.
1935 Laid up at Lake Union for three years due to the cost of meeting new U.S. fire and safety precautions.
1940 Reduced to cargo only.
1941-47 Operated by the U.S. War Administration for 46 Alaska cargo runs.
1952 She was laid up at Lake Washington owned by Dulien Steel Products.

The hull was still sound but her hatchways were too small to take containers.
1954 Purchased by Straits Towing & Salvage Co. Converted into a log carrying barge. R/n *Straits No. 27.*
1956 Sold to Japanese breakers. R/n *Straits Maru* and towed by *Sudbury* to Osaka. Oct 16: Arrived. 86 years old.

BATAVIA

62 **BATAVIA**
B 1870 Wm Denny & Bros, Dumbarton. **T** 2,593g, 1,828n.
D 327.3/99.77 x 39.3/11.96 x 28.4/8.66.
E Sgl scr, comp inv direct acting, surface condensers, 1,800 IHP; 60 psi. 2 blrs, 12 furnaces. 12 kts on 40 tons per day. By builder.
H Iron, 4 dks. Cargo 2,650 tons. Coal 655 tons.
P 54 1st, 51 2nd, 624 3rd.
1870 Feb 1: Launched having been purchased on the stocks. She was Denny's first compound engine building. Same owners as *Parthia.* Mar 29: Ready except for her boilers which delayed her for six weeks, P. & O's *Nemesis,* now owned by Peter Denny, was loaned for £5,000 until the delivery of *Batavia.* She was virtually a sister to *Siberia* (57). May 10: M/v Liverpool-New York. On the inbound leg her bowsprit carried away.
1880 Feb: Made one voyage Liverpool to Bombay for P. & O. Cunard actually wanted to test the route. Nothing came of the idea.
1883 Chartered to John Inman for one New York round sailing.
1884 Feb 2: Her final Cunard sailing before being taken over by John Elder & Co. in part payment for *Umbria* (81) and *Etruria* (82), Tpl exp. fitted and new blrs. Placed on Guion Line service.
1885 Operated the C.P.R's Transpacific route with *Abyssinia* and *Parthia.*
1893 Returned to Guion Line service as *Tacoma.*
1898 Sold to the North American Mail S.S. Co. Tacoma-Hong Kong route alongside of *Victoria* ex-*Parthia* (61).
1901 Owned by the Northwestern S.S. Co. Same service.
1904 Her owners became the North Western Commercial S.S. Co.
1905 Feb 4: During the Russo-Japanese war she sailed Tacoma-Vladivostok with relief food for Russia. March 15: Captured in an ice field of Hokkaido, became *Sheikotan Maru* (later *Shikotan Maru)*, R. Yamshina, Uraga.
1924 Oct 23: Stranded 60 miles from Shanghai, at Shaiweishan, inbound from Tsingtao. She was then Chinese owned but no owner is given in Lloyds. Salvaged and towed to Shanghai but condemned and scrapped there.

TRINIDAD, DEMERARA

63 **TRINIDAD**
B 1872 J. & G. Thomson & Co, Glasgow. **T** 1,900g, 1,230n.
D 307.5/93.73 x 34.1/10.39 x 24.5/7.47.
E Sgl scr, 2 cyl comp inv; 300 NHP; 2 blrs, 8 furn. 10½ kts on 22 tons per day. By builder. **H** Iron. 2 dks. Brig rig. Cargo 2,150 tons. Coal 400 tons. **P** 46 1st.
1872 Built for the new service Glasgow-West Indies. Placed initially on the Mediterranean routes for one year.
1873 Inaugurated the West Indies route which did not prove to be a venture which demanded the building up of a substantial fleet.

1880 Became a general steamer and served on most routes; cargo only.
1898 Sold for £3,985 to German owners.
Sept: Foundered in the China Sea.

64 **DEMERARA**
As *Trinidad* except: **T** 1,904g, 1,230n.
1872 Built for the same service as *Trinidad.* Served initially to the Med.
1873 West Indies service.
1880 Transferred to general cargo only duties.
1887 Dec 25: Left Liverpool for Gibraltar and disappeared.
Note. A third vessel, *Barbados,* was never delivered.

65 **BETA**
B 1873 Aitken & Mansel, Glasgow. **T** 1,070g, 677n.
D 235.1/71.66 x 28.5/8.69 x 14.6/4.44.
E Sgl scr, 2 cyl comp inv.; 160 NHP; 10 kts. By builder.
H Steel. 2 dks + spar dk, 3 masts.
1873 Nov: Delivered for the Halifax-Boston or winter New York-Bermuda feeder services. Owned by William Cunard, Sir Samuel's younger son. Registered office at 48 Cromwell Road, London where he lived.
1889 Sold to the Halifax & West India SS Co, Glasgow. Owned by W. A. Black with Pickford & Black as managers. Operated Halifax-West Indies. Her port of registry was later moved to Halifax. See *Alpha* (47).
1906 Broken up in Canada.
Note: This is actually Cunard's first steel hulled ship but this is never claimed by them for her.

NANTES, BREST

66 **NANTES**
B 1874 Blackwood & Gordon, Port Glasgow. **T** 1,473g, 949n.
D 238.3/72.62 x 32.2/9.8 x 26.5/8.08.
E Sgl scr, 2 cyl comp inv direct action, 160 NHP; 2 blrs, 6 furn, 65 psi; 10 kts on 15 tons per day. By builder.
H Iron. 1 dk. 3 masts; barque rig. Cargo 2,000 tons. Coal 240 tons. **P** 8 1st, 386 3rd.
1874 Liverpool-French Manche ports. These two vessels acted as emigrant feeder ships to connect with the Liverpool mail steamers. The French Line services to New York catered only for the French whereas there were many central Europeans wishing to emigrate.
1886 Nov 6: Lost 36 miles south east of the Lizard, en route Liverpool-Le Havre, after colliding with the *Theodore Ruger.* Three of the crew of *Nantes* jumped onto the sailing ship and when she too sank were landed with her 14 survivors. The remainder of the crew of the *Nantes* stayed with her. At 10.00 next day she suddenly sank and all but one were dragged down with her.

67 **BREST**
As *Nantes* except: **T** 1,472g, 949n.
1874 Built for the same services as her sister.
1879 Sept: Wrecked off Hot Point, Cornwall, in thick fog, en route to Le Havre.

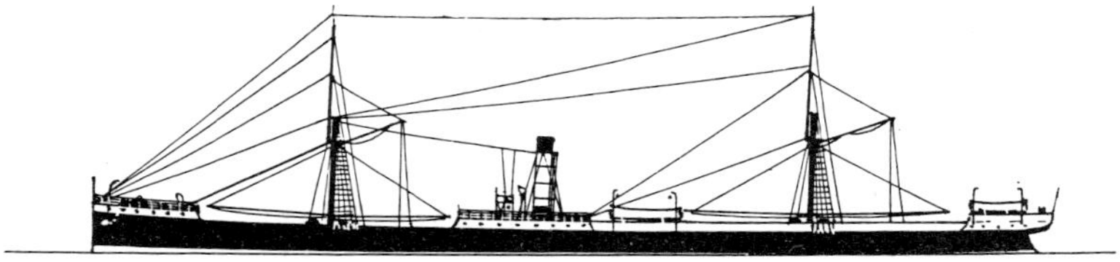

SARAGOSSA

68 **SARAGOSSA**
B 1874 J. & G. Thomson & Co, Glasgow. **T** 2,263g, 1,430n.
D 316.3/96.39 x 35.3/10.74 x 17.6/5.36.

E Sgl scr, 2 cyl comp direct acting; 300 NHP; 2 blrs, 12 furn, 70 psi; 11 kts on 26 tons per day. By builder.
H Iron. 1 dk. Cargo 2,500 tons. Coal 572 tons. **P** 74 1st, 548 3rd. Crew 34.
1874 May 5: Launched for the West Indies service. July 23: M/v to Boston. Remained on the route for three months and then switched to the Mediterranean. She remained on this service for the remainder of her career and never served the West Indies.
1909 Sold for £400 to Thos. W. Ward and broken up at Preston.

BOTHNIA (I), SCYTHIA (I), GALLIA

69 **BOTHNIA (I)**
B 1874 J. & G. Thomson & Co, Glasgow. **T** 4,535g, 2,923n.
D 422.3/128.7 x 42.2/12.85 x 34.5/10.52.
E Sgl scr, 2 cyl comp inv. surface condensers; 600 NHP; 8 blrs, 24 furnaces, 65 psi; 12½ kts at 50 rpm and on 75 tons per day. By builder.
H Iron, 2 dks + spar dk. Cargo 1,692 tons. Coal 1,016 tons.
P 200 1st, 1,100 3rd. Crew 150.
1874 Mar 4: Launched. These three ships were enlarged *Abyssinia* (59) class and with updated contemporary improvements. Her mizzen mast was of wood to avoid compass distortion. Aug 8: M/v to New York.
1885 Transferred to the Boston route. She also made a number of Naples-New York journeys.
1898 Sold; initially for further trading but then to breakers in Italy.
1899 Scrapped.

70 **SCYTHIA (I)**
Details as *Bothnia* except: **T** 4,557g, 2,907n. Length 420.7/128.22.
1874 Oct 28: Launched.
1875 May 1: M/v Saturday being the Mail service sailing day, to New York. July: After breaking a propeller blade when she struck a whale off Queenstown the ship had to put back into Liverpool for a new screw.
1884 July 9: With the advent of *Oregon* (78) she was placed on the Boston service. Remained predominantly on this route.
1898 Sept 20: Final Voyage Liverpool-New York.
1899 Broken up in Italy.

71 **GALLIA**
As *Bothnia* except: **B** 1879. **T** 4,809g, 3,801n. **D** 430.1/131.1 x 44.5/13.56.
E More powerful; 110 tons per day. **P** 300 1st, 1,200 3rd.
1878 Nov 12: Launched. Slightly larger than her sisters with more beam but still, despite the competition, an 'Old style' vessel. She was also the last ship built for the British & North American Royal Mail Steam Packet Co. before it officially became Cunard.
1879 Apr 5: M/v Liverpool-New York.
1886 Switched to the Boston route. She was by now greatly outclassed by new ships entering service.
1889 Placed on the Tuesday intermediate service to New York.
1895 When her propeller shaft snapped she was towed to Liverpool by the steamer *River Afton*. J. Little & Co.
1896 Chartered to Cia Trasatlantica for trooping to Cuba. R/n *Don Alvado de Bazan*.
1897 Oct 7: Made her final Boston voyage and then sold for £21,250 to D. & C. MacIver for operation by their Beaver Line of Associated Steamers. Nov 20: First Beaver sailing to Halifax and St Johns, New Brunswick. She was on the route for only four months.
1898 Transferred with the rest of the fleet to Elder Dempster but not used by them.
1900 Sold to the Allan Line, May 5: Left on her first sailing for them to Quebec and Montreal. May 18: Aground near to Sorel Point, Quebec. Salvaged and returned to Liverpool without passengers. Condemned and scrapped at Cherbourg.

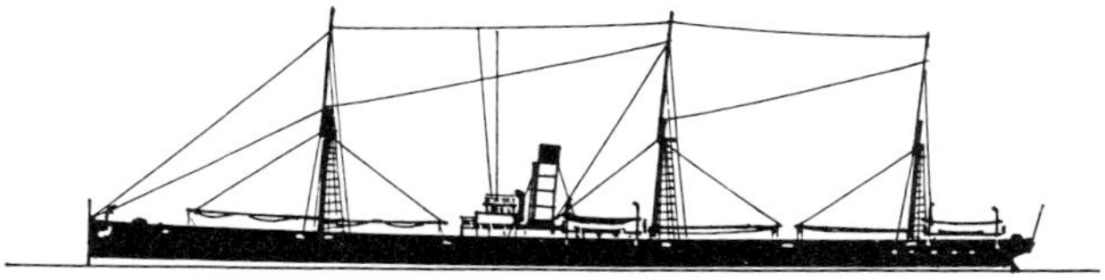

CHERBOURG

72 **CHERBOURG**
B 1875 J. & G. Thomson & Co, Glasgow. **T** 1,614g, 1,038n.
D 251.2/76.56 x 32.3/9.86 x 26.5/8.08.
E Sgl scr, 2 cyl comp vertical direct acting. 155 NHP; 2 blrs, 6 furn. 60 psi; 10 kts on 16 tons per day. By builder. **H** Iron 1 dk. cargo 2,121 tons. Coal 215 tons. **P** 4.
1875 Nov: Completed for short sea voyages to the French and Mediterranean ports; note her small bunker space and larger cargo capacity. Cost £30,886.
1900 Mizzen mast removed and a small lifeboat added abreast funnel. Rijeka Maritime Museum has an oil painting of her with the name altered to *Cherso*.
1909 Sold for £3,000 to Thos. W. Ward and broken up.

BRITISH QUEEN

73 **BRITISH QUEEN**
B 1849 Wm. Denny & Bros, Dumbarton, Yard No. 18. **T** 773g, 645n.
D 195/59.43 x 29.2/8.89 x 18/5.49
E Sgl scr, 1 cyl geared vertical direct acting; 140 NHP; 1 blr, 6 furn, 18 psi. 10 kts. By Caird & Co, Glasgow. **H** Iron. 2 dks. **P** 71 Saloon, 166 Steerage.
1849 Feb 12: Ordered by Brownlow, Pearson & Co, Hull.
1849 May 26: Completed for the Mediterranean trade. Cost 14,000.
1851 Operated by Charles MacIver & Co. The firm later became Burns & MacIver. The ship traded in conjunction with *Margaret* (8) and *Shamrock* (20).
1855 Transferred to the ownership of the British & Foreign S.N. Co on its formation.
1878 Owned by Cunard S.S. Co. She had been in their colours for years (but without the thin black bands because the Burns & MacIver funnel was also red). However until now had only traded within their fleet. Compounded by James Jack & Co, Liverpool. Placed on the Le Havre service with Nantes and Brest.
1898 Broken up after 49 years of unblemished service.

OTTER

74 **OTTER**
B 1880 Blackwood & Gordon, Port Glasgow. **T** 287g, 270n. **D** 142.2/43.3 x 23.2/7.06 x 10.2/3.1.
E Sgl scr, 2 cyl comp; 40 RHP; 9 kts. By builder.
H Iron. 1 dk.
1880 Water & Baggage tender at Liverpool. She worked in conjunction with *Skirmisher* (83) and can be seen alongside many Cunarders in early photographs. Originally had two steam deck cranes but later one with a midmast boom derrick.
1920 Sold to R. H. Rea & Co, Liverpool. Water barge.
1922 Sold to H. J. Cooper as a sand hopper. The firm was later renamed W. Cooper & Sons, Liverpool.
1963 Broken up at Garston 83 years old.

CATALONIA

75 **CATALONIA**
B 1881 J. & G. Thomson & Co, Glasgow. **T** 4,638g, 3,093n.
D 429.5/130.91 x 43/13.11 x 33.7/10.26.
E Sgl scr, 2 cyl comp inv direct acting. 500 NHP; 2 blrs 12 furn, 78 psi; 12 kts on 70 tons per day.
H Iron. 2 dks. Cargo 2,870 tons. Coal 975 tons.
P 308 1st in 85 staterooms, 680 3rd. Crew 118.
1881 May 14: Launched. The first of three ships intended for Boston, *Pavonia* and *Cephalonia* being the others. Aug 6: M/v Liverpool-New York.
1883 Apr 18: Transferred to the Boston service.
1895 June 12: Became the first steamer to berth alongside the new Princes Landing Stage inbound. *Germanic* (White Star) joined her to become the first to embark there. Until now the ships had embarked passengers in mid-river from tenders.
1899-1900 Chartered as a troopship for the Boer War at the rate of 15 shillings per ton per month.
1901 Sold for £10,305 to Thos W. Ward for demolition.

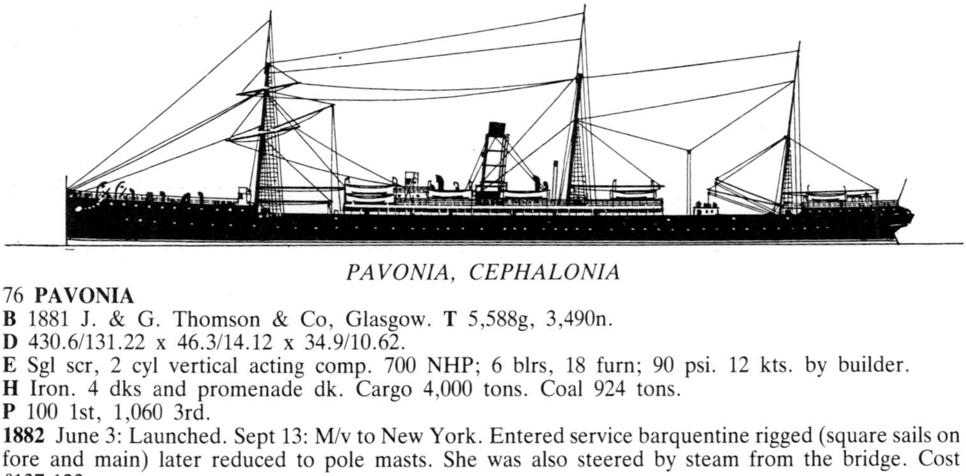

PAVONIA, CEPHALONIA

76 **PAVONIA**
B 1881 J. & G. Thomson & Co, Glasgow. **T** 5,588g, 3,490n.
D 430.6/131.22 x 46.3/14.12 x 34.9/10.62.
E Sgl scr, 2 cyl vertical acting comp. 700 NHP; 6 blrs, 18 furn; 90 psi. 12 kts. by builder.
H Iron. 4 dks and promenade dk. Cargo 4,000 tons. Coal 924 tons.
P 100 1st, 1,060 3rd.
1882 June 3: Launched. Sept 13: M/v to New York. Entered service barquentine rigged (square sails on fore and main) later reduced to pole masts. She was also steered by steam from the bridge. Cost £137,123.
1884 Apr 23: Transferred to Boston service being the last of the three for the route.
1892 Jan 19: Towed into Boston by Hamburg America's *Rhaetia* after her shaft had snapped off New England.
1899 Feb 18: In heavy weather her boilers were unseated and she put into the Azores. Towed to Liverpool for repairs. Aug 28: Made her final Transatlantic voyage to Boston. Up for disposal but in October the Boer War had begun and she was taken up for two trooping sailings.
1900 Sold for £13,250 to Thos. W. Ward and broken up.

77 **CEPHALONIA**
Details as *Pavonia* except: **B** Laird Bros, Birkenhead. **T** 5,606g, 3,515n.
1881 May 1: Keel laid in dry dock there being no slip long enough to take her. She was then the largest ship yet built on Merseyside.
1882 May 20; Launched. Aug 12: Trials off Anglesey. Cost £141,671. Aug 23: M/v Liverpool-Boston; her intended route.
1889 Sept 12: Her final Cunard sailing. Taken up as a Boer War transport. Made six voyages.

1900 Sold to the Eastern Railway Company, Shanghai for services in the Yellow Sea. R/n *Hai Lor* (sometimes spelled *Hailor)*
1904 Feb 8: The battle of Port Arthur was a pre-emptive strike (like Pearl Harbour) by the Japanese and started the Russo-Japanese war. After the battle a number of ships were sunk at Port Arthur as block ships: *Hai Lor* was one of these.

OREGON

78 **OREGON**
B 1883 John Elder & Co, Fairfield, Glasgow. **T** 7,017g, 3,529n.
D 520/158.5 oa, 501/152.7 x 54.2/16.51 x 36/10.97.
E Sgl scr, 3 cyls, 1 HP between 2 LP; 3,000 IHP, 9 blrs, 72 furn, 110 psi, 18½ kts on 268 tons per day at 64 rpm. 20 kts. by builder.
H Iron, 4 dks. 10 watertight compartments. Cargo 2,427 tons. Coal 2,357 tons.
P 472 Saloon in 155 staterooms, 1,000 3rd. Crew 255.
1883 June 23: Launched. Sept: Trials; averaged 20 kts. Designed by the Guion Line to be the finest ship on the Atlantic. Her delivery voyage to Liverpool was used as a shakedown cruise. Oct 7: M/v Liverpool-New York.
1884 Jan: Docked at Liverpool being too expensive to operate during the winter. June: After only four voyages for Guion the company were unable to keep up their payments to the builder who repossessed her. Cunard, who were aware of the potential of so fine a ship purchased her.
June 7: First Cunard sailing to New York. Same name. In August she made a record crossing Queenstown-Sandy Hook. 2,792 nautical miles in 6 days, 9 hours, 42 minutes at an average of 18.16 kts. (She lost the record to *Etruria* in the following year.)
1885 March: During the Russian war scare *Oregon* was taken over for Armed Merchant Cruiser duties and converted. June: Commissioned as a 'Scouting cruiser'. By now the crisis was passed but the ship was used to test the worth of such ships. Stationed at Berehaven, July: Decommissioned. Nov: Back to normal service.
1886 Mar 14: 1600 hrs. While approaching New York, 26 miles south east of Fire Island, *Oregon* was struck below the bridge by an unknown wooden schooner. Her watertight doors were clogged with coal dust and could not be properly shut; she thus slowly flooded and sank. All 641 passengers and 255 crew, together with 600 bags of mail, were taken aboard Norddeutscher Lloyd's steamer *Fulda*.
The unknown schooner is thought to have been the *Charles Morse* which disappeared with all hands on the same day.

SERVIA (I)

79 **SERVIA (I)**
B 1881 J. & G. Thomson & Co, Glasgow. **T** 7,391g, 3,971n.
D 515/156.97 x 52.1/15.88 x 37/11.28. Dft 26/7.92
E Sgl scr 3 cyl comp; 1 HP cyl between 2 LP. 10,000 1HP; 7 blrs with 38 Fox type furnaces. 16 kts on 190 tons per day. By builder.
H Siemen's mild steel. 4 dks. Cunard's first dbl bottom; to carry 741 tons ballast. 10 gun mountings.

Cargo 4,000 tons. Coal 1,800 tons. Cunard's first ship with electric lighting. Barque rigged with topgallant masts.
P 480 1st in 202 staterooms, 500 3rd. Crew 252 (105 being stewards).
1881 March 1: Launched. She was originally to have been *Sahara.* The only Cunarder designed on the Bibby long length to narrow beam formula. Cost £256,903. The mild steel saved 620 tons of metal. Just prior to her trials a crack was found in the crank shaft and completion was delayed while it was replaced. Nov 26: M/v to New York. Excepting the *Great Eastern* she was the largest ship afloat and only the second steel Transatlantic liner, after Allan's *Parisian* in March 1881. At this stage she had no boat deck; her boats were on projecting skids. With electricity she introduced the fcsle 'lighthouses'. Steered from under the poop whalebacking right aft.
1891 Towed into New York after her shaft snapped.
1892 Collided with the American sailing ship *Undaunted.* Both only grazed.
1893 June 7: Ran down the American sailing barque *A. McCallum.* During her winter refit a boat deck was added (as drawn) and her accommodation was re-modelled. **P** 400 1st, 200 2nd, 500 3rd. Crew 380.
1899 Nov: Became *H.M.T. No 31* for Boer War trooping. Chartered at 21 shillings per ton per month.
1900 June 9: Resumed her service to New York.
1901 Sept 17: Final sailing. *Ivernia* (94) took her place.
1902 Jan: Sold for £15,625 to Thos. W. Ward. She was stripped to a hulk at Barrow-in-Furness and then demolished at Preston.

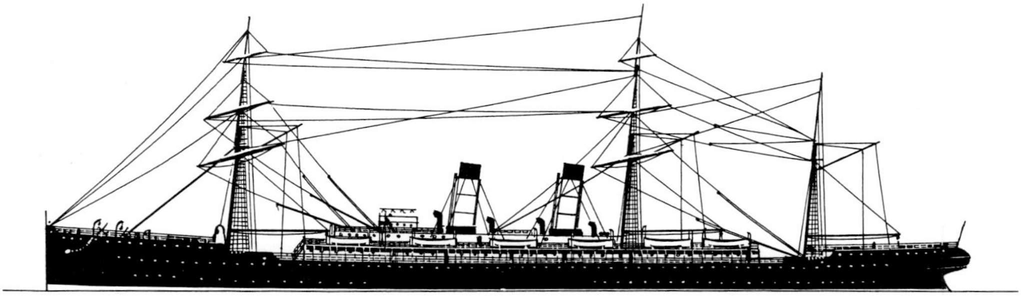

AURANIA (I)

80 **AURANIA (I)**
B 1883 J. & G. Thomson & Co, Glasgow. **T** 7,269g, 4,030n.
D 470/143.26 x 57.2/17.42 x 37.2/11.33.
E Sgl scr, 3 cyl similar to *Servia* but with 42 furnaces using 205 tons.
H Steel, 2 dks + 2 pt dks. Cargo 2,755 tons. Coal 2,282 tons.
P 500 1st, in 213 staterooms, 2-berth cabins, named 'Bridal Suites' were introduced; 700 3rd. Crew 275.
1882 Dec 26: Launched to partner *Servia.* Coming from the same yard it is odd that these two consorts were in no way sisters. In fact despite her 5 ft extra beam *Aurania* rolled badly and was not as popular as *Servia.*
1883 June 23: M/v to New York. Nearing New York, off Montauk, the engines failed due to overheating, which had plagued the crossing. The connecting rod snapped and punctured the casing. She continued under sail and was towed up to New York by three tugs. July 4: Docked. The ship returned to her builders, without passengers, using her LP cylinders only.
1884 April 12: Back in service. May: Went ashore off Bull Head, Ireland. Suffered bow bottom damage that put her out of action for three months.
1885 On charter to Inman Line. Scraped White Star's *Republic* with only minor damage to either.
1897 Towed by Thos. Wilson's *Marino* into Queenstown, inbound, with a snapped shaft.
1899 Oct: Boer War Transport *H.M.T. No 20.* Chartered at 16/6d per ton/month. Served 36 months and carried 30,000 men.
1903 Feb: Returned to Cunard, Apr 14: Resumed the New York intermediate service.
P 2nd and 3rd only. Square rigged foremast only. Nov 10: Inaugurated the Fiume-Trieste-Venice-Palermo-New York route which immediately proved to be very popular. Cunard lay plans for the expansion of this service.
1905 Feb: Sold at Fiume for £14,850 and scrapped at Genoa.

UMBRIA, ETRURIA

81 **UMBRIA**
B 1884 John Elder & Co, Fairfield. **T** 8,128g, 3,699n, 13,000 disp.
D 519/158.19 oa, 501.5/152.86 x 57.2/17.42 x 38.2/11.63.
E Sgl scr, 3 cyl, 1 HP, 2LP; 14,500 IHP, 9 blrs, 36 furn, 110 psi. 19 kts (21 on trials) on 315 tons per day at 68 rpm. By builder.
H Steel. 4 dks. F 112/34.14. Turtle decked poop 75/22.85. Cellular dbl bottom. **P** 550 1st. 800 2nd.
1884 June 26: Launched. The last two Cunarders with auxiliary sail. The order was given to John Elder because of the satisfaction with *Oregon. Umbria* was 'the most powerful steamer in the world' said John Burns but by now the compound engine was being outmoded by triple expansion. Nov 1: M/v to New York. At full speed (21 knots) she was found to vibrate excessively but was smooth just a fraction below this setting. Since her service speed was only 19 knots this was not regarded as a builder's problem.
1885 Chartered for six months as an Armed Merchant Cruiser.
1887 May: Took the record from *Oregon* (78).
1889 Square rigged only on the foremast.
1890 Apr 16: Rescued the crew in mid Atlantic of the barque *Magdalena.*
1892 Her 82nd crossing was her fastest at 19.57 kts. She logged 461, 502, 427, 502 and 388 miles per day.
1892 The winter overhaul saw her passenger carrying amended to 500 1st, 160 2nd, 800 3rd. The aftermost three pairs of lifeboats were double banked and the yardarms removed except for a gaff on the fore. At this time her topgallant masts were also taken out.
1893 Dec 23: Her propeller shaft snapped; taken in tow by HAPAG's *Bohemia* but the line snapped. *Umbria* drifted, sailless by now, for three days before temporary repairs brought her into New York on Dec 31.
1896 Her shaft again snapped.
1900 Jan 2: Entered Boer War trooping service.
1901 July 27: Resumed New York service. Pole masts only.
1903 In New York a case of dynamite was used in an attempt to blow her up. It was discovered before it could be used.
1908 Oct: Laid up at Liverpool.
1909 *Umbria* made three autumn relief sailings. Then up for sale.
1910 Feb 2: Sold for £20,000 to Forth Shipbreaking Co. Scrapped at Bo'ness.

82 **ETRURIA**
Sister of *Umbria* except: **B** 1885. **T** 8,120g, 3,690n.
1884 Sept 20: Launched.
1885 March: Her trials were followed by a shakedown delivery cruise to Liverpool. After her arrival at her home port she was hurriedly prepared for possible use as an Armed Merchant Cruiser but the order to install guns was cancelled and she was returned to Cunard.
Apr 24: M/v to New York. In service she was found to be the slightly faster of the two. May: Took the record Queenstown-Sandy Hook.
1887 March: Again became the record holder.
1888 May: *Etruria* once more became the fastest ship on the Atlantic routes.
1893 Her accommodation and rig was altered similarly to *Umbria*
1897 Attended Queen Victoria's Diamond Jubilee 'Pageant of Shipping' in the Mersey.
1901 Fitted with wireless.
1902 Lost her propeller. Using only stay sails she set course for the Azores. Frederick Leyland's *William Cliff,* West India & Pacific SS. Co. took her in tow to Fayal, Salvage of £11,000 being awarded. Cunard chartered Royal Mail's *Ebro* to bring home the passengers while the ship was herself towed to Liverpool.
1906 Oct: *Etruria* left New York in worsening fog with Atlantic Transport's *Minnehaha* astern. When *Etruria* was forced to anchor, with her bells tolling, she was gashed in the stern by *Minnehaha.*
1909 Sep 9: Made her final round voyage to New York then laid up at Liverpool. Nov: Sold for £16,750 and scrapped at Preston.

SKIRMISHER

83 **SKIRMISHER**
B 1884 J. & G. Thomson & Co, Glasgow, **T** 612g, 194n
D 165/50.29 x 32.2/9.8 x 15/4.57.
E Tw scr; 2 x 2 cyl comp. 168 NHP; 10 kts by builder.
H Steel. 1 dk. **P** 1,000 plus their cabin baggage. *Otter* took the hold baggage.
1884 Cunard tender at Liverpool. Their first twin screw. At this time Cunard ships anchored in mid-Mersey for embarkation.
1894 May 25: Acted as escort to Queen Victoria's Royal Yacht at the opening of the Manchester Ship Canal.
1895 June 12: With the opening of Prince's Landing Stage ships now berthed alongside for the first time and the Riverside Station permitted boat trains to run right to the shipside. (See *Catalonia,* 75). *Skirmisher* was still used to control the positioning of every Cunarder.
1897 Acted as tender to *Campania* (84) at the Diamond Jubilee Spithead Naval Review. She also visited Fishguard at this time.
1899 Oct: Acted during the whole of the Boer War as the Liverpool embarkation ship. The troopships mainly anchored in the river and were stored and provisioned by a medley of small craft.
1907 With the advent of *Lusitania* an extra deck was added (as drawn) to enable her gangways to reach the hull doors.
1914 Went to the Clyde to attend the launching of *Aquitania.* (116).
1917 When U-boats were reported off the Mersey she was berthed across Gladstone dock gate in case of an attempt to destroy it by torpedo.
1922 Spent the summer acting as tender to Anchor Line sailings.
1932 West to Dublin as tender to the Cunarders bringing American delegates to the Eucharistic Congress.
1939-45: Equipped as a fire fighter; 100 tons of water per minute.
1944 Went to Fishguard to disembark Winston Churchill from *Queen Mary* after the Quebec Conference. Bad weather forced *Queen Mary* to sail straight to the Clyde.
1945 Oct: Withdrawn aged 61. Dismantled in Langton Branch Dock.
1947 Mar 28: Towed to Gaston for final demolition.
She is said to have moved more passengers than any other Cunard vessel.

84 **CAMPANIA**
B 1893 Fairfield S.B. Co, Glasgow. **T** 12,950g, 4,974n.
D 620/188.98 oa, 601/183.18 x 65.2/19.96 x 37.7/11.48. Dft 29.7/9.05.
E Tw scr, tpl exp, 2 x 5 cyls, 2 HP, 1 MP, 2 LP, in tandem, 30,000 IHP, 12 blrs, 96 furn, 165 psi, 21 kts at 12 tons per hour each eng. By builder.
H Steel. 4 dks. F 120/36.58. P 75/22.86. These were later extended to give a continuous upper deck (as drawn).
P 60 1st, 400 2nd, 1,000 3rd. Crew 400.
1892 Sept 8: Launched. The largest vessel except for *Great Eastern.*
1893 March 30: Trials. 23.18 kts. Her machinery was the most powerful yet installed. She was a reply to *City of New York* and *Teutonic* but better.
Apr 22: M/v to New York. Captain Haines. Cost £650,000.
May: On her second voyage took the Blue Riband Sandy Hook-Queenstown.
1894 Aug: Made her fastest crossing in 5 days, 9 hours, 21 minutes at an average of 21.59 kts. She had been rather wet forward until now but the modified upper deck, as drawn, gave her the extra speed.
1897 July 26: At the Diamond Jubilee Spithead review with Members of Parliament. She was classed as an Armed Merchant Cruiser.
1900 Ran down and sank a small sailing vessel in St Georges Channel, 11 lost.
1901 June: Fitted with Marconi wireless; it had a range only of 30 miles.
1904 Hit by a wall of water which washed 5 overboard and injured 30.
1914 Apr: Completed her 250th voyage and retired. May 25: Chartered to Anchor line for 5 sailings. Completed 2 before the war began. When *Aquitania* was taken up for trooping *Campania* replaced her (Aug 15) on Liverpool-New York. Oct 15: Sold for scrap to Thos. W. Ward following the release back of *Aquitania.*
Nov 27: Acquired by the Admiralty for use as an AMC. Conversion began at Cammell Laird. 8 x 4.7 in guns. It was then decided to add a flight platform forward. The foremast was removed, a slope added plus a hanger on the bridge top.

1915 Completed. In practice the flight deck was not long enough.
Nov: Returned to Cammel Laird. Fore funnel split (as drawn) and the flight deck extended to 240ft/73.15m with a hanger beneath for 10 Sopwith Schneider or Short 184 seaplanes. The after part was cleared for use by observation balloons. Back in service she proved to be a useful scouting adjunct to the fleet.
1918 Nov 5: During a gale in the Firth of Forth she broke from her moorings and gashed her hull open on the ram bow of the battleship *Revenge* and sank. All were saved.

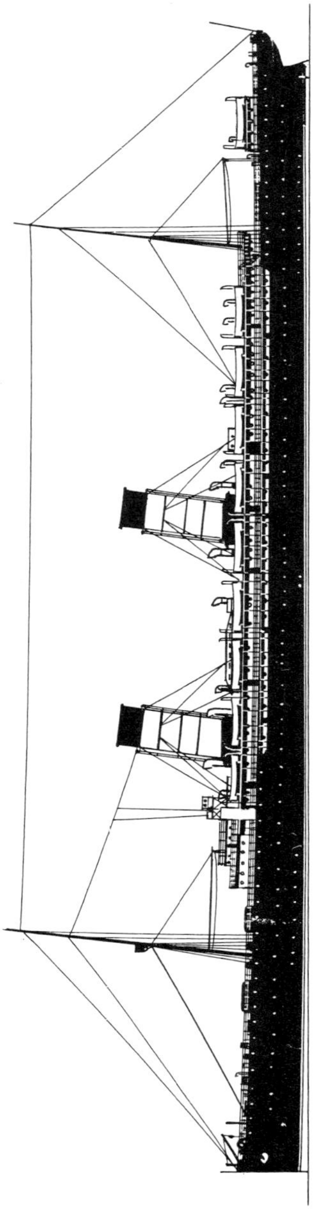

CAMPANIA (I), LUCANIA

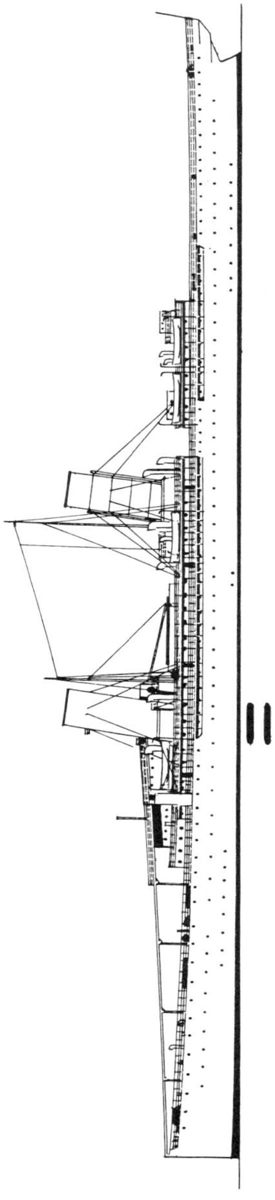

CAMPANIA

85 **LUCANIA**
As *Campania* except: **T** 12,952g, 4,975n.
1893 Feb 2: Launched. Sept 2: M/v to New York. Captain H. Mackay. Oct: Took the Atlantic record from her sister. In service she was slightly the faster of the two.
1894 Aug, Sept and Oct, broke the record, held by *Campania,* on three occasions with average speeds of 21.49 21.66 and 21.75 kts.
1897 The Atlantic speed record went to N.D.L.'s *Kaiser Wilhelm der Grosse.*
1901 June 15: Marconi wireless fitted; Cunard's first. The shore end was aboard the Mersey training ship *H.M.S. Conway.*
1903 Oct 10: On this crossing she became the first liner to publish the Cunard bulletin made up from radio news.
1909 During the year she made only one voyage being mainly laid up. Aug 14: Burnt out at Huskisson Dock, Liverpool, and settled on the bottom. Sold to Thos. W. Ward for breaking up at Swansea. The raised *Lucania* steamed there under her own power and made 17 kts.

SYLVANIA (I)

86 **SYLVANIA (I)**
B 1895 London & Glasgow S.B.&E. Co, Glasgow. **T** 5,508g, 3,623n.
D 445/135.63 x 49/14.93 x 31.9/9.7.
E Tw scr, 2 x tpl exp, 766 NHP, 3 blrs, 14 furn, 180 psi, 13½ kts. By builder. Coal 768 tons.
H Steel, 3 dks. F 84/25.6. B 163/49.68. P 98/29.87. Cargo 6,232 tons.
1895 Jan 24: Launched for North Atlantic cargo services.
Apr 24: M/v Liverpool-New York. These two ships proved to be rather too large in service. Turn round time in port was slow.
1910 Broken up in Italy.

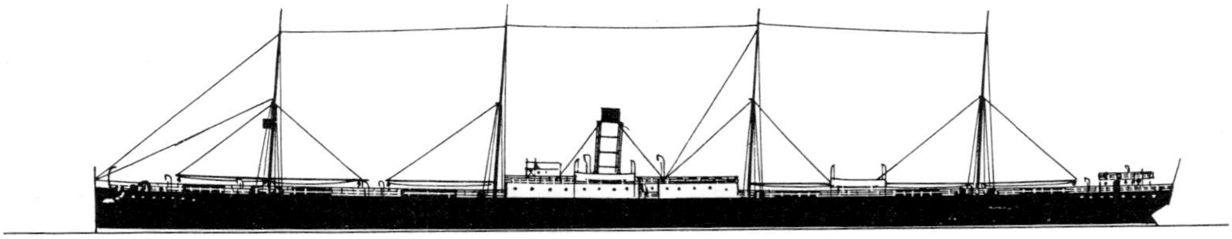

CARINTHIA (I)

87 **CARINTHIA (I)**
As *Sylvania* except: **T** 5,598. H P 88/26.82.
1895 May 24: Launched Oct 24: M/v Liverpool-Boston.
1899 Nov: Taken over for the carriage of mules to South Africa for Boer war service.
1900 July 15: Final sailing. July 30: Stranded off Cape Gravois, Haiti, on her way to load a cargo of mules in Mexico. No lives lost.

PAVIA (I), TYRIA, CYPRIA

88 **PAVIA (I)**
B 1897 Workman Clark & Co, Belfast. **T** 2,945g, 1,885n.
D 332. 1/101.22 x 45.7/13.89 x 15/4.57.
E Sgl scr, tpl exp, 354 NHP, 2 blrs, 6 furnaces, 200 psi; 10½ kts on 10 tons per day. By Barclay, Curle & Co, Glasgow.

H Steel. 1 dk+ spar dk. F 33/10.06. B 76/23.16. p 25/7.62. cargo 2,500 tons. Coal 480 tons.
1897 June: Delivered for service to the Mediterranean.
1912 When Cunard linked with Anchor Line this trio included Glasgow as their U.K. terminus and were frequently seen in the Continental Dutch, Belgium and French ports.
1914-18 Served as supply and general purpose vessels to the Eastern Mediterranean.
1917 May 29: Missed by a torpedo off southern Ireland inbound for Liverpool.
1928 Broken up.

89 **TYRIA**
As *Pavia* except: **T** 2,936g, 1,884n.
1897 Aug: Delivered. Served in parallel with her sister throughout her career.
1928 Sold to Niger Company (Motto Ars Jus Pax). R/n *Ars*; their first ship.
1930 Scrapped.

90 **CYPRIA**
Third of the *Pavia* class **B** 1898. **T** 2,936g, 1,884n. **E** By builder.
1898 Jan: Completed for the Mediterranean routage.
1916 June 2: An Austrian submarine surfaced and opened fire. *Cypria* was defensively armed and a running duel took place. When *Cypria's* shots became too accurate for safety the submarine submerged.
1928 Broken up.

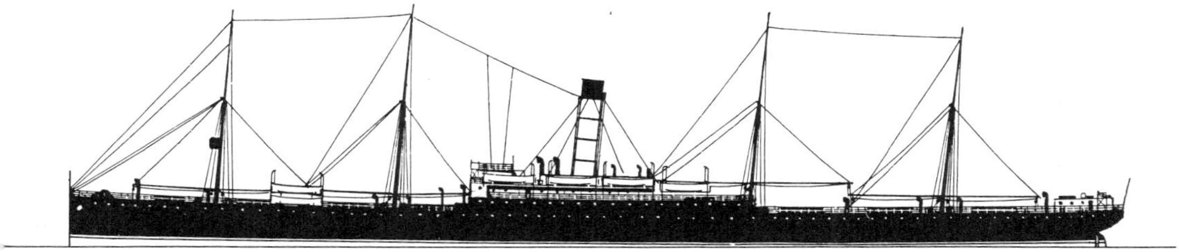

ULTONIA

91 **ULTONIA**
B 1898 C. S. Swan & Hunter, Newcastle. **T** 8,845g, 5,748n.
D 500/152.4 x 57.4/17.5 x 33.9/10.31.
E Tw scr, 2 x tpl exp. 863 NHP, 5 blrs, 15 furnaces, 200 psi, 12½ kts. By Sir Christopher Furness, Westgarth & Co, Middlesbrough.
H Steel. 2 dks. B 140/42.67. **P** 12.
1898 June 4: Launched for Sir Christopher Furness. Purchased on the stocks. Nov: Entered Cunard service on the cattle trade for which she had main deck stalls fitted.
1899 Jan: Third class accommodation for 675 was added aft. Cattle no longer carried. Feb 28: Placed on the Boston emigrant service.
1904 Cunard obtained a ten year Hungarian Government contract to operate between Trieste and New York. Cunard placed four ships on the route: *Ultonia, Slavonia, Pannonia* and the better *Carpathia. Ultonia's* passengers now became 120 2nd, 2,100 3rd.
Apr: 29: First sailing Trieste-Fiume-Naples-New York. Apart from one summer on the St Lawrence run *Ultonia* remained on this route until 1914.
1915-16 St Nazaire-New York.
1917 June 27: Torpedoed by *U-53* 350 miles west of Land's End. 2 lost.

VERIA, BRESCIA (I)

92 **VERIA**
B 1899 Armstrong Whitworth & Co, Newcastle. **T** 3,229g, 2,064n.
D 330.6/100.74 x 45.2/13.77 x 16.8/5.11.
E Sgl scr, tpl exp; 361 NHP, 2 blrs, 6 furnaces, 200 psi, 10½ kts. By Wallsend Slipway Co, Newcastle.
H Steel. 1 dk + spar dk. F 42/12.8. B 78/23.77. P 41/12.5.
1899 April: Delivered for the Mediterranean routes.
1915 Dec 17: Stopped in the mid-Mediterranean by an Austrian submarine and sunk by four bombs which were suspended on each side along the waterline. It was, said the commander, cheaper than a torpedo.

93 **BRESCIA (I)**
Sister to *Veria* except: **B** 1903 J. L. Thompson & Co, Sunderland. **T** 3,255g 2,058n. **D** 330/100.58. **H F** 39/11.89. B 80/24.38. P 39/11.89.
1903 May: Delivered.
1929 Laid up out of service.
1931 Sold for breaking up. Actual date of demolition not known; so many ships were unwanted during the depression.

Scale 1: 1360 except where shown

IVERNIA (I),

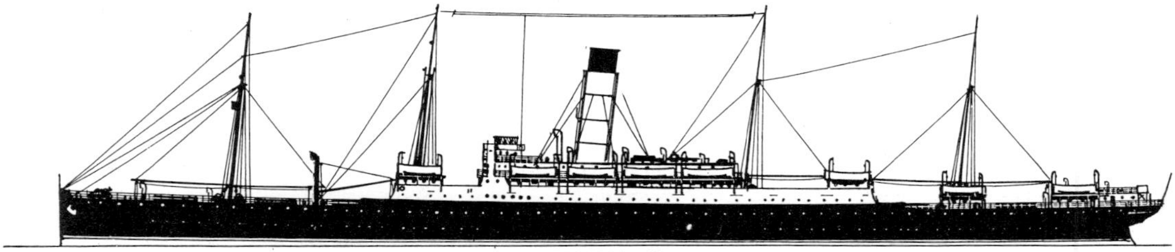

SAXONIA (I)

94 **IVERNIA (I)**
B 1900 C. S. Swan & Hunter, Newcastle. **T** 14,067g, 9,058n, 12,770dwt.
D 598/182.27 oa, 582/177.39 x 64.9/19.76 x 37.7/11.48.
E Tw scr, 2 x quad exp; 1,668 NHP, 9 blrs, 27 furn, 210 psi, 16 kts on 152 tons per day. By Wallsend Slipway Co, Newcastle.
H Steel, 3 dks, 7 holds. B 275/83.82. Cargo 14,000 tons. Coal 2,280 tons.
P 164 1st, 200 2nd, 1,600 3rd. Troop capacity 3,000.
1899 Sept 21: Launched. Cost £400,000. Intended for the Boston service.
The funnels of these two ships were the tallest ever installed: 106/32.31 from main deck to rim (the outer casing from the boat deck to the rim, being some feet less).
1900 Apr 14: M/v Liverpool-New York because of the disruption caused by the Boer War trooping contracts.
1911 May 24: Hit Daunt's Rock, Queenstown. Out of service for four months. During this time her accommodation became: 485 Cabin, 978 3rd.
Dec 21: Made her first sailing Trieste-New York.
1912 March: Took a summer season Trieste-New York. Nov 30: Back to Liverpool-Boston.
1913 April 24: Again on the Trieste berth for the summer.
1914 Sept: Taken over as a troopship. Was in the Eastern Mediterranean theatre for much of the time.
1917 Jan 1: Torpedoed by *UB-47* 58 miles off Cape Matapan, Greece, on her way to Alexandria with 2,400 Scottish troops aboard; of these 85 were drowned together with 36 crew. The escorting destroyer *HMS Rifleman* took off 650 and then the remainder of the survivors were towed in their lifeboats by armed trawlers to Crete.
UB-47 had been sent overland to Pola and re-assembled there. Four days earlier she had sunk the French battleship *Gaulois*.

95 **SAXONIA (I)**
Sister to *Ivernia* except: **B** & **E** John Brown & Co, Glasgow (formerly J. & G. Thomson). **T** 14,281g, 9,100n.
1899 Dec 16: Launched. Despite being a sister she had the 'John Brown' look to her. Note the ventilator derricks forward.
1900 May 22: M/v to Boston. Remained on this, her design route.
1909 Winter: New York-Mediterranean, to Trieste.
1910 Oct: Towed HAPAG's *Scotia,* broken shaft, 170 miles to the Azores.
1912 Fiume-New York service with *Ivernia.*

1914 July 8: *Saxonia* made the first Patras passenger call. Aug 29: Sailed Liverpool-New York then, because the war had started on Aug 4, to Quebec for Canadian troops.
1914-15 Used as a German prisoner-of-war ship in the Thames.
1915 May: Back to the Liverpool-New York service.
1917 March: Commenced to sail to New York under the Liner requisition Scheme. By April, with the U.S.A. in the war, she was trooping eastbound.
1918 Dec 14: Her first post-war voyage was London-New York.
1919 Jan 25: Liverpool-New York. May 14: Switched to the London route.
1920 Refitted. **P** 471 Cabin, 978 3rd. Funnel shortened by 15ft/4.57m.
When she re-entered service she was London based and also made journeys out of Hamburg with calls always at Cherbourg or Le Havre en route to New York.
1924 Nov: Laid up at the Tilbury buoy.
1925 March: Sold for £47,000 and broken up at Hendrik Ido Ambacht.

CARPATHIA

96 **CARPATHIA**
B 1902 C. S. Swan & Hunter, Newcastle. **T** 13,603g, 8,660n.
D 540/164.59 x 64.3/19.66 x 37.2/11.34.
E Tw scr, 2 x quad exp. 1,341 NHP, 7 blrs, 21 furn, 210 psi, 17 kts. By Wallsend Slipway Co, Newcastle.
H Steel, 3 dks. B 290/88.39.
P 204 2nd, 1,500 3rd (486 in rooms, the rest in dormitories).
1902 Aug 6: Launched. A smaller edition of *Ivernia* built with the Mediterranean in mind.
1903 May 4: M/v to Boston as running mate to *Aurania.* (80).
Nov 24: Placed on the Trieste service to New York.
1904 May 17: Commenced her summer Liverpool-New York stint. Nov: 29: Back to the Trieste winter run.
1905 May: The same annual pattern again. Oct 27: Her final sailing thence for her annual winter overhaul and refitted to **P** 100 1st, 200 2nd, 2,250 3rd. This mixture of routes became her normal programme and calls at the Azores were added to the Trieste service according to need.
1912 April 14: En route New York-Trieste *Carpathia,* Captain A. H. Rostron, picked up distress calls from the sinking *Titanic.* The ship was 58 miles away and despite increasing ice and a sea bespeckled with icebergs and growlers *Carpathia* made the scene of the horrific disaster by 04.00. Green Verey lights guided the ship to a cluster of lifeboats and in all 705 survivors were lifted from the sea. Captain Rostron did not leave the scene until every chance of others surviving had gone. He then sped back to New York before continuing his journey. Enormous insurance claims resulted from the tragedy but in the vast list the name of Cunard did not once appear. Perhaps this one episode best demonstrates what is meant by 'greatness'.
1915 *Carpathia* was allocated the task of maintaining a Liverpool-New York service under wartime conditions.
1918 July 17: Outbound for New York, sunk in convoy by three torpedoes from *U-55* 170 miles west of Bishop's Rock. 215 (57 passengers) were saved by *H.M.S. Snowdrop.* 5 engine room staff were killed in the initial explosion.

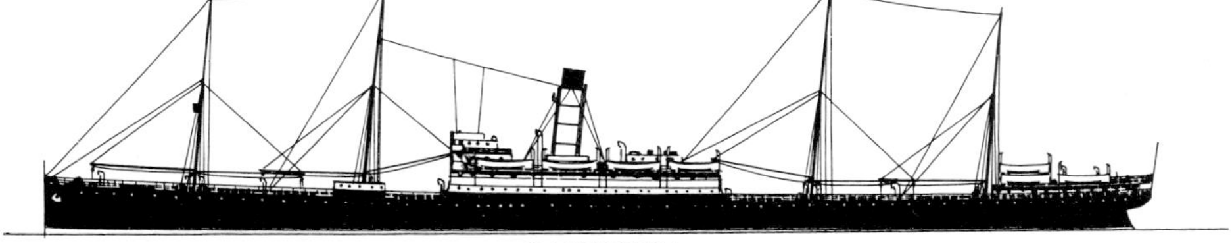

PANNONIA

97 **PANNONIA**
B 1903 John Brown & Co, Clydebank, Glasgow. **T** 9,851g, 6,210n.
D 486.5/148.28 x 59.3/18.06 x 33/10.06.
E Tw scr, tpl exp, 2 x 3 cyls, 811 NHP, 4 blrs, 18 furn, 190 psi; 12½ kts.

By builder. Efficient engines with only a 4ft stroke.
H Steel. 2 dks + shelter dk. B 120/36.58.
P 91 1st, 71 2nd, 2,066 3rd, in dormitories.
1902 Laid down for Sir Christopher Furness. Purchased on the stocks.
Sept 5: Launched
1903 May 15: Positioned Glasgow-Trieste.
May 28: First voyage Trieste-Fiume-Palermo-New York.
1914 Oct 3: To replace vessels taken up as AMC's commenced 4 Glasgow-New York voyages for Anchor.
1915-19 Operated London-New York.
1919 March 29: Final London sailing, May 18: Reverted to her pre-war programme.
1921 Sept 17: Her final Mediterranean voyage. She then replaced Liverpool-New York vessels on overhaul during the winter; continued through the summer awaiting the delivery of new buildings.
1922 April 18: Final voyage New York-Hamburg; laid up there. Oct: Scrapped.

SLAVONIA

98 **SLAVONIA**
B 1903 Sir James Laing & Co, Sunderland. **T** 10,606g, 6,725n,
D 510/155.45 x 59.5/18.14 x 34.6/10.54.
E Tw scr, tpl exp 2 x 3 cyls, 929 NHP, 6 blrs, 18 furn, 200 psi, 12½ kts. By Wallsend Slipway Co, Wallsend.
H Steel. 3 dks. B 184/56.08.
P 71 1st, 74 2nd, 1,954 3rd, emigrants in dormitories.
1903 Nov 15: Launched as *Yamuna,* British India S.N.Co. The longest ship ever built by Laings. Cost £50,000. Had to be brought down below the Tyne bridges to have her masts stepped.
1904 Jan: Made one voyage to the Far East for British India but found to be much too large for service beyond India. Almost all the passengers disembarked there and the onwards boarding was 'a handful'. Inbound was the same. And, of course, B.I. had adequate tonnage on their India routes. Sold to Cunard with delivery at Trieste. R/n *Slavonia* for the Trieste route. March 17: First sailing.
1909 June 3: Left New York for Trieste, 100 Cabin, 273 steerage and 225 crew. June 11: 02.30. Went ashore near Velos, southwestern tip of Flores, Azores. Her distress signal was picked up by *Princess Irene,* M. Langland & Sons. The small ship set off for the scene and brought with her HAPAG's *Batavia.* Between them all aboard were taken off but *Slavonia* was beyond salvage.

99 **CARONIA (I)** (Drawing page 59)
B 1905 John Brown & Co, Glasgow. **T** 19,687g, 10,306n.
D 675/205.74 oa, 650/198.12 x 72.2/22 x 40.2/12.24.
E Tw scr, quad exp. 2 x 4 cyls, 21,000 NHP, 13 blrs. 63 furn, 210 psi, 18 kts (trials 19½). By builder.
H Steel, 3 dks + shelter dk, B 400/121.92. The first Cunarder to be fitted with Stone-Lloyd bridge controlled watertight door closing system, C 389,000/10.015cu g in 7 holds.
P 300 1st, 350 2nd, 1,100 3rd.
1904 July 13: Launched. She and her sister were the company's largest ships but were intended to be second line vessels because of the building of *Lusitania* and *Mauretania* (101/2).
1905 Feb 4: Reached 19½ knots on the Skilmorlie mile.
Feb 25: M/v Liverpool-New York. Completed with single decked lifeboats and house only at mainmast. Also no derrick posts forward. On her third voyage stranded at Sandy Hook.
1906 Jan: Cruised from New Work to the Mediterranean. The success of the venture led to many more in the future.
1914 June: Commenced a summer of sailings to Boston but after two she was taken over for AMC duties. Armed with 8 x 4.7 in. old style guns. Aug 10: Commissioned.
1915 Re-armed with 8 x 6 in. modern weapons.
1916 Aug: Transferred to trooping duties.
1919 Jan 11: Resumed Liverpool-New York sailings.
1920 June: Converted to oil fuel then became the largest ship sailing out of London-New York.
1922 Apr 27: Commenced Hamburg-Southampton-New York. Nov: Reverted to Liverpool-New York.

1924 Passenger accommodation re-modelled at Barrow. Given new funnels. Her boats were also double banked.**P** 425 Cabin, 365 tst, 650 3rd. May 1: On the Liverpool-Quebec-Montreal service.
1926 Oct: Following the arrival of the 'A' class ships served out of London with winter cruising New York-Havana.
1931 Laid up off Sheerness, all the dock berths being full. Sold to Hughes Bolckow for £39,000 for scrapping.

100 **CARMANIA (I)**
Details as *Caronia* except; **T** 19,524g, 9,982n, **D** 650.3/198.22.
E Tpl scr, in place of quad exp. 3 direct action turbs, HP centre shaft, 2 LP wing shafts and astern. Installed to test the effectiveness of each in service. *Carmania* was better than ½ kt faster but flow line tests indicted that it was more to do with the stern design for tpl scr than the actual machinery itself.
1905 Feb 21: Launched. Nov: Trials with Admiralty officials present. Found not to be as manoeuvrable when going astern.
Dec 2: M/v Liverpool-New York. The opposition was White Star Line's *Celtic* class.
1912 June 4: Caught fire at Liverpool; not seriously damaged.
1913 Oct 9: One of the nine ships which took part in the rescue of survivors from the Canadian Northern's burning *Volturno.* But for the intervention of Anglo-American's tanker *Narrangansett,* which poured oil onto the wild seas, it was probable that more than 133 out of the 654 aboard would have lost their lives.
1914 Aug 6: Arrived at Fishguard to unload £2½ million gold; then to Liverpool. Aug 15: Taken over for conversion to an AMC. Fitted with 8 x 4.7 in. old style guns, range 9,300 yards/8,504m., Aug 29: Left Bermuda, Captain Noel Grant RN, to scout the area of Trinidad Island, 1,750 miles north east of Montevideo. Any ships were to be reported to *H.M.S. Bristol.* Sept 14: At Trinidad Island Hamburg Sud Amerika's *Cap Trafalgar* had just finished coaling from *Eleonore Woermann* and was armed only with two 4.1 in guns (range 7,000 yards/6,400m) and six heavy machine guns taken from the German gunboat *Eber.* Her aftermost funnel had been removed and she had disguised herself as *Carmania,* the very ship now approaching, *Carmania* fired a shot across *Cap Trafalgar's* bows but the enemy joined battle with accurate shooting. Nevertheless the odds were impossible and she sank under a deluge of shot. Even so *Carmania* was hit 29 times and was on fire as the German ship sank and her collier picked up the survivors. *Carmania* lost 9 killed and 26 wounded. From the scene of the battle she went for repairs to Gibraltar.
1916 Nov 11: Resumed her New York service.
1921 Oct 22: Placed on the Southampton-New York run.
1922 May 3: Reverted to Liverpool-New York.
1923 Dec: Converted to oil burning. Renovated at the same time; **P** 425 Cabin, 365 tst, 650 3rd. Boats double banked and extra pairs abreast the mainmast on a deck house (as drawn).
1924 May 15: Re-entered service Liverpool-Quebec; she was too deep to sail up to Montreal. Winter: Back to the New York route.
1926 May: Located onto the London-New York service.
1927 Oct: Overhauled by Cammell Laird then used for winter cruises out of New York to Havana.
1931 July 25: Final Cunard sailing then laid up off Sheerness.
1932 Broken up by Hughes Bolckow at Blyth.

101 **LUSITANIA** (Drawing page 59)
B 1907 John Brown & Co, Clydebank. **T** 31,550g, 9.145n.
D 790/240.79 oa, 762.2/232.31 x 87.8/26.75 x 56.4/17.2.
E Quad scr, 4 direct acting Parson's turbines, 2 HP + 2 LP, 68,000 SHP, 23 dbl and 2 sgl blrs, all 3-abreast; 195 psi, 25 kts on 850 tons per day. By builder.
H Steel, 5 dks + shelter dk, F 305/92.96.
P 563 1st, 464 2nd, 1,186 3rd, Crew 802.
To accommodate the ship and her sister, *Mauretania,* the Mersey Docks & Harbour Board had to remove 200,000 tons of sand from abreast the Liverpool landing stage which also had to have elevated platforms erected from which the gangways could reach the entrance hallways. Special buoys were installed at the Sloyne in mid river at which they could safely anchor. Finally *Skirmisher* (83) had her extra deck added so that she too could reach to service them.
1905 May: Contracted. Designed as AMC's under Admiralty supervision.
1906 June 7: Launched by Lady Inverclyde. She was always known as 'The Lucy'. Given a Government operating subsidy. Her appearance differed from her sister; being less cluttered.
1907 June 29: Trials; she reached 26.45 kts. Sept 7: M/v Liverpool-New York; Captain James Watt. Oct: On her second voyage she took the Atlantic record from N.D.L.'s *Kaiser Wilhelm II,* Queenstown — Sandy Hook averaging 23.99 kts. The passage time being 4 days, 19 hours, 52 minutes. Great Britain was to hold the record for the next 22 years.

1908 During the winter both sisters had machinery adjustments.
1909 Given a new set of propellers.
1914 Aug 4: Left New York for Liverpool on the day that war broke out. It was decided that she would remain in service sailing at monthly intervals. A point of interest is that between voyages neither ship docked at Liverpool but anchored at the Sloyne and were serviced by *Skirmisher* and *Otter* until coming alongside Princes landing Stage to embark passengers.
1915 May 1: Left New York, Captain J. W. Turner, with 1,257 passengers and 702 crew. On that morning German Embassy advertisements had appeared in the local press warning against using the vessel because she was sailing into the war zone. May 7: 14.15 torpedoed once, according to the submarine's log, between the third and fourth funnels, by *U-20* off the Old Head of Kinsale while approaching Queenstown. The ship had slowed to 18½ knots and with way on her heeled over to starboard sinking in less than eighteen minutes. 1,198 were drowned including 291 women, 94 children and 124 U.S. citizens, 761 were saved, many by the trawlers *Bluebell* and *Peel.* Controversy followed the sinking. Admiralty warnings had been given which the captain, who survived, was said to have largely ignored. He hugged the coast instead of going wide. He slowed down to enable him to catch the tide at Liverpool (in case of attack in the Mersey estuary) but paramount was a second explosion which was internal and, it was said, caused her to sink so disasterously quickly in sight of land. This was either a boiler or, as the Germans claimed, proof that she was a munitions carrier. The outcome was public outrage on both sides of the Atlantic which had a great effect on anti-German feeling world wide.

102 **MAURETANIA (I)** (Drawing page 60)
Sister to *Lusitania* except: **B** Swan, Hunter & Wigham Richardson, Newcastle.
T: 31,938g, 12,797n, 12,280dwt. **E** By Wallsend Slipway, Wallsend.
1906 Sept 20: Launched. Very distinctively different due to the pronounced deck ventilators and thicker steam pipes to the funnels.
1907 Sept 17: Builder's trials off Flamborough Head. Reached 27 knots.
Nov 16: M/v Liverpool-Queenstown-New York. Entered service as drawn with no white strake to the fcsle. On the return leg she took the record from *Lusitania* in 4 days, 22 hours, 29 minutes at 23.69 kts average.
1908 Jan: On her second sailing the forward derricks unshipped in a gale and smashed the bridge front windows. Firmer holding stanchions were fitted to both ships. During the year she lost the record to *Lusitania.*
1909 New propellers were fitted; extra speed with less vibration aft. July crossed in 4 days, 17 hours, 20 minutes at 25.89 kts and held the record until 1929 when Norddeutscher Lloyd's *Bremen* took it from her.
1910 Dec 10: Left Liverpool on an advertised attempt to do New York and back in 12 days; 600 passengers were landed at Fishguard but she still reached Liverpool on Dec 23.
1913 July 11: Present at the opening of Liverpool's Gladstone Dock by King George V. The ship was inspected by the King and Queen Mary.
Oct 5: Became the first Cunarder to use the Gladstone graving dock for her winter overhaul.
1914 October 10: Last sailing to New York before war service then three trooping trips out of Halifax.
1915 March: Commissioned as a troop transport for 3 voyages to the Dardenelles with 10,390 men.
Sept: Converted into a hospital ship, white livery, yellow funnels and looked magnificent.
1916 Laid up at Greenock. Autumn: Painted in camouflage dazzle grey.
1917-18 Employed Halifax-Liverpool with troops then, May, after the American entry into the war, brought U.S. soldiers to Liverpool. Carried 33,610 men.
1919 June 28: Resumed Liverpool-New York route.
1920 March 6: After a refit by the builder made her first Southampton-New York departure. This became her base and Liverpool lost prime position.
1921 July 25: Damaged by fire at Southampton, repaired and converted by builder to oil fuel. **T** 30,696. P 589 1st, 400 2nd, 767 3rd. To replace her P. & O's *Kaiser-i-Hind,* which was advertised by Cunard as the *Emperor of India,* and Canadian Pacific's *Empress of India* were chartered for one and three voyages respectively.
1922 Mar 25: Returned to service.
1924 Aug 20: Made a record crossing Ambrose Light to Cherbourg in 5 days, 1 hour, 49 mins at 26.25 kts. This was the eighth time that she had achieved this distinction; a performance unsurpassed by any other ship. (Although *United States* made scheduled sailings in a lesser time).
1930 Hull painted white for cruising. Her nickname changed from 'The Maurie' to 'The Grand Old Lady'. By now she was making very few Atlantic crossings.
1934 Sept 26: On the very day that *Queen Mary* was launched *Mauretania* left New York on her final voyage after five cruises from that port.
1935 Sold to Metal Industries for scrap. July 1: Left Southampton for Rosyth, Firth of Forth and demolition. To enable her to pass under the Forth Bridge her masts had to be cut off at funnel height. Thus passed one of the most loved ships of all time.

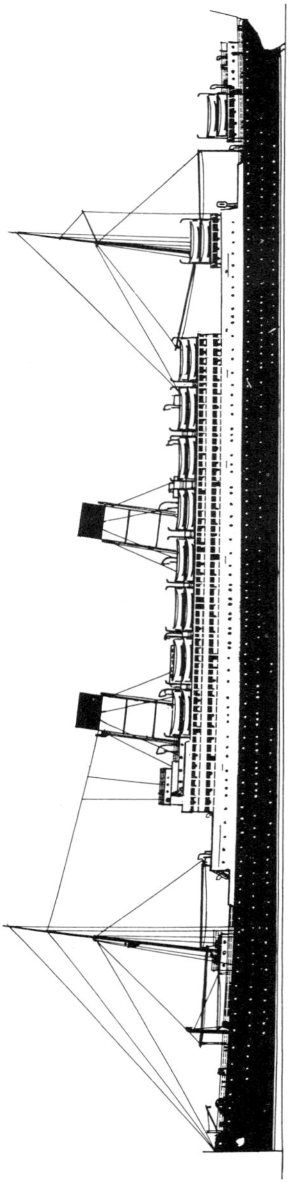

99/100 *CARONIA (I) CARMANIA (I)*

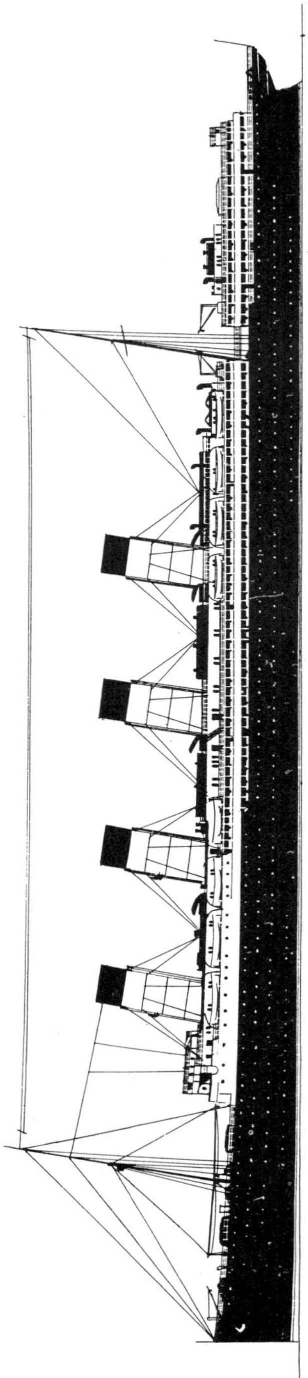

101 *LUSITANIA*

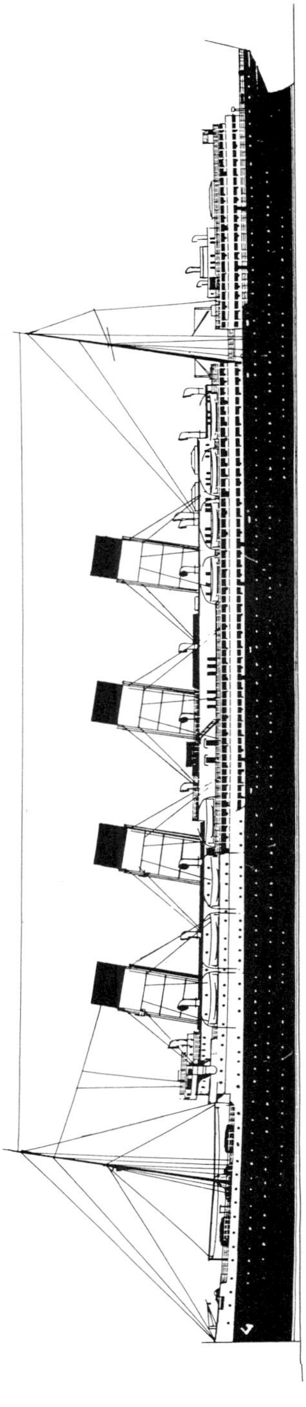

102 *MAURETANIA (I)*

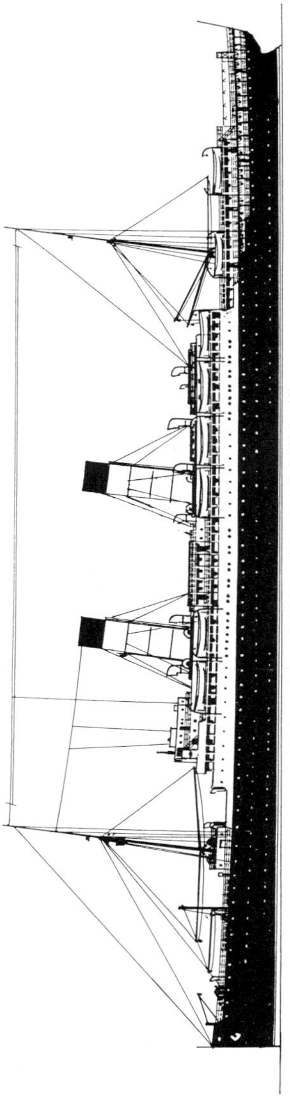

106/7 *FRANCONIA (I), LACONIA (I)*

PHRYGIA (I)

103 **PHRYGIA (I)**
B 1900 Sir Raylton Dixon & Co., Middlesbrough. **T** 3,352g, 2,147n.
D 340/103.63 x 47.1/14.36 x 15.4/4.7.
E Sgl scr, tpl exp, 3 cycls, 337 NHP, 2 blrs, 180 psi, 10 kts. By Sir Christopher Furness & Westgarth & Co., Middlesbrough.
H Steel. 1 dk + spar dk. F 36/10.97. B 78/23.77. P 30/9.14.
1900 Built as *Oro* for the Plate S.S. Co., London; owned by Gellatley, Hankey & Co. Service to the River Plate.
1909 Acquired by Cunard; r/n *Phrygia.* General cargo duties.
1915 Rammed and sank a U-boat. The German records list no attack and the number of the U-boat is unknown.
1916 March 24: Attacked by U-boat shelling 110 miles west of Fastnet. The enemy was driven off by gunfire. May 1: Again chased by a submarine, this time in the Bay of Biscay, escaped by speed and gunfire.
1928 Sold to F. L. Dawson, Liverpool. Mediterranean trade.
1933 Broken up.

THRACIA, LYCIA (I)

104 **THRACIA**
B 1895 Sir Raylton Dixon & Co., Middlesbrough. **T** 2,891g, 1,850n.
D 310/94.49 x 44.1/13.44 x 15.6/4.75.
E Sgl scr. tpl exp, 3 cyls, 258 NHP, 2 blrs, 180 psi, 10 kts. By T. Richardson & Sons, Hartlepool.
H Steel. 1 dk. F 34/10.36. B 74/22.56. P 30/9.14.
1895 Completed as *Orono* for Gellatley Hankey's Plate S.S. Co., London.
1909 Purchased and r/n *Thracia.* Mediterranean service.
1917 Mar 27: Torpedoed off Belle Isle, Brittany carrying iron ore from Bilbao, 2 survived.

105 **LYCIA (I)**
As *Thracia* except; **B** 1896. T 2,715g, 1,739n. **D** 308/93.88 x 43.3/13.21.
E By North East Marine, Newcastle.
1896 Built as *Oceano,* Plate S.S. Co., Gellatley, Hankey & Co., London.
1909 Acquired for the Mediterranean routes. R/n *Lycia.*
1917 Feb 11: Torpedoed off the South Bishop Light.

106 **FRANCONIA (I)** (Drawing page 60)
B 1911 Swan, Hunter & Wigham Richardson, Newcastle. **T** 18,150g, 11,247n.
D 625/190.5 oa, 600.2/182.96 x 71.2/21.72 x 40.4/12.32.
E Tw scr, quad exp, 2 x 4 cyls, 2,170 NHP, 6 blrs, 48 furnaces, 210 psi, 17 kts. by Wallsend Slipway & Engineering Co., Newcastle.
H Steel. 3 dks + shelter dk. F & B 491/149.66. Both ships were fitted with Frahm anti-rolling tanks.
1909 Oct 8: Keel laid. To replace *Ivernia* and *Saxonia.*
1910 July 23: Launched for the Boston route. Designed to counter the Leyland and White Star competition on this service.

1911 Jan 23: Handed over. Feb 25: M/v but to New York not Boston. Her next sailing was to Boston and she then kept to this route. In the winter she replaced *Ultonia* on the New York-Trieste service.
1913 A call at Fishguard was introduced in each direction.
1914 May 3: Picked up one boat of survivors from Leyland's *Colombian* which had been lost by fire en route Antwerp-Boston.
1915 Feb 15: Requisitioned for use as a troopship.
1916 Oct 4: Torpedoed and sunk by *UB-47* 200 miles south east of Malta en-route Alexandria (where 2,700 troops had been disembarked)-Salonika. 12 lost.

107 **LACONIA (I)**
Details as *Franconia* except: **T** 18,099g, 11,226n.
1911 July 27: Launched. Dec 10: Left the Tyne.
1912 Jan 20: M/v to New York then onto the Boston service with winter service to Trieste.
1914 Nov 1: Requisitioned and converted into an Armed Merchant Cruiser. Used as the headquarters ship in Tanganyika during the operations against the German light cruiser *Konigsberg* in the Rufigi River estuary.
1916 Sept 9: Returned to commercial service to New York.
1917 Feb 25: Sunk by *U-50* 160 miles from Fastnet, Ireland. The first torpedo failed to sink her but a second exploded in the engine room. Out of 292 persons aboard only six passengers and six crew were lost.

CARIA

108 **CARIA**
B 1900 Tyne Iron S.B. Co., Newcastle. **T** 3,032g, 1,928n.
D 318/96.93 x 43/13.1 x 25.2/7.67.
E Sgl scr, tpl exp, 3 cyls, 265 NHP, 10 kts. By Wallsend Slipway Co.
H Steel. 1 dk. F 35/10.67. B 30/9.14. P 29/8.84.
1900 Built as *Clematis,* Societe Anonyme d'Entreposage & de Transports, Antwerp.
1911 Acquired became *Caria.*
1915 Nov 6: Sunk by U-boat gunfire 120 miles south east of Cape Martello en-route Naples-Alexandria in ballast.

ASCANIA (I)

109 **ASCANIA (I)**
B 1911 Swan, Hunter & Wigham Richardson, Newcastle. **T** 9,111g, 5,699n.
D 466.5/142.19 x 56.1/17.1 x 29.4/8.97.
E Tw scr, tpl exp; 2 x 3 cyls, 900 NHP, 4 blrs, 180 psi, 13 kts. By Palmer's Co., Jarrow.
H Steel. 2 dks + shelter dk. F 52/15.85. B 187/57. P 60/18.29.
P 200 1st, 1,500 3rd.
1911 Laid down as *Gerona* for Cairns, Noble & Co's Thomson Line for their Canadian services. With Cunard's re-entry onto the route the Line was purchased together with the ships owned. *Gerona* was, therefore acquired on the stocks. March 3: Launched as *Ascania* thereby commencing the tradition that 'A' named ships were for the Canadian service. May 23: M/v Southampton-Quebec-Montreal.
1918 June 13: Wrecked 20 miles east of Cape Ray, Newfoundland, en-route Liverpool-Montreal in ballast. No lives lost.

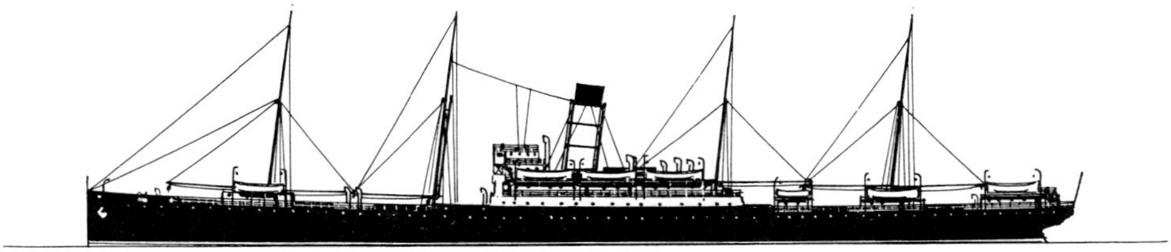

AUSONIA (I)

110 **AUSONIA (I)**
B 1909 Swan, Hunter & Wigham Richardson, Newcastle. **T** 7,907g, 955n.
D 464/141.42 oa, 450.5/137.31 x 54.2/16.51 x 29.1/8.89.
E Tw scr, tpl exp, 3 cyls, 888 NHP, 180 psi, 12 kts. By Palmer's Co., Jarrow.
H Steel. 2 dks + shelter dk. B 117/35.66. 7 holds. **P** 37 1st, 1,100 3rd.
1909 Aug 18: Launched as *Tortona,* Thomson Line. She had been announced as being for an Italy-Canada service. Oct 18: M/v Newcastle-Canada.
1911 March: Acquired with the Thomson Line. R/n *Ausonia.* May 16: Made the first voyage for Cunard on their new service to Canada. London-Southampton-Quebec-Montreal. Shortly afterwards she was rebuilt by extending the bridgedeck forward to the fore mast. **T** 8,153g, 5,111n.
1914 Aug 8: Commenced 6 voyages for Anchor Glasgow-Moville-New York.
1915 Feb: Commenced ballast outwards and Canadian trooping inbound.
1916 May: Resumed normal service.
1917 June 11: Torpedoed en-route Montreal-Avonmouth but made port.
1918 May 30: Torpedoed and then sunk by gunfire from *U-55* off Fastnet outbound Liverpool-Montreal. 44 lost. The survivors were in the boats for 8 days before being picked up by *H.M.S. Zinnia.*

ALBANIA (I)

111 **ALBANIA (I)**
B 1900 C. S. Swan & Hunter, Newcastle. **T** 7,682g, 5,012n, 9,200dwt.
D 461.6/140.67 x 52.1/15.88 x 38.7/11.79.
E Tw scr, tpl exp, 2 x 3 cyls, 783 NHP, 4 blrs, 200 psi, 12 kts. By T. Richardson & Sons, Hartlepool.
H Steel. 2 dks + shelter dk. **P** (as built) 12.
1900 Feb 2: Launched as *Consuelo* for Thomas Wilson & Co., Hull. Cattle carrier with cattle stalls on the main deck. June: Entered service Hull-New York.
1908 April: Sold for £69,000 to the Thomson Line (Cairns, Noble & Co.). R/n *Cairnrona* for the Newcastle-London-Canada route. Refitted **T** 7640g. **P** 50 1st, 300 3rd.
1910 Apr 7: Her coal bunkers caught fire off Beachy Head, 879 passengers were transferred to two ships standing by. *Cairnrona* then returned to London for repairs. 1 death. Aug: Commenced the London-Southampton-Quebec-Montreal passenger service with *Tortona. Gerona* (109) was awaited.
1911 March: Cunard bought the fleet and its trading connections but not Cairns, Noble. R/n *Albania* for the Canadian routes. The ship was not up to Cunard standards and was to last less than six months. May 2: First Cunard sailing on the London-Canada route which they had taken over.
Oct: After arriving at London she was laid up off Southend 'for sale'. Chartered by Royal Mail Line for their River Plate service.
1912 Sold for £21,000 to Andrew Weir's Bank Line and renamed *Poleric.*
1916 Used on Government service.
1919 Overhauled on the Clyde; given new blrs and converted to oil burning. Cost was £100,000.
1920 Apr: Resumed Weir service.
1921 Feb: Caught fire off Ponta Delgada, Azores en-route to U.K. Ended up in Rotterdam for repairs.
1925 Nov: On voyage Vancouver-Shanghai with grain her cargo shifted during a storm. Found by the tug *Salvage King,* Straits Towing, and taken to Vancouver.
1927 May: Laid up at Shanghai. Eventually sold to Japanese breakers for £17,000. She is reported to have served with Osaka Syosen but does not appear in their fleet lists.
1929 Broken up as Osaka.

ANDANIA (I), ALAUNIA (I)

112 **ANDANIA (I)**
B 1913 Scotts S.B. & E. Co, Greenock. **T** 13,405g, 8,464n, 9,450 dwt.
D 520.4/158.62 x 64.7/19.71 x 42.5/12.95.
E Tw scr, tpl exp, 2 x 3 cyls, 8,500 IHP, 2 blrs, 32 furn, 180 psi, 14½ kts. By builder.
H Steel, 3 dks. B 243/74.07. **P** 520 2nd, 150 3rd.
1913 March 22: Launched. The first of three ships ordered for the Canadian route to Montreal as replacements for the Thomson ships.
July 17: M/v London-Southampton-Quebec-Montreal.
1914 Jan: Took three voyages on the Liverpool-Boston run.
1915 Carried Canadian troops inbound. She also served as an accommodation ship for German prisoners of war in the Thames.
1916 March 18: Joined *Alaunia* on the London-New York route.
1918 Jan 27: 10.00. Torpedoed by *U-46* near to Rathlin Lighthouse, 7 men were lost by the explosion. 12 Officers and men stayed aboard. 16.00: Again abandoned as bulkheads gave way. A tug then arrived and, in an effort to beach her, she was taken in tow but at 19.30, when less than four miles from safety, she suddenly fell onto her side and sank.

113 **ALAUNIA** (I)
Details as *Andania* except: **T** 13,405g, 8,464n, 9,450dwt. **E** Quad exp.
1913 June 9: Launched. Nov 27: Delivery voyage. Dec 3: M/v Liverpool-Portland, Maine.
1914 April: London sailings; firstly to Portland and then to Montreal. Aug: Commenced to carry troops inbound for 10 voyages.
1915 Trooped to India. Something rare for Cunard.
1916 May 10: Initiated sailings London-Falmouth. Plymouth-New York.
Oct 19: After landing her passengers at Falmouth she hit a mine 2 miles from the Royal Sovereign lightship, 2 dead. An attempt to beach her was made and power got her underway but *Alaunia* sank soon afterwards.

TRANSYLVANIA (I)

114 **TRANSYLVANIA (I)**
B 1914 Scotts S.B. & E.Co, Greenock. **T** 14,315g, 8,620n.
D 549.3/167.43 x 66.5/20.27 x 45.4/13.84.
E Tw scr, 2 Parson's sgl reduction geared steam turbines, 9,000 IHP, 16 kts. By builder.
H Steel. 4 dks. **P** 305 1st, 216 2nd, 1,858 3rd.
1914 May 23: Launched, the first geared turbine liner on the North Atlantic. Designed for an intended Mediterranean Cunard-Anchor Joint Service which, because of the war, failed to materialise.
Nov 7: Maiden voyage Liverpool-New York via Queenstown. Cunard owned and in their livery. Her sister *Tuscania* was delivered to Anchor.
1915 Feb 4: Acquired by Anchor. March 23: First Anchor sailing Glasgow-Liverpool-Queenstown-New York. Anchor livery.
May: Taken over for trooping. Capacity 200 Officers and 2,860 men.
1917 May 3: Left Marseilles for Alexandria with a full complement and escorted by the Japanese destroyers *Matsu* and *Sakaki*.

May 4: Torpedoed in the engine room by *U-63*. The ship was zig-zagging at 14 kts some 2½ miles from Cape Vado, Gulf of Genoa. *Transylvania* at once headed for the shore while *Matsu* came alongside and commenced to take off the troops. *Sakaki* circled to force the submarine to remain submerged. A second torpedo was seen heading amidships of *Matsu,* which was still alongside and by now crowded with men. With great skill *Matsu* went full astern and got clear by a split second. The second torpedo hit *Transylvania* which settled and sank immediately. The whole attack had taken a little over half an hour. Her commander, Lt. Brennel, R.N.R., 11 crew, 29 Officers and 373 men were killed or drowned; 413 in all.

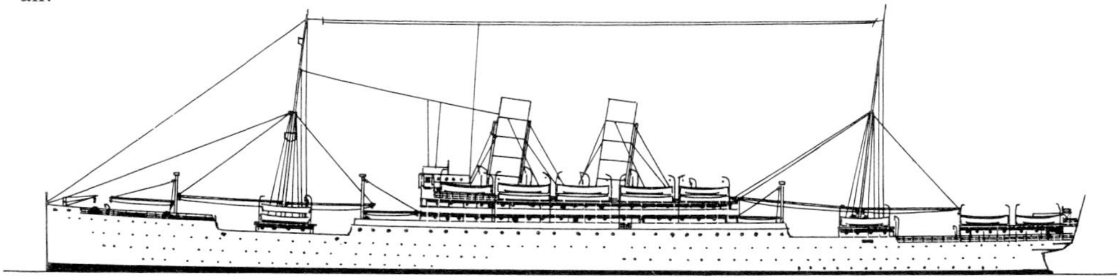

AURANIA (II)

115 **AURANIA (II)**
Details as *Andania* (112) except: **B** 1917 Swan, Hunter & Wigham Richardson, Newcastle. **T** 13,936g, 8,499n. **E** 4 dbl reduction turbines (from 17,000 to 100 rpm) by Wallsend Slipway Co. **H** F 86/26.22.
1914 laid down. Given a fclse and had taller funnels when delivered.
1916 July 16: Launched. Grey painted as drawn; never in Cunard livery.
1917 March 28: M/v Tyne-New York-Liverpool. Troopship duties.
1918 Feb 4: Torpedoed by *UB-67* on only her eighth voyage 15 miles north west of Inishtrahull, Donegal. 8 killed. Taken in tow by an armed trawler, but, in heavy weather, the tow broke and *Aurania* went ashore near to Tobermory and was wrecked.

116 **AQUITANIA** (Drawing page 66)
B 1914 John Brown & Co, Clydebank. **T** 45,647g 21,998n, 14,400dwt.
D 901/274.62 oa, 868.6/264.74 x 97/29.57 x 49.7/15.14.
E Quad scr, 4 Parsons-Brown direct acting turbines, 3 HP + 1 LP, 56,000 SHP, at 195 pps. 23 kts on 680 tons coal per day. By builder.
H Steel 4 dks + shelter dk. B 524/159.71. C 141,000/3,993 cu g.
P 597 1st, 614 2nd, 2,052 3rd.
1910 Dec 8: Ordered. Designed to run a weekly service with *Lusitania* and *Mauretania.* No Government subsidy; therefore she had to have 50% more carrying capacity in order to become an economic proposition.
1911 June 5: Keel laid. Before this the Mersey Docks & Harbour Board had to amend the plans for their new Gladstone Dock by lengthening it to 1,050 ft/320m and widening the entrance to 120ft/36.58m. John Brown's yard also had to lengthen and strengthen the slip to take her.
1913 Apr 21: Launched. The Clyde Navigation Trustees had to deepen the river and the dockyard berth to accept her.
1914 May 10: Her trials began. 24 kts was reached. May 30: M/v Liverpool-New York. Captain W. T. Turner. Tragically on May 29 the Canadian Pacific *Empress of Ireland* had been sunk in the St Lawrence with the loss of 1,023 lives and this overshadowed her debut. Before the outbreak of World War I she had only completed three voyages.
Aug: Taken over at Liverpool, with *Caronia* (99), and converted into an AMC; flew the White Ensign.
Aug 8: Left the Mersey armed with 6 x 6in guns. Unwieldy, she at once hit her escort off Anglesey and returned to port. Sept: Laid up at Liverpool, having been judged too large and vulnerable for AMC duties.
1915 May: Dazzle painted she was used to troop a total of 30,000 men to the Dardenelles.
1916 Aug: In white livery she became a hospital ship carrying 25,000 patients from the Turkish war zone. Dec: Laid up at Liverpool.
1917 At Liverpool all year.
1918 March: In 9 voyages she brought 60,000 U.S. troops to Europe and then continued to work to repatriate them after the ending of hostilities.
1919 Feb 19: Her first post war sailing was Liverpool-New York.
May: Commodore Sir James Charles took her out of Southampton without the aid of tugs due to their being on strike.
1919 Dec: Converted to oil burning by Swan, Hunter & Wigham Richardson, Newcastle. Bunkers 8,638 tons. Fitted with gyro compass.

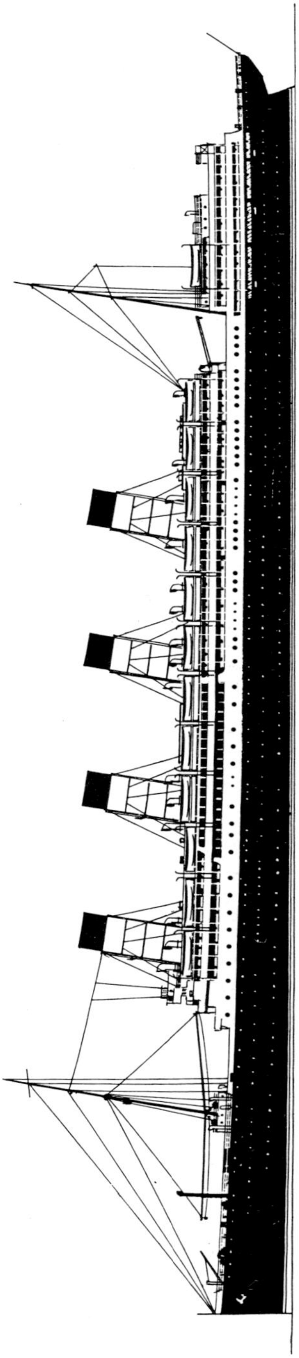

116 *AQUITANIA*
(Scale 1:1600)

1920 July 17: Resumed service alongside *Mauretania* and *Berengaria* (136), the post war replacement for *Lusitania.*
1921 May: During a strike by stewards 2,750 passengers were carried being served by office staff and volunteers. Her crossing was her fastest.
1924 The reduction in permitted immigrants into the U.S.A. led to a drive to encourage tourists and in winter to cruising out of New York.
1936 When she ran in conjunction with *Queen Mary* she had to average 24.87 kts to maintain the schedule which she achieved.
1938 Her master Sir James Charles on his final voyage before retirement collapsed at Cherbourg and died after the ship arrived at Southampton. Sailors, who are superstitious, drew their own conclusions.
1939 Nov 21: Requisitioned as a troopship at the end of her 582nd crossing and 1,746,000 miles. Nov 29: Left for Halifax.
1940 Trooped from Sydney to the Middle East covering 526,264 miles.
1941 Nov 23: Picked up raft with 26 survivors from German raider *Kormoran* which had sunk H.M.A.S. *Sydney*. Kept radio silence unaware of *Sydney*'s loss. 318 survived from *Kormoran*. 645 lost in the *Sydney*.
1948 Used to repatriate U.S. troops. In all during hostilities she carried 384,586 personnel travelling unescorted on the high seas.
May 25: She commenced 25 austerity voyages for the Canadian Government Southampton-Halifax.
1949 Nov 24: Her final sailing was Halifax-Southampton arriving on Dec 1.
1950 Feb: Sold to the British Iron and Steel Corp. Feb 19: Delivered by a crew of 250 to the Gareloch and broken up at Faslane. During her career she had steamed over 3 million miles and carried 1,200,000 people.

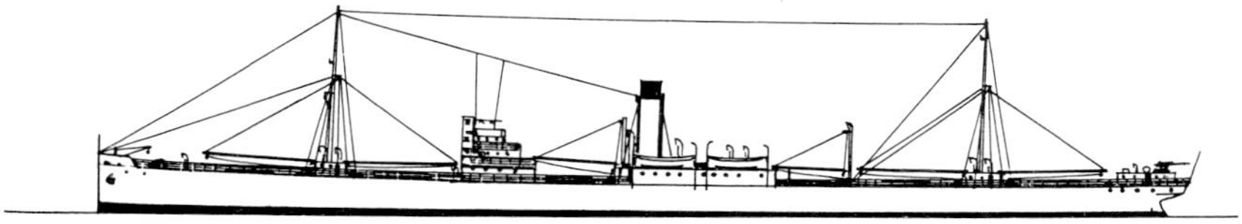

VINOVIA, VANDALIA (I)

117 **VINOVIA**
B 1906 Short Bros, Sunderland. **T** 7,046g, 4,545n.
D 418.2/127.46 x 54.4/16.59 x 37.2/11.33.
E Sgl scr, quad exp, 4 cyls, 539 NHP, 3 blrs, 9 furn, 220 psi, 12 kts. By North East Marine Engine Co, Newcastle. **H** Steel. 2 dks.
1906 Nov: Delivered as *Anglo-Bolivian,* Lawther, Latta & Co, London.
1915 Purchased by Cunard. R/n *Vinovia.* This started their 'V' style nomenclature for North Atlantic U.S.A. cargo vessels.
1917 Dec 19: Torpedoed in the English Channel, 8 miles south of Wolf Rock. 9 killed.

118 **VANDALIA (1)**
Details as *Vinovia* except: **B** 1912, **T** 7,333g, 4,618n.
D 425/129.54 x 56.3/17.15 **H** 2 dks + shelter dk.
1912 Built for Lawther, Latta & Co. London as *Anglo-Californian.*
1915 Purchased and renamed *Vandalia.*
1918 June 9: Torpedoed 18 miles west north west of the Smalls. All saved after taking to the boats.

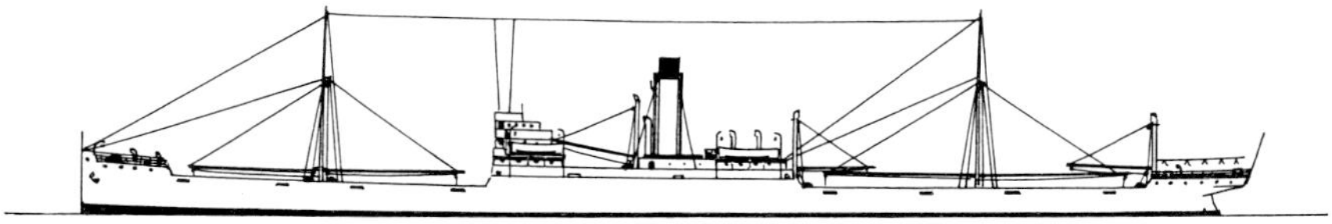

VALERIA, VOLODIA

119 **VALERIA**
B 1913 Russell & Co, Port Glasgow. **T** 5,865g, 3,055n.
D 423.2/129.98 x 56.2/17.12 x 34.5/10.52.
E Sgl scr, tpl exp, 3 cyls, 540 NHP, 3 blrs, 9 furn. 200 psi. 12 kts. By Rankin & Blackmore, Greenock. **H** Steel, 2 dks.
1913 Built as *Den of Airlie* for Charles Barrie, Dundee.
1915 Acquired and r/n *Valeria.* Drawn grey painted; never in Cunard livery.
1918 March 21; Caught fire and grounded on Taylor's Bank, River Mersey. Burnt out and became a constructive total loss.

120 **VOLODIA**
Sister of *Valeria except:* T 5,689g, 3,010n.
1913 Built as *Den of Ogil,* Charles Barrie, Dundee.
1915 Purchased and r/n *Volodia.* Atlantic service.
1917 Aug 21: Torpedoed 285 miles west of Ushant, 10 killed by the explosion.

ROYAL GEORGE

121 **ROYAL GEORGE**
B 1907 Fairfield Co. Glasgow. **T** 11,146g, 5,685n.
D 541.5/165 oa, 525.7/160.22 x 60.2/18.34 x 27/8.23. Dft 25.6/7.8.
E Tpl scr, 3 turbines, 8 blrs, 48 furnaces, 180 psi, 18 kts on 170 tons per day. By builder. Achieved 19¾ knots on her trials.
H Steel. 3 dks. F 70/21.33. B 308/93.88. Cargo 4,000 tons.
P 344 1st, 210 2nd, 560 3rd.
1907 May 28: Launched for the Egyptian Mail S.S.Co. Nov 6: Completed for a new express service Marseilles-Alexandria bearing the name *Heliopolis.* Her sister ship was *Cairo* which later became *Royal Edward* and was lost in 1915 off Gallipoli. The ships cost £350,000 each.
1909 May 9: The service proved to be uneconomic and after this last sailing she was laid up at Marseilles.
1910 Acquired by Canadian Northern Steamship Co, Toronto. R/n *Royal George* for a service Avonmouth-Quebec-Montreal. Known as the Royal Line. Refitted by builder for Atlantic service. May 26: First sailing. At Montreal it was realised that she coaled through side ports and a special coal barge was converted out of a grain elevator.
1912 Nov 5: As the St Lawrence commenced to freeze she grounded outbound on Orleans Island and was ashore for two weeks before salvage. Temporarily repaired at Halifax. Dec 12: Back at Liverpool for more repairs, which took six months, at Cammell Laird.
1913 June 17: Resumed service.
1914 Sept: Taken over with her sister for trooping. Their places being taken by *Campanello* (122) and *Principello.* (124). For 33 months she trooped Marseilles-Salonika and Durban-Persian Gulf.
1916 Cunard took over the five Canadian Northern ships. Of the five only *Royal George* retained her name.
1919 Feb 8: Her first post war voyage was Liverpool-New York. Known as the 'Rolling George', her tophamper was reduced by lowering her boats by one deck onto slung davits (as drawn).
1920 June: Became a depot ship at Cherbourg for emigrants awaiting passage. At the end of the summer she was laid up at Falmouth.
1922 July: Sold. Aug 7: Towed to Wilhelmshaven and scrapped.

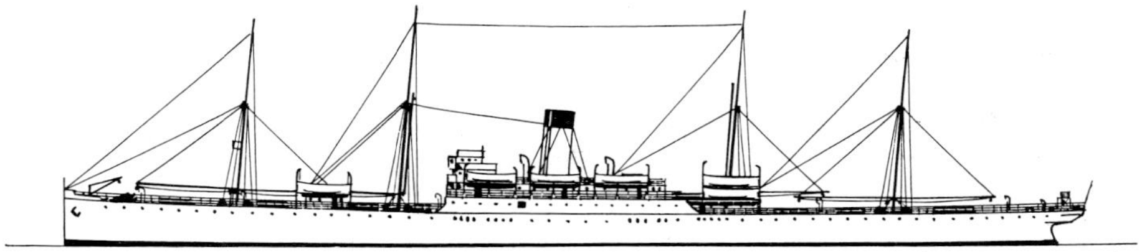

FLAVIA

122 **FLAVIA**
B 1902 Palmer's Co, Jarrow. **T** 9,285g, 4,693n.
D 470/143.26 x 56.8/17.3 x 32.1/9.78.
E Tw scr, tpl exp, 2 x 3 cyls, 795 NHP, 190 psi, 13½ kts. By builder.
H Steel, 2 dks + shelter dk. B 110/33.53. **P** 125 1st, 900 3rd.
1901 Sept 29: Launched as *British Empire* for British Shipowners Co.

1902 Entered service Liverpool-New Zealand on charter. Her owners had made a practice for many years of building fine ships that spent much of their lives on charter to established lines who were temporarily in need of extra tonnage. Several ships owned by them were purchased cum-charter.
1907 Sold to Navegazione Generale Italiana, Genoa. R/n *Campania* for the Genoa-Naples-New York service.
1909 Jan: Chartered to the Northwest Transport Line, London, (owned by the Canadian Northern Railway Co) Feb 16: Hamburg-Rotterdam-New York route.
1910 April: Transferred at Rotterdam to the Uranium S.S. Co; the company's new title. To avoid confusion with Cunard's *Campania* (and at their insistence) r/n *Campanello.* When taken over it was found that 2,000 passengers awaited her and the ship was forced to sail for New York 48 hours later on a voyage that all would have preferred to forget.
1914 Aug: Due to the war the Hamburg-Rotterdam-New York service ceased. Oct: The ship now joined the Royal Line service out of Avonmouth.
1916 Acquired by Cunard. R/n *Flavia.* Same service.
1918 Aug 24: Struck by two torpedoes from *U-107* off Tory Island, Ulster. 1 lost. She remained afloat for over two hours.

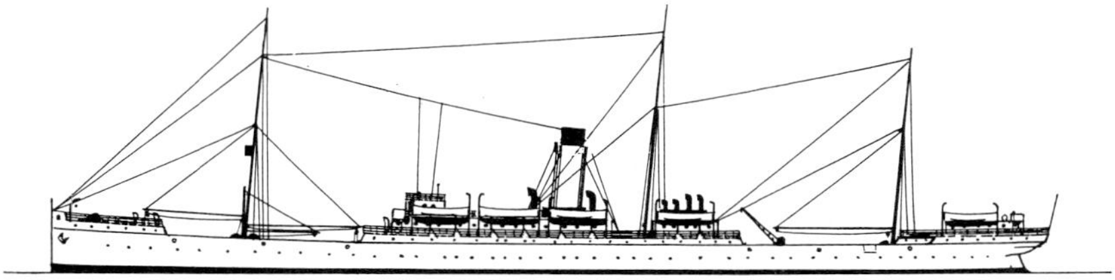

FELTRIA

123 **FELTRIA**
B 1891 Wm Denny & Bros, Dumbarton. **T** 5,254g, 3,287n, 6,090 dwt.
D 420/128.02 x 48.2/14.68 x 30/9.14.
E Sgl scr, quad exp (2 crank compound type) 666 NHP, 3 blrs, 8 furn, 180 psi, 13 kts with left hand rotating screw. By builder.
H Steel. 2 dks. F 49/14.93. B 165/50.29. P 45/13.72. **P** (as built) 400 3rd.
1890 Aug 13: Ordered as *Avoca* for British India Associated Steamers.
1891 June 9: Launched. Aug 25: M/v to Calcutta then, Sept 14, on Torres Strait route to Brisbane. The ship cost £102,167.
1896 Chartered to Cia Trasatlantica for Cuba trooping. R/n *San Fernando.* Late in the year reverted to B.I.A.S. and *Avoca.*
1907 June: Sold to the East Asiatic Co, Copenhagen for use as the royal yacht for the visit of the King and Queen of Denmark to Greenland. Overhauled and white painted. R/n *Atlanta.*
1908 Became *Avoca* of the New York & Continental Line (Robertson, Shankland & Co). During the year the company was wound up and the ship was sold to the Northwest Transport Line. R/n *Uranium.*
1910 Her owners became Uranium S.S. Co who acquired her for £35,000.
1916 May: Taken over by Cunard with the fleet of the Uranium Co. as a war loss and war service replacement. R/n *Feltria.*
1917 May 5: Torpedoed 8 miles off Mine Head, Waterford, 45 lost.

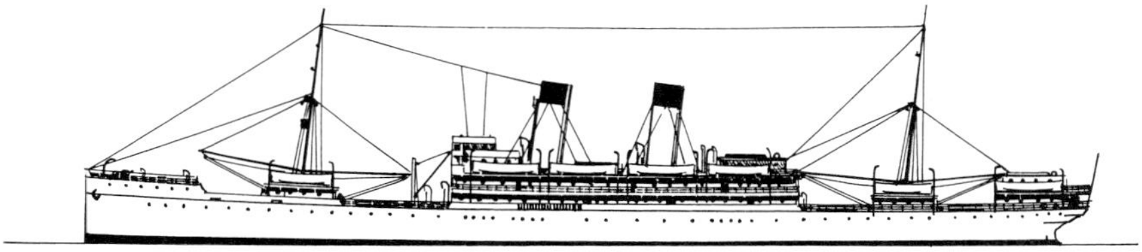

FOLIA

124 **FOLIA**
B 1907 James Laing & Co. Sunderland. **T** 6,704g, 4,211n.
D 430/131.06 x 52.6/16.03 x 25/7.62.
E Tw scr, tpl exp, 2 x 3 cyls, 807 NHP, 5 blrs, 12 furn, 180 psi, 14 Kts. By George Clark & Co, Sunderland.
H Steel. 2 dks + shelter dk. F 35/10.67. **P** 120 1st, 50 2nd, 1,500 3rd.
1907 Feb 28: launched as *Principe di Piemonte* for Lloyd Sabaudo. June 19: M/v Genoa-Naples-Palermo-Gibraltar-New York.

1913 Following the loss of their *Volturno* the Uranium S.S.Co acquired her for £95,000. R/n *Principello.* Rotterdam-New York route.
1916 Acquired with the remainder of the fleet by Cunard. R/n *Folia.* Served Avonmouth-New York. At this stage she was cargo only.
1917 Mar 11: Inbound for Avonmouth torpedoed off Waterford. The submarine surfaced to finish her off with gunfire and a further torpedo. 11 lost.

VALACIA (1)

125 **VALACIA (1)**
B 1910 Russell & Co. Port Glasgow. **T** 6,526g, 4,100n.
D 460/140.2 x 57/17.37 x 28.9/8.79.
E Sgl scr, tpl exp, 3 cyls, 690 NHP, 180 psi. 13 Kts. By Rankin & Blackmore, Greenock. **H** Steel. 2 dks + shelter dk.
1910 Oct: Built for Andrew Weir's Bank Line as *Luceric.*
1916 May: Bought by Cunard. R/n *Valacia.* New York cargo service.
1931 Sold to Italian shipbreakers.

VIRGILIA

126 **VIRGILIA**
B 1918 Russell & Co, Port Glasgow. **T** 5,697g, 3,619n.
D 423.3/129.01 x 56/17.07 x 28.6/8.71.
E Sgl scr, tpl exp, 3 cyls, 550 NHP, 3 blrs, 180 psi, 12 kts. By J. G. Kincaid, Greenock.
H Steel, 2 dks. F 43/13.11. B 123/37.49. P 38/11.58.
1918 Nov: Completed for Cunard S.S. Co. Her design was basically one of the standard 'A' type but she was custom built. In fact Russell & Co did not construct standard ships.
1925 Sold to the Lancashire Shipping Co., James Chambers & Co., Liverpool. R/n *Corby Castle.*
1927 Sold to Tatsuuma Kisen K.K. became *Tatsuha Maru.*
1944 War loss.

VELLAVIA, VITELLIA, VENNONIA, VENUSIA, VERENTIA

127 **VELLAVIA**
B 1918 Armstrong, Whitworth & Co., Newcastle. **T** 5,272g, 3,195n.
D 400.2/121.97 x 52.3/15.95 x 28.4/8.66.
E Sgl scr, tpl exp, 3 cyls, 517 NHP, 3 blrs, 180 psi, 12 kts. By G. Clark, Sunderland.
H Steel, 2 dks, F 39/11.89. B 112/34.14. P 49/14.94.
1918 June: Built as *War Setter.* Narrow goal post masts. Standard B type.
1919 Became *Vellavia,* Cunard.
1925 R/n *River Tigris,* America-Levant Line, S. & J. Thompson, London.
1931 May: R/n *Ines Corrado,* Soc. Anon di Nav. Corrado, Genoa.
1941 Dec: Seized by Argentina, R/n *Rio Diamante.* State operated.
1946 Reverted to Corrado and *Ines Corrado.*
1951 July 26: Scuttled in Porto Vecchio bay when the cargo of coal took fire. Refloated and repaired.
1959 Apr: Broken up at Tokio.

128 **VITELLIA**
As *Vellavia* except: **B** 1918 Earles Co., Hull. **D** 375.6/114.45 x 51.7/15.9.
E By builder. **H** P 41/12.5.
1918 Nov: Completed as *War Pintail,* Standard E type for the Shipping Controller. Liverpool-Glasgow-New York. Managed by Cunard. Pole masts with lattice derricks. Type E were of shorter dimensions.
1919 June: Acquired and r/n *Vitellia.* June 5: Transferred to Anchor Line ownership when Cunard dropped the Glasgow call in favour of Anchor.
1923 Dec 13: Sold to Scindia S.N. Co., Bombay; r/n *Jalarashmi.*
1953 Sold to Jhajharia Trading Co., Bombay, R/n *Asha.*
1954 Jan 23: Arrived at Singapore with a cargo of scrap metal for Osaka. The crew left her as being unseaworthy. Laid up 'unfit for sea'. Apr 22: R/n *Asha Maru* and towed to Hirahata, Japan.
1955 Broken up.

129 **VENNONIA**
As *Vellavia* except: **B** & **E** Caledon SB & E Co., Dundee. **T** 5,225g, 3,193n.
1918 Nov: Bt for the Shipping Controller as *War Carp;* type B standard ship. Type B were 2 deckers; A's were sgl decked.
1919 Jan: Became *Vennonia* for Cunard.
1923 May: Sold to America-Levant, S. & J. Thompson R/n *River Hudson.*
1931 Became *Zeffiro,* Soc. Anon. di Nav, Corrado, Genoa.
1941 May 20: Torpedoed by H. M. Submarine *Urge* near to Cape Bon.

130 **VENUSIA**
Details as *Vellavia* but: **B.** & **E.** Harland & Wolff, Belfast. **T** 5,222g, 3,173n.
1918 Aug: Built as *War Snake,* Shipping Controller. Type B. Sept: Purchased by Cunard. R/n *Venusia.* Like all the standard ships purchased they were intended only as war loss replacements pending the outcome of the Company's post war planning.
1923 Sold to S. & J. Thompson's America-Levant Line, R/n *River Delaware.*
1931 Sold with her sister to Corrado. R/n *Rina Corrado.*
1941 Nov 11: Sunk by British naval gunfire east of Syracuse. Employed in the carriage of war supplies to Rommel's forces in North Africa.

131 **VERENTIA**
As *Venusia.* **T** 5,185g, 3,152n.
1918 May: Completed for the Shipping Controller as *War Lemur.* Type B.
1919 Jan: Became Cunard's *Verentia.* Atlantic cargo services.
Had the narrow style of goal post masts.
1926 Acquired by Cree Investments, Andrew Weir; r/n *Foreric.*
1927 Jan: Transferred to Bank Line ownership. Resold to Buenos Aires & Great Southern Railway Co. London. Arthur Holland & Co. managers. Collier duties from South Wales to Buenos Aires. R/n *Galvan* (one of 5 purchased). Lattice girder derricks were replaced pole type.
1935 Sold to Kaye, Sons & Co. Same name.
1937 Passed to Pedder, Mylchreest for delivery to the Far East owners Nisshin Kaiun Shokai who kept her name while they sold her to Chang Shu Chang, Tsingtao, R/n *Pei Tai.*
1938 Sold to Kitagawa Sangyo Kaiun, Osaka. R/n *Hokutai Maru.*
1944 Mar 30: Sunk by U.S. air attack of Pelew Islands, Pacific.

VARDULIA (I), VASCONIA (I), VERBANIA

132 **VARDULIA (I)**
B 1917 Russell & Co., Port Glasgow. **T** 5,691g, 3,613n.
D 423.2/129 x 56/17.07 x 28.7/8.74.
E Sgl scr, tpl exp, 3 cyls, 564 NHP, 3 blrs, 180 psi, 12 kts. By Rankin & Blackmore, Greenock.
H Steel. 2 dks. F 43/13.11. B 123/37.49. P 38/11.58.
1917 March: Built as *Verdun* for Gow, Harrison & Co., London.
1918 March: Purchased by Cunard S.S. Co. R/n *Vardulia.*
1929 Sold to Donaldson Bros, Glasgow. Same name. Canadian routes.
1935 Oct: Lost with all hands en route West Hartlepool-St John. N.B. with a cargo of coal. Two radio messages were picked up: 'Dangerous list' and 'Am abandoning ship'.

133 **VASCONIA (I)**
As *Vardulia* except: **T** 5,680g, 3,613n.
1918 Aug: Completed as *Valverda.* Gow Harrison & Co. Taken over by Cunard and renamed *Vasconia.*
1927 Sold to Tatsuuma (later spelled Tatuuma) Kisen K., Nishinomiya. R/n *Shiraha Maru.*
1944 war loss.

134 **VERBANIA**
As *Vardulia* except: **B** R. Duncan & Co., Port Glasgow. **T** 5,021g, 3,180n.
D 405.3/123.55 x 53/16.15 x 27.3/8.33. **E** By J. G. Kincaid, Greenock.
1918 March: Built as *Trafalgar* for Lawrence Glen & Co., Glasgow. She has a slightly more pronounced rake than the drawing of *Vardulia.*
1919 Purchased by Cunard. R/n *Verbania.*
1926 To the Lyle Shipping Co, Glasgow. R/n *Cape Cornwall.* Cost £25,000.
1931 Broken up at Shanghai.

SATELLITE (II)

135 **SATELLITE (II)**
B 1896 J. Scott & Co., Kinghorn, Fife. **T** 333g, 132n.
D 160/48.77 x 27.1 x 9.8/2.3.
E Pad, comp 2 cyl, 164 NHP, 10 kts. By builder.
H Steel 1 dk. **P** 1,200 or 800 with baggage.
1896 Built as the Mersey ferry *John Herron* for the Wallasey Corporation.
1920 Acquired for use as a tender at Cherbourg. R/n *Satellite.* Her owners were registered as Societe Maritime de Transbordment, Cherbourg.
1924 Replaced by *Lotharingia* (150) and broken up locally.

136 **BERENGARIA**
B 1913 Vulkan Werke, Hamburg. **T** 52,226g, 21,506n, 51,000disp.
D 899/274 oa, 883.5/269.29 x 97.3/29.7 x 57.1/17.4.
E Quad scr, 4 Curtis-AEG Vulkan-Parsons turbs 62,000 SHP (HP and Intermediate drove inner screws, 2 x LP the outer pair), 46 water tube blrs, 228 psi, 23½ kts at 185 rpm, bunkers 8,500 tons coal. By builder.
H Steel. 10 dks in all. Dbl bottom 6ft/1.82 deep. Funnels were eliptical 82ft/25m high. Entered service with eagle figure head.
P 970 1st, 830 2nd, 1,000 3rd, Crew 1,180.
1910 June: Keel laid as *Europa.*
1912 May 23: Names *Imperator* in honour of the Kaiser who launched her for the Hamburg America Line. The largest ship in the world at the time.
1913 Apr: Trials after which she stranded in the Elbe without damage. Then a minor explosion delayed her first sailing by three days.
June 10: M/v Cuxhaven-Southampton-Cherbourg-New York.
In service the ship was found to be top heavy and tender. She exhibited the trait that passengers disliked most. She hung over at the end of a roll as if the next wave might capsize her. When, at New York, a fire broke out the water used to extinguish it almost turned her over in dock. Returned to her builder who took 10ft/3.05m off her funnels and all the ornate heavy wooden panelling on the upper decks was replaced with light sheeting. The marble grill room was converted into a verandah lounge with garden type furniture. This cured her. The removal of the dummy third funnel was considered but it contained the ventilating equipment which could not be re-located.
Because of the *Titanic* her lifeboats, 83 in all, had some carried on the lower Promenade deck. This had been done to reduce top-hamper.
1914 July 31: Arrived at Hamburg. War broke out within days and she was laid up in the River Elbe.
1919 May: Allocated to the United States; used for troop repatriation. Aug: Laid up at New York because the U.S. had taken *Vaterland/Leviathan.*
1920 Feb: Taken over by the Shipping Controller with Cunard as managers. Feb 21: First Cunard managed sailing Liverpool-New York as *Imperator.*
May: Cunard with White Star jointly purchased *Imperator* and *Bismarck/Majestic* and they were jointly owned for the next decade.
June 6: Transferred to Southampton-New York route; remained there.
1921 Apr 16: R/n *Berengaria* for the Southampton-New York service. Her consorts were *Mauretania* and *Aquitania.* Sept: Six month overhaul by Armstrong, Whitworth, Walker on Tyne. Converted to oil fuel. Bunkers 6,500 tons. Her lifeboats were black and some were on the boat deck aft.
1922 Apr 26: Left the Tyne. May: Back in service. **T** 52,226g.
1926 May: **P** 972 1st, 630 2nd, 515 3rd.

1934 Transferred to Cunard White Star ownership.
1935 Accommodation rated as Cabin, Tourist and Third. All boats now on boat deck; still black but shortly afterwards painted white. With her return to service *Olympic* was retired.
1936 Oct: Several cabins were burnt out at Southampton.
1938 March 3: Damaged by fire at New York. Left next day without passengers for Southampton. Uneconomic to repair. Nov 7: Sold for scrapping at Jarrow.
1946 The war had stopped the work at waterline level, now 7 tugs towed the fore part, 535ft/163.07m, to Rosyth for final dismantling.

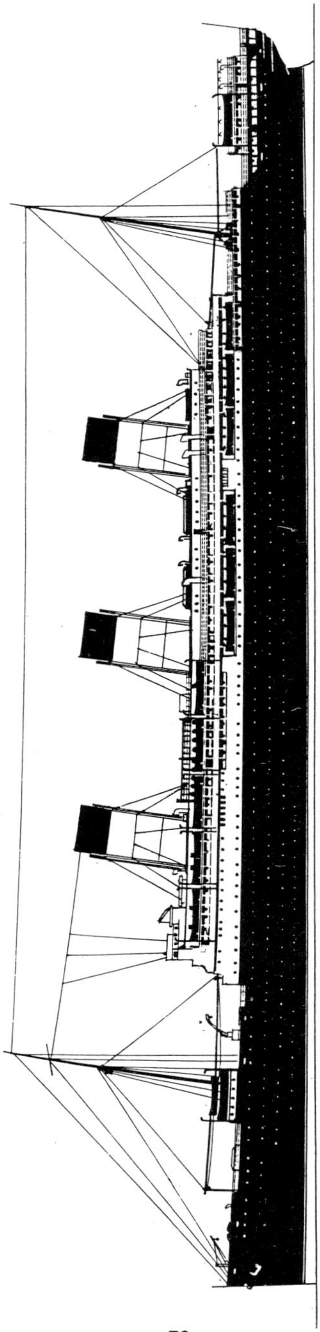

BERENGARIA
(Scale 1:1600)

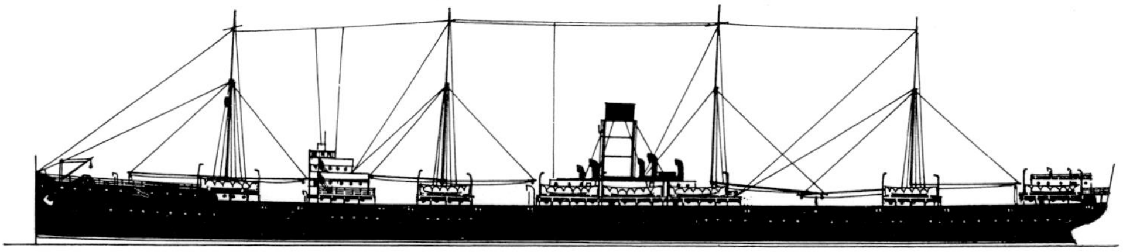

ALBANIA (II)

137 **ALBANIA (II)**
B 1921 Scotts S.B. & E. Co, Greenock. **T** 12,767g, 7,519n, 12,170dwt.
D 523.1/159.44 x 64/19.51 x 43.8/13.36.
E Tw scr, 4 dbl red, geared turbs, 1,340 NHP, 3 blrs, 18 furn, 200 psi, 13 kts. By builder.
H Steel. 2 dks + shelter dk, F 86/26.22. **P** 480 Cabin.
1914 Laid down as sister to *Aurania* (114) but work suspended due to the war. Later work to complete her as a cargo ship started.
1920 Apr 17: Launched.
1921 Jan 18: M/v Liverpool-New York.
1922 Apr 20: Transferred to the Canadian route for which her 'A' name intended her. With the freezing of the St Lawrence she went onto the Boston service.
1925 At the close of a summer on the London-New York route she was laid up. As a Liner she had not been successful due to her large cargo capacity which prevented her keeping to a passenger schedule. But she had served as a stop-gap until the new 'A' ships arrived.
1930 March: Sold to Soc. Anon. di Nav. Libera Triestina and renamed *California* for their Trieste-North Pacific ports service. Rebuilt with a better profile. **P** 130 1st, 30 2nd. Dec 11: First sailing to Seattle.
1935 Jan: Taken over as a hospital ship for the Italo-Abyssinian war.
1935 With the Government reorganisation of Italian shipping into four major groups *California* was transferred to Lloyd Triestino.
1941 Aug 11: Sunk by air attack at Syracuse, Sicily. She was eventually refloated but was broken up.

SCYTHIA (II), SAMARIA (II), LACONIA (II)

138 **SCYTHIA (II)**
B 1921 Vickers Ltd, Barrow-in-Furness. **T** 19,730g, 11,938n, 12,500dwt.
D 625/190.5 oa, 600.7/183.08 x 73.8/22.48 x 40.7/12.4.
E Tw scr, 2 x 3 dbl reduc. geared turbs, 2,528 NHP, 6 blrs, 36 furn, 220 psi, 16 kts, Oil burner; the largest yet so designed. By builder.
H Steel, 2 dks. B 284/86.56. **P** 350 1st, 350 2nd, 1,500 3rd, Crew 434.
1920 March 23: Launched. The first of five; 3 for Liverpool-New York and 2 for Liverpool-Boston.
1921 March: Due to a strike by the joiners her accommodation had to be completed at Lorient. Aug 20: M/v Liverpool-New York. Served for 18 years.
1922 March: Turbine damage caused delays to some voyages.
1928 King Amanulla of Afghanistan and his Queen visited Liverpool and were accommodated on *Scythia* alongside Princes landing stage. Later for the Welsh Eisteddfod she carried Americans to Cardiff.
1934 Hit the Isle of Man steamer *Viking* while berthing at Liverpool.
1939 Aug 5: Final sailing to New York and then three trips to take home U.S. citizens and to evacuate children. Nov: Taken over for trooping and converted at Glasgow.
1942 Nov 23: Severely damaged at Algiers by aerial torpedo during Operation Torch. She sank at her quayside berth in the harbour and was used as a naval transit camp. Dec: pumped out and patched.
1943 Jan 7: Went to Gibraltar and then on to New York for repairs.

1946 Feb 21: Her turbo feed pumps failed off White Head, Bangor Bay. Harland & Wolff repaired her there. Apr 7: Brought 2,500 German prisoners of war back to Liverpool from Canada. July: Trooped back from India.
1948 Chartered by the International Refugee Organisation and made 10 voyages to carry displaced persons from Germany to Canada.
1949 Nov: Refitted by John Brown, Clydebank for 9 months. **T** 19,930g, 11,927n. **P** 248 1st, 630 Tst. More superstructure glassed in.
1950 Aug 17: Resumed service Liverpool-Quebec. Her draught was too great to go up river to Montreal.
1951 Apr 10: Made the first Southampton-Quebec sailing for Cunard since 1939.
1952 June 5: Hit by the Canadian steamer *Wabana* in the St Lawrence.
1957 Nov: On Canadian Government service Rotterdam-Quebec. Then Liverpool-New York.
Dec 11: Left Halifax for Southampton and then out of service. John McLelland, a crew member, had served in her all her life — 36 years.
1958 Jan 1: Left Southampton and broken up at Inverkeithing by Wards.

139 **SAMARIA (II)**
Details as *Scythia* except; **B** 1921 Cammell Laird & Co, Birkenhead.
T 19,597g, 11,834n, **D** 601.5/183.34. Brown-Curtis turbines by builder.
1920 Nov 27: Launched. The largest ship yet built on Merseyside. Her launch was delayed for six months by strikes at a cost of £250,000.
1922 Apr 8: Trials. Apr 19: M/v Liverpool-Boston.
June: Returned to Liverpool with engine trouble. Her passengers were transferred to *Laconia.* Nov 2: Resumed service.
1923 Jan 24-June 22: Took the Thomas Cook 'Round the World' cruise from New York. Worked on a one class basis.
1924 Repeated the 'Round the World' cruise. Was the first Cunarder through the Panama Canal.
1928 Jan: To New York for cruising. July: Became the largest ship to visit Galway, Ireland when she embarked cruise pilgrims for Lourdes and Fatima.
1934 Winter: Overhauls relief ship with summer cruises out of London.
1939 Dec 16: Left Liverpool for New York but struck her escorting warship and had to put back.
1940-48 Trooping and Government service. June 6: First trooping voyage to Suez.
1946 Her livery, and that of other company troopships, was grey with Cunard funnel.
1948 Sept: Carried Canadian troops and their dependants from Cuxhaven to Quebec.
1950 Oct: To John Brown, Clydebank, for full overhaul. **P** 250 1st, 650 Tst.
1951 June 14: Liverpool-Quebec then to Southampton to join *Scythia* on the Southampton-Le Havre-Quebec route.
1952 Grounded near to Quebec. Her draught was almost that of the river. She, and her sisters, were designed for New York or Boston.
1953 June 15: Represented Cunard among the 260 vessels at the Coronation Naval Review at Spithead.
1955 Dec 3: Arrived at Southampton and laid up pending disposal.
1956 June 26: Sold for breaking up to BISCO and allocated to Thos W. Ward at Inverkeithing.

140 **LACONIA (II)**
As *Scythia* except: **B** 1922 Swan, Hunter & Wigham Richardson, Wallsend. **T** 19,695g, 11,804n. **D** 601.3/183.29. **E** By Wallsend Slipway, Wallsend.
1921 Apr 9: Launched. Last of the New York trio.
1922 May 25: M/v Southampton-New York then back to her Liverpool berth.
1923 Made a number of summer voyages out of Hamburg to New York.
1928 Refitted to Cabin, Tourist and Third.
1930-39: Used frequently for cruising ex-U.K. or New York.
1939 Sept: Converted into an Armed merchant Cruiser at Southampton.
1941: Reclassified to Troopship.
1942 Sept 12: The 'Laconia Incident'. 08.00 she was torpedoed by *U-156* 360 miles north of Ascension. The U-boat commander, Werner Hartenstein, then discovered that out of 2,200 aboard 1,800 were Italian prisoners of war. With the agreement of Admiral Doenitz from Paris Hartenstein stayed with the survivors; rounding up the lifeboats and distributing food and water. He collected so many survivors on his deck that he could not dive. For the first time in the war a U-boat sent an open message saying that help should be sent and that unless attacked he would not retaliate. The French at Casablanca sent the cruiser *Gloire* and the sloops *Dumont d'Urville* and *Annamite, U-506* and *U-507* arrived to help him by ferrying survivors to the approaching French warships. On Sept 16 an American Liberator aircraft appeared and, from 200 feet bombed *U-156* which was towing a string of overcrowded lifeboats. Hartenstein was forced to jettison over 200 survivors, many of whom had been injured. Next day *U-506,* with 142 survivors on her decks was also bombed. Her commander, Schacht, put all non-Italians into the

lifeboats (except for two British officers held as witnesses). Hitler was furious and Admiral Doenitz issued the order that U-boats, for their own safety, should not attempt to assist survivors (later, at his trial in Nuremburg, he was acquitted of the charge that this order was a war crime).
Larconia's losses were, nevertheless, 1,275. Only 450 Italians were saved. The U.S.A.F., from Ascension, claimed that they understood from the radio messages that only Italians were being picked up. For the record only one case is recorded of a U-boat destroying survivors (from the Greek *Peleus*, March 13, 1944) and *U-852's* commander Heinz Eck (and his officers) was executed on Nov 30 1945.

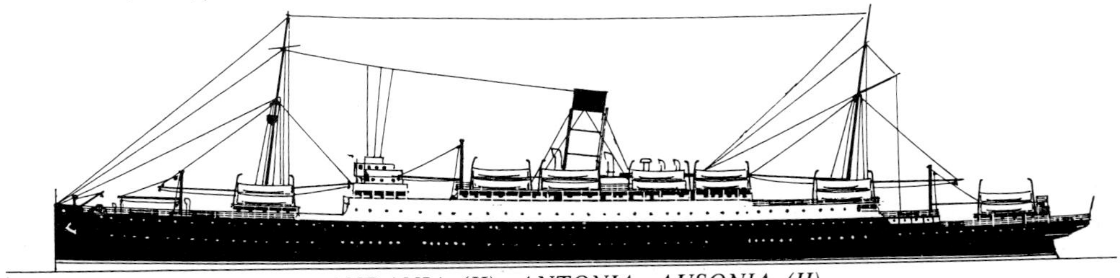

ANDANIA (II), ANTONIA, AUSONIA (II)

141 **ANDANIA (II)**
B 1922 Hawthorn, Leslie & Co, Hebburn-on-Tyne. **T** 13,950g, 8,391n.
D 520.2/158.55 x 65.3/19.91 x 39.2/11.94.
E Tw scr, 2 dbl reduction geared turbs, 1,660 NHP; 2 brs, 24 furn, 220 psi 15 kts. By builder.
H Steel. 2 dks + shelter dk. F & B 426/129.84. 7 hatches, 20 derricks.
P 500 1st, 1,200 3rd. Crew 270.
1921 Nov 1: Launched for the Canadian routes. Six modified *Andania* (I) (112) class were ordered. Four for Liverpool and two for London.
1922 June 1: M/v London-Southampton-Quebec-Montreal; her permanent intended route with Halifax in the winter.
1925 Nov: commenced 20 voyages with Hamburg as the starting port.
1927 Apr 29: Joined with the Anchor-Donaldson service Liverpool-Glasgow-Belfast-Canada. Her masts were cut and fidded topmasts fitted.
1939 Aug 11: Made her last voyage and then taken over for use as an AMC.
1940 June 16: Torpedoed by the U-boat *UA* (so named because she had been under construction for Turkey when taken over) 70 miles from Reykjavik. Only two men were injured and it was not until the next day that, despite all efforts, she finally sank.

142 **ANTONIA**
As *Andania* except: **B** Vickers Armstrong, Barrow. **T** 13,867g, 8,445n.
1921 March 3: Launched.
1922 June 15: London-Southampton (embarked passengers)—Canada.
1928 Apr 14: Transferred to the joint Anchor-Donaldson sailings alongside *Andania*. Stayed on this route until 1939.
1939 Aug 26: Her final commercial voyage although she remained on the North Atlantic trooping inbound with Canadians.
1940 Oct: Earmarked for conversion into an AMC but immediately took 2,000 men to Iceland due to intelligence that the Germans were about to seize the island. (This threat was eventually removed when Churchill persuaded President Roosevelt to use U.S. troops as a garrison.)
Nov: Converted to an AMC at Portsmouth to release a cruiser for Mediterranean work resulting from the loss to the Allies of the French fleet.
1941 May: Entered service. Her completion had now taken a low priority.
1942 Mar 24: Purchased by the Admiralty for conversion into a fleet Repair Ship. R/n *Wayland*. Four 'A's were used for this purpose.
1948 Broken up at Troon.

143 **AUSONIA (II)**
As *Andania* except: **B & E** Armstrong, Whitworth & Co, Newcastle. **T** 13,912g, 8,527n.
1921 March 22: Launched.
1922 Aug 31: M/v Liverpool-Canada.
1923 Apr: Transferred to the London-Canada route.
1927 June: After an overhaul her accommodation became Cabin, Tourist and Third. This change ran across most Cunarders at this time.
1939 Sept 2: Requisitioned by the Admiralty. Sept 16: Returned to her builder and converted into an AMC.
1942 June: Purchased by the Navy and converted into a Heavy Repair Ship. Her name was, however, not changed.

1948 Re-boilered using spare admiralty destroyer 'V' type.
1964 Sept: Decommissioned.
1965 Aug: Broken up at Castellon, Spain.

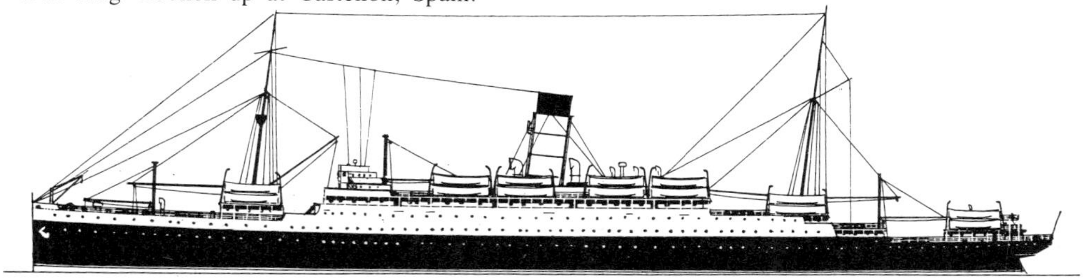

AURANIA (III), ALAUNIA (II), ASCANIA (II)

144 **AURANIA (III)**
As *Andania* except: **B** 1924 Swan, Hunter & Wigham Richardson, Newcastle.
T 13,984g, 8,473n. **E** By Wallsend Slipway Co, Wallsend.
1924 Feb 6: Launched. Sept 9: Delivered. Sept 13: M/v Liverpool-New York. The last three of the series different as drawn and looked better.
1925 Apr 17: Operated as the third of the Cunarders on the Anchor-Donaldson joint service out of Liverpool.
1928 Apr 13: Transferred to the London berth.
1939 Aug 27: At London from where she went back to her builders for conversion into an AMC. Like the other 'A's the work was so extensive that the ships were no longer capable of being used as troopships. Used on convoy escort duties.
1941 July: Collided with an iceberg between Iceland and Halifax while convoying. Not seriously damaged. Oct: Torpedoed but reached Rothesay. Laid up temporarily.
1942 Feb: Taken over permanently by the Admiralty; repaired and converted into a Heavy Repair Ship. R/n *Artifex.*
1948 Reboilered like her sister ship.
1961 Jan: Sold and broken up at La Spezia.

145 **ASCANIA (II)**
Details as *Andania* except: **B** Armstrong, Whitworth, Newcastle. **T** 14,013g, 8,437n, 9,750dwt.
D 520/158.49.
1923 Dec 20: Launched. Work on her was suspended.
1925 May 22: After a delayed completion M/v London-Canada.
1927 Accommodation regraded 520 Cabin, 928 3rd.
1928 Took one Anchor sailing Glasgow-New York.
1934 Oct 3: Went to the aid of Ropner's *Millpool* but she had gone down with all hands. *Ascania* searched the area for 21 hours. Dec 14: Went to the assistance of *Usworth,* R.S. Dalgliesh, which was sinking in mid Atlantic with a 23 degree list. Battling to save her was the Belgian *Jean Jadot* (Maritime Belge). *Ascania* stood close to windward, only 100ft/30.5m away, and both ships drifted oil to enable lifeboats to reach the ship. Eventually *Ascania* rescued nine men and *Jean Jadot* two, 15 died plus two from *Jean Jadot.*
1938 Went ashore at Bic Harbour, 150 miles below Quebec.
1939 Sept 4: Taken over for use as an AMC. Given 8 x 6in, and 2 x 3in anti-aircraft guns. Oct 16: Commissioned.
1942 Converted at Southampton into a Landing Ship (Infantry) Large.
1943 July 9: Took part in the invasion of Sicily (580 warships and 1,124 landing ships took part landing 478,000 men in 24 hours) and then the Anzio landings.
1944 Reverted to trooping.
1947 Dec 20: With austerity accommodation re-entered Liverpool-Halifax service. **P** 257 1st, 522 Tst.
1949 Went to Alex. Stephen & Sons for reconditioning. **P** 200 1st, 500 Tst.
1950 Apr 21: Resumed service Liverpool-Quebec-Montreal.
1956 Nov 23: Trooped to Cyprus during the Suez crisis. Dec 30: sold.
1957 Broken up by J. Cashmore, Newport, South Wales.

146 **ALAUNIA (II)**
As *Andania* except: **B & E** 1925 John Brown, Clydebank. **T** 14,030g, 8,448n.
D 538.5/164.13 oa, 519.5/158.34.
1925 Feb 7: Launched, July 24 M/v Liverpool-Montreal-Quebec.
1926 May 28: Transferred to the London-Canada route. Had to put into Plymouth where a boy Roy Nielson, with his abductor, was taken off by the police.

1927 Diverted into Belfast where a booking of 221 passengers, made by one person, were boarded.
1932 Nov: Collided with Canadian Pacific's *Duchess of Richmond* off Sorel, Quebec.
1933 At the height of the depression she made weekend cruises Liverpool-London for £4.
1939 Aug 24: After arriving at London earlier she was taken over on a T98A type charter and converted into an AMC at Gibraltar. 6 x 6in guns.
1944 May: Taken in hand for conversion into a Heavy Repair Ship for the Pacific Fleet train. Aug: Completed. Crew 700. Dec: Purchased by the Admiralty and stationed at Devonport as a Fleet Repair Ship. She later became a Depot Ship. Same name.
1957 Sept 10: Arrived at Blyth and broken up there by Hughes Bolckow.

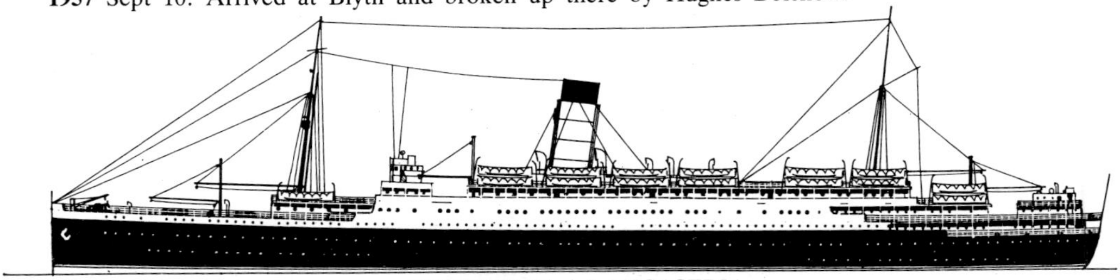

TYRRHENIA / LANCASTRIA

147 **TYRRHENIA / LANCASTRIA**
B 1922 Wm. Beardmore & Co, Dalmuir, Glasgow. **T** 16,243g, 9,645n, 11,200dwt.
D 522.7/168.45 x 70.4/21.46 x 38.8/11.81 Dft 29/8.84.
E Tw scr, 2 x 3 Brown-Curtis DRG turbs; 6 blrs, 36 furn, 220 psi, 16½ kts at 80 rpm. By builder.
H Steel, 2 dks + shelter dk. B 455/138.68. 7 holds. Oil: 1,380 tons.
P 265 1st, 355/370 2nd. 1,150/1,256 3rd. Crew 300/310.
1920 May 31: Launched. A sister to Anchor's *Cameronia* and planned as a running mate to their *Tuscania* hence her original (and unpopular) name.
1922 Completion was delayed by a strike of joiners. June 13: M/v Glasgow-Quebec-Montreal then onto the Liverpool-Canada route until the arrival of the new 'A' class in the following year.
1923 Feb 21: Started on the Hamburg-New York service.
1924 Refitted during her winter overhaul for the New York service. **P** 580 Cabin, 1,000 3rd, R/n *Lancastria*. March 22: First sailing from Liverpool.
1926 June 21: Commenced on the London-New York run with two 'A' class.
1936 Given a white hull for cruising which enhanced her popularity. She was openly described as 'beautiful'. Oct 19: Aground in the Mersey at Egremont during a gale, no damage.
1939 March 3: Positioned to New York for the New York-Bermuda route.
1940 Stripped for trooping. April: Allocated to the Norwegian campaign for the evacuation from Narvik. May: Back at Liverpool awaiting developments in France which the Germans were over running.
June 16: At St Nazaire, with several other ships, to evacuate troops and refugees. Four transports left with 4,000 and all morning *Lancastria* embarked. She then lay in the roadstead waiting for escort. Air attacks were incessant. Orient's *Oronsay* was hit. At 14.00 *Lancastria* came under concentrated attack. At 16.30 a stick of bombs hit her causing internal carnage and ripping open her hull so that she sank within 20 minutes. Only two lifeboats had left when incendiary bullets from the machine gunning aircraft set fire to her surface floating oil fuel. Many small craft put out to pick up survivors. The armed trawler *Cambridgeshire* picked up 1,000 and put them aboard the *John Holt* (John Holt & Co) which landed them at Falmouth. However out of some 5,300 or more only 2,477 were accounted for. No one knows the exact number but some 3,000 died.

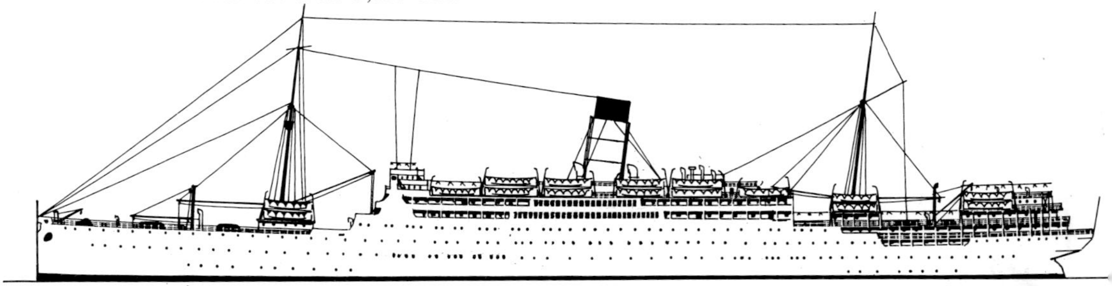

FRANCONIA (II), SERVIA (II)/CARINTHIA (II)

148 **FRANCONIA (II)**

B 1923 John Brown & Co, Clydebank, Glasgow. **T** 20,175g, 12,162n.
D 625/190.5 oa, 601.2/183.26 x 73.7/22.45 x 40.5/12.34.
E Tw scr, 2 x 3 DRG turbs; 2,562 NHP, 6 blrs, 36 furn, 220psi, 16½ kts. By builder.
H Steel. 2 dks + shelter dk. Prom. dk 419/127.71.
P 330 1st, 420 2nd, 1,500 3rd. Crew 435.
1922 Oct 21: Launched. Had a continuous superstructure.
1923 June 23: M/v Liverpool-New York. Winter cruising for which she had a swimming pool abaft the bridge.
1925 Spring: Due to gales a call at Queenstown had to be omitted.
1926 While cruising to the West Indies from New York went aground at San Juan, Puerto Rico, The tug *Grebe* got her off.
1930 May: After her winter refit emerged with 1st, tst and 3rd classes.
1931 June: Chartered for 6 months to Furness-Bermuda Line to replace their burnt out *Bermuda.*
1933 Given a white hull, as drawn, for her world cruise out of New York.
1934 June 26: Transferred to London-New York route.
1935 June: Back to Liverpool-New York.
1938 Her world cruise covered 37 ports and 41,727 miles.
1939 Sept: Refitted at Liverpool for trooping; 1,301 men. Sailed for Malta. Oct 5: Enroute collided minimally with Royal Mail's *Alcantara.* Next she took 700 Polish troops to Marseilles.
1940 June: As part of Group One, escorted by *H.M.S. Vindictive,* she evacuated forces from northern Norway. June 16: During the evacuation of France she was bombed in Quiberon Bay, Brittany. The near misses unseated her engine gearing. In all she rescued 8,000 troops and civilians.
1941-42 Trooped to Middle East including 'Operation Collar' to Malta and via the Cape to Suez. She was also at Diego Suarez, Madagascar.
1943 July 9: Took part in the invasion of Sicily.
1945 Used as the headquarters ship for the Crimean Yalta Conference between Churchill, Rooseveldt and Stalin. She was the first British ship to go through the Dardenelles in four years and all personnel, because of Turkish neutrality, wore civilian clothes for the passage.
1946 March: Troop repatriation work commenced.
1948 July: Paid off. Carried 149,239 personnel and steamed 319,284 miles.
1949 June 2: Resumed Liverpool-Canada service. **P** 250 1st, 600 Tst.
1950 July 12: Aground on Orleans Island, Quebec. Off 4 days later; repairs needed dry-docking.
1954 Apr: Engine failure put her back into Southampton. Escorted by *Asia* (164). *Queen Mary* took her 669 passengers. Repairs took 2 months.
1956 After a summer of New York cruising she made her final voyage.
Dec 14: Left Liverpool for Inverkeithing. Scrapped by Thos. W. Ward.

149 **SERVIA (II) / CARINTHIA (II)**
As *Franconia* except: **B & E:** 1925 Vickers Armstrong & Co, Barrow.
T 20,277g, 12,086n. **D** 600.6/183.06.
1924 Laid down as *Servia.* The work was suspended for some months. Because of the seaman's habit of name distortion (whereby *Tyrrhenia* became Tureenia or the soup tureen) *Servia* was already 'serve-ya right'.
1925 Feb 24: Given a name change and launched as *Carinthia.* Aug 22 M/v Liverpool-New York. Remained on this route with winter cruising.
1930 Chartered to Furness-Bermuda Line for three months to cover the gap caused by their destroyed *Bermuda.* See *Franconia* (148).
1934 May 25: Transferred to London-New York service.
1935 Given a white hull for her winter cruising out of New York.
1939 Sept 3: Left New York for Liverpool on the day Britain entered the war with Germany. Converted at Liverpool into an AMC, 6 x 6in. guns.
1940 June 6: West of Ireland she was torpedoed by *U-46,* four of her crew being killed by the explosion. Although clearly doomed and incapable of being towed to port the ship stayed afloat for 35 hours and all aboard were safely taken off by her escort. She sank on June 7.

LOTHARINGIA, ALSATIA (I)

150 **LOTHARINGIA**
B 1923 Wm. Hamilton & Co, Port Glasgow. **T** 1,256g, 598n.
D 199.8/60.91 x 38.1/11.61 x 15.5/4.72.

E Tw scr, tpl exp, 2 x 3 cyls, 170 NHP, 2 blrs, 6 furn. 180 psi, 12 kts.
By D. Rowan & Co, Glasgow.
H Steel. 1 dk. B 95/28.95. P 1,200 plus baggage.
1923 Replaced *Satellite* (135) as the Cunard tender at Cherbourg.
Registered as owned by Compagnie Nord Atlantique.
1933 Sold to Société Cherbourgeoise de Remorquage et de Sauvetage.
R/n *Alexis de Tocqueville.* (Black funnel red band). Continued to handle Cunard at Cherbourg.
1940 July: Taken over by the Germans. Became a war loss.

151 **ALSATIA (I)**
As *Lotharingia* except: **B** Coaster Construction Co, Montrose. **T** 1,310g, 632n.
1923 Tender at Cherbourg; same owners as her sister.
1933 Transferred to the same new owners. R/n *Ingenieur Cachin.*
1940 June: Escaped to Falmouth ahead of the German entry into the port.
1942 R/n *Volontaire.* Owned by the Ministry of War Transport, managed by the London, Midland & Scottish Railway Co.
1946 Back to France as *Volontaire.*
1947 Reverted to *Ingenieur Cachin.*
1960 Laid up with survey overdue and then scrapped.

BACTRIA, BANTRIA, BOSNIA BOTHNIA (II)

152 **BACTRIA.**
B 1928 J.L. Thompson & Co, Sunderland. **T** 2,407g, 1,209n.
D 292.3/89.1 x 45/13.72 x 20.2/6.17.
E Sgl scr, tpl exp, 3 cyls, 403 NHP, 2 blrs, 8 furn; 180 psi, 12 kts. By J. Dickinson & Sons, Sunderland. Bunkers: 114 tons coal.
H Steel, 2 dks. F 28/8.53. B 129/39.32. C 200,000/5,663 cu g. Crew 30.
1928 April: Delivered for the Mediterranean trade. All for Cunard's America-Levant Line S & J Thompson as managers.
1934 These three ships were not transferred to Cunard-White Star.
1940-46 Mainly north Atlantic cargo.
1954 Sold to Cia Isla Bella, Puerto Limon, Costa Rica, R/n *Theo*
1958 Became *Catalina S,* Capital S.A., Panama.
1961 Owned by Bahamas Pearl Co, Freeport, Same Name.
1963 Broken up.

153 **BANTRIA**
As *Bactria.* **T** 2,402 g, 1,209n.
1928 June: Completed for Mediterranean services.
1939-46 War service without incident.
1954 Sold to Costa Line, Genoa. R/n *Giorgina Celli.*
1955 Sold to Lauro & Montella, Naples. R/n *Sacrum Cor.* She was later registered in the name of the partner Gennaro Montella.
1968 Feb: Broken up at Vado.

154 **BOSNIA**
as *Bactria.* **T** 2,402g, 1,209n.
1928 March: completed. Mediterranean services.
1939 Sept 5: Sunk two days after the outbreak of war by Prien's *U-47* in the Bay of Biscay. She was the second war loss, after Donaldson's *Athenia.* Warning was given and all aboard got safely away.

155 **BOTHNIA (II)**
As *Bactria.* **T** 2,402g, 1,209n.
1928 May: Trials. June: Delivered. Mediterranean service.
1956 Sold to Vivalet Shipping & Trading Co. S. A. Panama. R/n *Emily.*
1958 Sold to Alexander G. Sigalas, Beirut; managers G. Sigalas & Sons. R/n *Capetan Manolis.*
1962 Broken up (Sigalas gave the same name to a new purchase in 1962).

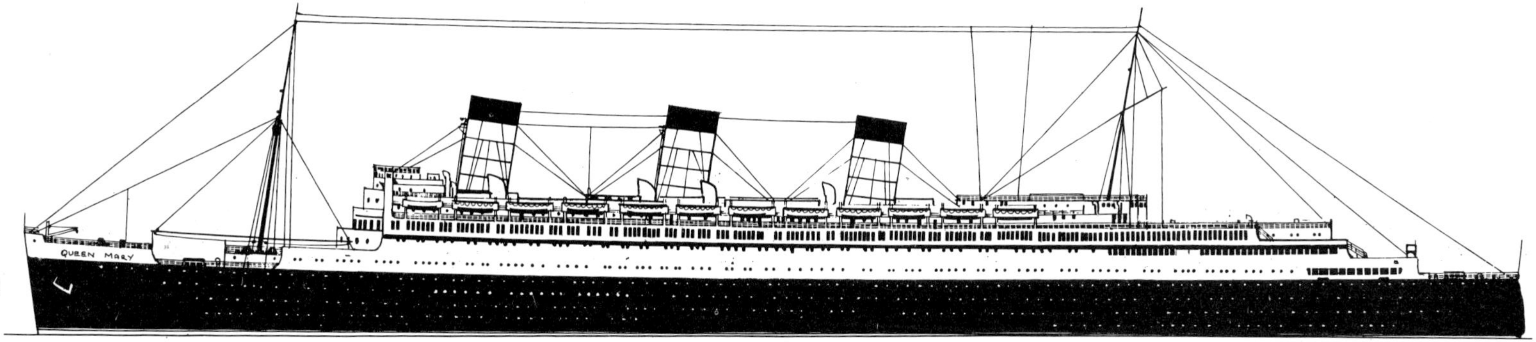

156 *QUEEN MARY*
(Scale 1:1600)

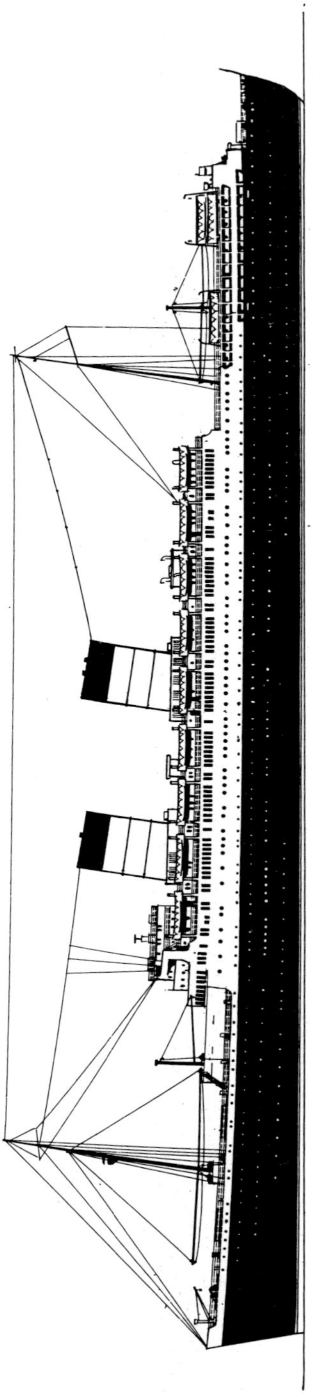

157 *MAURETANIA (II)*

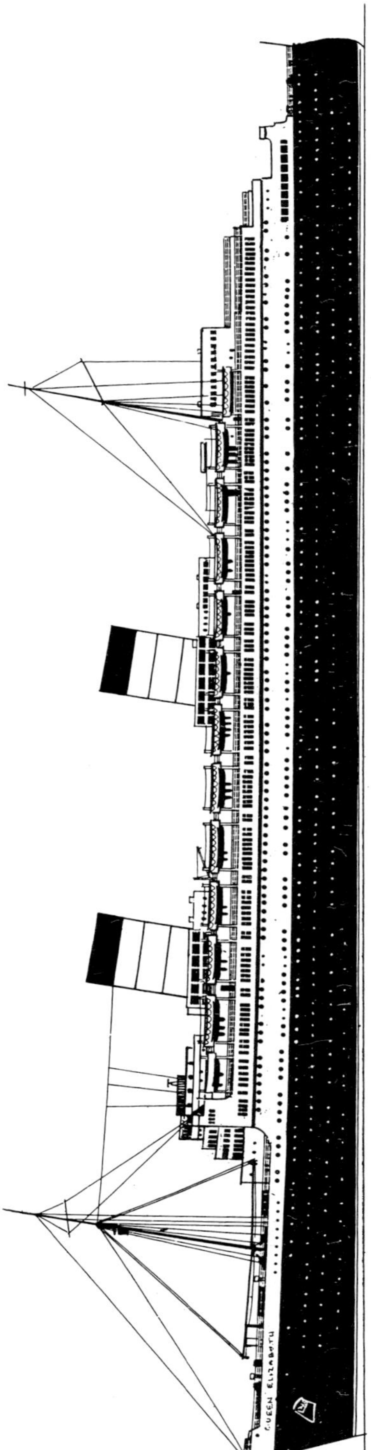

158 *QUEEN ELIZABETH*
(Scale 1:1600)

156 **QUEEN MARY** (Drawing page 81)
B 1936 John Brown & Co., Clydebank. **T** 81,235g, 34,120n.
D 1,019.5/310.74 oa 975.2/297.23 x 112.6/34.29 x 68.6 20.88.
E Quad scr, 4 x4 turbs (4 stages + 1 intermediate stage at 1,530 rpm, 2nd intermediate + LP at 1,030 rpm) sgl reduc. geared to 180 rpm at 40,000 SHP each, 24 blrs 446 psi, 29 kts. By builder.
H Steel 12 dks in all. F 93/28.35. B 715/217.93. Upper B 540/164.59. Keel to base of funnel: 125/38.1. Keel to top of foremast 184/56.08. Fore funnel height: 60/18.29.
P 711 1st. 707 Cabin, 577 Tst, Crew 1, 285.
1930 Dec 27: Laid down as yard number 534 with the name *Victoria* pencilled in.
The leading designers were G. McLeod Paterson and L. McEwan.
1931 Dec: Due to the depression work ceased.
The ship was designed to complete a crossing within a week and to do 44 per annum. This only permitted 112 hours steaming time Cherbourg to Ambrose Light plus 45-50 hours turn round at either end. This required an average of 29 knots in all weathers and at least 158,000 SHP from the engines to achieve this. Actual SHP was 160,000.
It was, for crew numbers, required that the three dining rooms should be capable of a one sitting service with all the galleys on one level. 'C' Deck was the lowest that could meet this need. Cunard also wanted the design to include outside portholes for 90% of First Class cabins. Safety was pre-eminent. Her stress, fire and flooding limits were of a higher standard than on any vessel afloat. Against flooding her machinery was in two self contained compartments. The forward one drove the two outer propellers and the after one the inboard pair. Also each turbine could be isolated and within each the four pressure stages could be shut down independently. To eliminate any propeller shaft oscillation at high speed, which would cause vibration that would whip the turbine blades and shed them, electro-magnets were used. The rudder was of particular interest. Because of the speed and frequency with which she would use congested estuaries this was enlarged and driven by the most powerful electro-hydraulic gear in existence. There were four driving rams instead of two and every control was duplicated against failure. The pressure was designed at 3,500 torque-tons per square foot. On her trials, travelling at 29 knots, the wheel was spun fully over to 35° without the working design being exceeded.
To reduce vibration and noise every moving part, turbine blades, gear wheels, couplings, pinions and propeller shafts were balanced to the nth degree and then rebalanced so that none re-acted with any other. It was found, for instance, that vibration frequencies did occur at 51,89,151,224 and 292 rpm on the inner shafts but on the outer pair the 292 became 296 rpm. The machinery controls were designed to pass over these resonance rpms without lingering. In passing it has to be remembered that the teeth of the gearing, engaging at 1,530 and 1,030 rpm had to be accurate to an unimaginable degree. For *Queen Mary* this was achieved by making a soft cast iron blank of the gears which was then run in until perfect. The hard metal gears were then cut from these. The resultant gearing was thus already run-in and silent. The old way of matching gears was to paint both with a thin coat of red lead paint then hand turn them and rub down any spots where the paint had come off. The process continuing until a perfect mesh was achieved. Next the process was repeated using a friction brake to simulate actual conditions. The whole being again repeated until the turbines were able to run 'smooth as silk'. Nevertheless when *Queen Mary* entered service a turbine engineer met her at Southampton at the end of each voyage and serviced the gears for 'rub'. It was seven months before perfection was achieved.
1934 Apr: Following Government aid and the formation of Cunard-White Star Ltd work restarted. Sept 26: Launched by Queen Mary. The story is not true that the name was changed due to King George V misunderstanding the desire to name the ship after his grandmother, Queen Victoria and not his wife. Chairman Sir John Brocklebank told me that the King was asked if the name Queen Mary could be used. The reason, he said, was that in the thirties Victoriana denoted to the Board old fashionedness not modernity. The name *Victoria* was never seriously intended.
1936 March 26: Left John Brown's yard. It took 4 hours 28 minutes to reach her Gareloch anchorage with *Skirmisher* (83) leading the way. May 25: King Edward VIII with Queen Mary visited her at Southampton. May 27: M/v Southampton-New York. Commodore Sir Edgar Britten in command. Aug: Took the westbound Blue Riband from her year old competitor *Normandie* in 4 days 27 minutes at 30.14 kts average and then eastbound in 3 days 23 hours 57 minutes at 30.63 kts.
1938 Oct. Commodore R.B. Irving berthed her at Southampton without tugs.
1939 Aug 25: With war clouds looming she left Southampton with her largest number of fare paying passengers. Then laid up at New York for six months.
1940 March 20: Left for Sydney, via Singapore; converted into a troopship. Apr 17: First trooping voyage with 5,000 Australians.
1942 Oct 2: While zig-zagging at speed 20 miles N.W. of Bloody Foreland, Northern Ireland she cut into her escorting cruiser *Curacao,* rolled the ship over and sank her. *Curacao's* straight line course met with that of *Queen Mary* and the venturi effect as the two came close together lost steering way on the warship. 338 were drowned; only 26 being saved. *Queen Mary* dared not stop because she had 15,000 U.S. troops aboard and a submarine alert was in being, the Courts later found in favour of Cunard-White Star. An escorting vessel is the give way ship and is required to act accordingly. *Queen*

Mary was right to obey her zig-zag course and right to expect that the other ship would give way.
1943 Aug 5: Carried Prime Minister Winston Churchill (he was also Minister for Defence) and his staff of over 200 from the Clyde to Halifax for the Quebec conference. He took with him to meet President Roosevelt Wing Commander Guy Gibson whose uniform bore only three ribbons (compared to some twenty or so on the American generals). These were the Victoria Cross, Distinguished Service Order and bar and Distinguished Flying Cross and bar (Bar was a small crown on the ribbon to denote that the medal had been awarded again for a second time). A totally unique set of awards.
1946 Sept 24: Final trooping voyage Halifax-Southampton. In all she carried 810,730 personnel. Went back to builder for overhaul.
1947 July 31: Resumed service.
1952 The *United States* took the Blue Riband from her with 35 kts.
1958 Fitted with twin Denny-Brown stabilisers. These were delayed because they intruded into the boiler space and re-design was needed.
1967 Sept 22: Left New York for the last time. Sept 27: Ended her 1,000th crossing. Carried 2,112,000 passengers, steamed 3,792,277 miles and, although registered there, never once visited her home port of Liverpool. Oct 31: Left for Long Beach, California having been acquired by the city for $3,450,000. Dec 9: Arrived. She carried 1,000 passengers on her 39 day final cruise via Cape Horn (too big for the Panama Canal).
1971 May 10: Conversion completed and opened as a museum, hotel and convention centre. Her machinery had been removed.
1978 Apr: With losses of $2 million per year the City put her up for sale. She was acquired by a new consortium and re-vitalised.
1987 Still afloat at Long Beach.

157 **MAURETANIA (II)** (Drawing page 82)
B 1939 Cammell Laird & Co. Birkenhead. **T** 35,739g, 20,170n.
D 771.8/23.23 oa, 739.3/225.33 x 89.3/27.23 x 57.7/17.58.
E Tw scr, 2 x 3 SRG turbines, 8,373 NHP, 6 blrs, 465 psi, 23 kts. By builder. **H** Steel, 5 dks, F & B 614/187.15. Upper B 381/116.13. **P** 475 1st, 390 Cabin, 304 Tst. Crew 593.
1937 May 24: Keel laid; the first liner for Cunard-White Star Ltd. She was also at that time the largest liner to be built in England. There was no Government subsidy. Her speed was designed so that she could relieve *Queen Mary* if necessary taking less than 24 hours longer.
1938 July 28: Launched; their third ship for Cunard. The previous building by Cammell Laird for the company had been *Samaria* (139) in 1921 and she also was launched from Slipway no 6. *Mauretania's* large cargo capacity was seldom used but was never converted to any other use.
1939 March 31: Acceptance trials off the Clyde averaged 22 kts.
June 17: M/v Liverpool-New York: Captain A. T. Brown, who had taken *Mauretania (I)* to the breakers. There were also four passengers aboard who had been on *Mauretania (I)'s* maiden voyage.
Aug: Transferred to the London-New York service. Aug 6: Became the largest liner to use the King George V dock. Aug 12: First sailing
Sept 14: Voyaged Southampton-New York-Liverpool. Made one more round trip with Americans returning from the war zone then Liverpool back to New York and laid up.
1940 March 6: Taken over as a troopship. March 20: New York-Panama-Honolulu-Sydney for conversion. At Honolulu the Liverpudlian crew drew wry comment in the Press. They asked not how the war was going but which horse had won the Grand National. Apr 14: Arrived Sydney. Stripped and all fittings stored there. May 5: Sydney-Clyde with 2,000 troops.
1946 Aug 2: Arrived at Liverpool. She had made 48 trooping voyages covering 540,000 miles and carried over 355,000 troops. Overhauled in Gladstone Dry Dock by her builders.
1947 April 18: Left on a 2½ day shake down cruise which ran into such foul weather that it was 5½ days before she re-docked.
Apr 26: Resumed service Liverpool-New York then to the Southampton berth.
1948 Jan-March: Cruised out of New York. Oct: Her fastest crossing ever averaged 23.85 knots.
1957 Oct: Winter overhaul and fitted with air conditioning throughout.
1958 Jan 17: To New York for world cruising. Then Southampton-New York.
1962 Sept: Given 'Caronia' green cruising livery which did not suit her.
P 406 1st, 364 Cabin, 357 Tst. Crew 560.
1963 March 28: On New York-Cannes-Genoa-Naples service plus cruising. She was now becoming increasingly unprofitable to operate.
1965 Sept 15: Final sailing New York-Mediterranean cruise-Southampton.
Oct 5: Disposal announced. Nov 10: Paid off at Southampton. Nov 23: Arrived at Inverkeithing, still in green livery, and scrapped by Thos. W. Ward.

158 **QUEEN ELIZABETH** (Drawing page 83)
B 1940 John Brown & Co., Clydebank. **T** 83,673g, 42,011n.
D 1,030/313.94 oa, 987/300.84 x 118.5/36.12 x 68.3/20.83.

E Quad scr, 4 x 4 SRG turbines,160,00 SHP, 12 blrs (against 24 in Queen Mary which reduced the funnels to two), 450 psi, 29 kts. By builder.
H Steel. 12 dks. F & B 875/266.7. Upper B 567/172.82. Keel to top of fore funnel 187/57. Keel to foremast top 233/71.02 Funnels 71/21.64.
P 823 1st, 662 Cabin, 798 Tst, Crew 1,296.
1936 Dec 4: Laid down, Consort to *Queen Mary*. Her basic design omitted the break at the fcsle which was proving to be rather wet in service.
1938 Sept 27: Launched by Queen Elizabeth (The Queen Mother).
1940 March 2: Completed but not furnished to Atlantic standards. Sailed without trials, Captain J. C. Townley, to New York. Laid up. Speed 24½ kts. Enroute, observing radio silence, she met her namesake battleship. From the bridge of the warship a signal lamp flashed one word 'Snap'.
July: Her fittings were moved by rail and stored in San Francisco.
Nov: Sent to Singapore and fitted for trooping. Initially for 5,000 troops but finally 20,000 were carried living in 4 shifts. She carried in all 811,324 and steamed 492,635 miles.
1944 Feb 16: A freak wave, enroute to New York for U.S. troops, submerged her so deeply that the wheel house windows were smashed by it.
1946 Feb: Decommissioned. The hull was refitted at Glasgow and the furnishings installed at Southampton. Oct. 16: Made her maiden commercial crossing to New York. She was the largest liner afloat. Only *France* was to exceed her in length. Crossing was 4 days, 5 hours, 3 minutes at 29.77 kts. She never held the Blue Riband which Cunard never officially recognised.
1955 March: Fitted with two sets of Denny-Brown stabilisers. Inbound in a 54 mile gale she was 'steady as a rock'.
1965 Dec: Air conditioned and up-dated. Swimming pool added aft. **T** 82,998g.
1968 Nov 4: Sold, after 907 crossings, for £3.23 million and a mandatory name change. Nov. 28: Sailed for Fort Lauderdale to become a tourist attraction. R/n *The Elizabeth,* Elizabeth Corp.
1969 Feb 14: Opened. After a few months her owners went into liquidation. July: Sold to The Queen Ltd. Inc. Port Everglades. Same name. When they too failed Cunard were still owed £2.1 million of the sale price.
1970 Sept 9: Acquired at auction by C. Y. Tung (Overseas Container Line) for £1,333,000.
1971 Feb 10: Left Port Everglades for Hong Kong. Arrived July 16. There she was converted at a cost of £5 million into a floating university cruise ship. R/n *Seawise University* (viz. C.Y.'s University). Owned by Island Navigation Corp.
1972 Jan: Completed; anchored in the harbour. Jan 9: Caught fire and, despite fire fighting from all available craft, fell onto her starboard side. 200 were on her at the time but no lives were lost. Total loss.

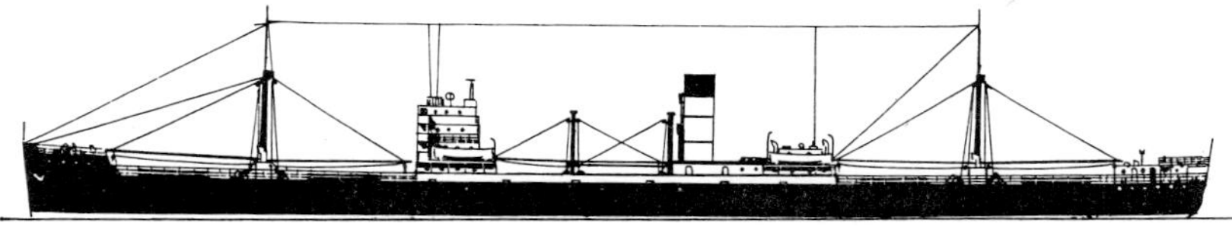

VALACIA, VASCONIA (II)

159 **VALACIA**
B 1943 Short Bros., Sunderland. **T** 7,052g, 4,760 n.
D 446.5/136.09 oa, x 56.3/17.17 x 35.2/10.71.
E Sgl scr, tpl exp, 542 NHP, 2 blrs, 9 furn, oil, 220 psi, 9½ kts. By North East Marine Eng. Co. (1938), Newcastle.
H Steel. 1 dk. 5 hatches. F 40/12.19.
1943 Oct: Completed as *Empire Camp*, Ministry of War Transport; managed by Cunard.
1946 Acquired. R/n *Valacia.* North Atlantic cargo services. Her name revived the use of 'V' names for such services; out of use since 1931.
1950 Sold to Charles Hill & Co., Bristol. R/n *New York City.*
1955 Became *Loch Morar,* Maclay, McIntyre, Glasgow.
1959 Sold to Lufti Yelkenci Evatlari Donatma Istiraki, Istanbul. Renamed *Yelkenci.*
1971 Feb 2: Arrived Istanbul for breaking up.

160 **VASCONIA (II)**
As *Valacia* except: **B** 1944. **T** 7,058g, 4,757n.
1944 June: Completed as *Empire Pendennis* for M.O.W.T. Ellerman Lines as managers.
1946 Acquired by Cunard (Correctly Cunard-White Star Ltd) R/n *Vasconia.*
1950 Sold to the Blue Star Line. Became *Fresno Star.*

1957 Transferred on bare boat charter to Lamport & Holt, Liverpool as *Millais*.
1960 Sold to the Grosvenor Shipping Co, Hong Kong, R/n *Grosvenor Navigator*.
1966 Sept 9: Arrived at Kaohsiung for demolition.

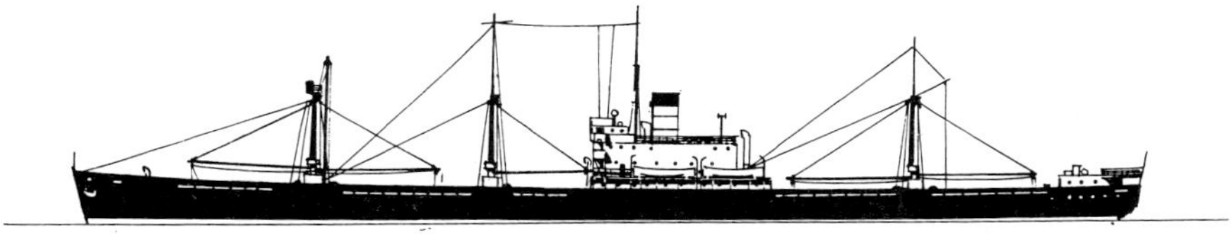

VARDULIA (II) VANDALIA (II)

161 **VARDULIA (II)**
B 1944 J. A. Jones Construction Co, Brunswick, Georgia. **T** 7,276g, 4,483n.
D 422.7/128.83 x 57/17.37 x 34.7/10.57.
E Sgl scr, tpl exp, 3 cyls, 2,500 IHP at 76 rpm, 2 blrs, 270 psi. 10 kts. By Filer & Stowell Co, Milwaukee, Wisconsin.
H Steel. 1 dk. C 562,608/15,931.4cu g. Crew 45.
1944 March: Completed at a cost of $1,992,000 as *Samfoyle* for M.O.W.T. with Cunard as managers. Liberty ship type.
1947 Purchased and renamed *Vardulia*.
1954 Sold to Nueva Valencia Cia, Nav; Panama. R/n *Valencia*.
1968 Dec: Broken up at Hong Kong.

162 **VANDALIA (II)**
As 161 except: **B** 1945 California Shipbuilding Corp, Los Angeles.
E Johsua Henry Ironworks, Sunnyvale, California.
1945 Ordered as *Granville Stewart*. July: Completed as *Samaritan*. Ministry of War Transport, Cunard-White star as managers.
1947 Purchased, R/n *Vandalia*.
1954 Became *Sideris*, Marine Transport Co, S.A. Monrovia.
1969 Owned by Transmarine Carriers Corp, Liberia.
1971 May 7: At Barcelona for scrapping.
Note Cunard-White Star also managed for the Ministry of War Transport the Liberty ships *Sambre, Samholt, Samouse, Samson* and *Samsurf*.

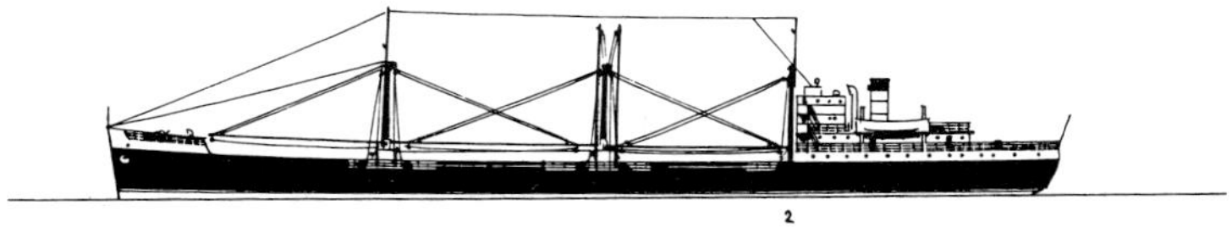

BRESCIA (II)

163 **BRESCIA (II)**
B 1945 Consolidated Steel Corp, Wilmington, Cal. **T** 3,834g, 2,124n.
D 323.9/98.7 x 51.1/15.58 x 26.5/8.08.
E Sgl scr, 6 cyl oil 12 kts. By Nordberg Manufacturing Co. Milwaukee, Wis.
H Steel, 1 dk. F 38/11.58. P 90/27.43.
1945 July: Built as *Hickory Isle*. Standard C1-MAV type. Bare boat charter to M.O.W.T. Managed by Common Bros.
1947 Acquired. R/n *Brescia*. Mediterranean service. Owned by Cunard S.S. Co.
1966 Became *Timber One*. Timber Shipping Co, Panama.
1970 Converted into an oceanographic research and mining vessel. Used for the recovery of mineral nodules from the seabed in order to ascertain the dredging potential. R/n *Deepsea Miner*. Owned by Deepsea Miner Inc, Panama. Employed on charter work to mining companies.
1974 Jan: Broken up at Santander.

ASIA (II), ARABIA (III), ASSYRIA

164 **ASIA (II)**
B 1947 Sir James Laing and Sons, Sunderland. **T** 8,723g, 5,077n, 11,000dwt.
D 508.7/155.04 oa, 488.5/14.83 x 64.1/19.54 x 32.3/9.83.
E Sgl scr, 2 SRG tubs, 2 blrs, 475 psi, 15½ kts. By Richardson, Westgarth & Co, Hartlepool.
H Steel. 2 dks. F 54/16.46. B 168/51.2. P 44/13.41. 6 holds. C 430,500/12,190. 4 cu g + 130,00/3,681 cu ref. **P** 12 1st.
1946 Sept 12: Launched, the first post-war construction for Cunard-White Star and their first actual cargo vessel building.
1947 Apr 15: M/v to Canada being an 'A' class ship for these routes.
1963 May 17: Sold to Eddie Steamship Co. Taipeh. R/n *Shirley*. Operated by Waywiser Nav. Corp., Keelung.
1968 Dec 16: Paid off at Osaka. Sold for scrap.
1969 Jan 14: Arrived at Kaohsiung.

165 **ARABIA (III)**
As *Asia* except: **B** 1948. **T** 8,632g, 4,949n.
1947 July 18: Launched.
1948 Jan 8: M/v Liverpool-Halifax.
1963 March: Sold to the International Marine Corp, Panama, R/n *Onshun*. Operated by the Neptune Marine Corp, Monrovia.
1966 Sold to joint owners; Cosmos Marine Development Corp and Shaw Shipping Co.
1972 May 10: At Kaohsiung, Scrapped by Jui Long Steel & Copper Works.

166 **ASSYRIA**
As *Asia* except: **B** 1950 Swan, Hunter & Wigham Richardson, Wallsend. **T** 8,530g, 4,856n. **H** Her cargo capacity differed slightly. F 57/17.37.
1950 Jan 19: Launched. She completed Cunard's 90,000 ton post-war five ship rebuilding programme for the Canadian services.
Aug 24: M/v Liverpool-Boston-New York. In service the ships covered all the eastern seaboard ports of U.S.A. and Canada.
1963 Sept: Sold to N. J. Vlassopulos, R/n *Laertis*. Managed by Stala Cia. Nav. S.A., Monrovia. Greek flag.
1970 Sold to Ambelos Development Corp, Greece, R/n *Holy Trinity*.
1973 Broken up.

MEDIA (I). PARTHIA (II)

167 **MEDIA (I)**
B 1947 John Brown & Co, Clydebank. **T** 13,345g, 7,480n.
D 531.4/161.97 oa, 500/152.4 x 70.3/21.44 x 46/14.02.
E Tw scr, 2 DRG turbs, 15,000 SHP, 2 blrs, 450 psi, 17 kts. by builder.
H Steel. 3 dks. F 46/14.02. B 202/61.57. C 371,430/10,517. 8cg g + 60,050/1,700cu ref. **P** 250 1st.
1946 Dec 12: Launched. The first post-war building for the company.
1947 Aug 20: M/v Liverpool-New York.
1952 Feb: Fitted with stabilisers. Her promenade deck was glazed in.
1961 During her winter overhaul there was a strike of the Amalgamated Engineering Union members which kept her in Gladstone graving dock for some months. Both ships were uneconomic cargo-passenger crossbreeds and it was decided to sell them. Sept: Final sailing Liverpool-Quebec-

Montreal with 145 passengers. During the voyage she aided the German *Bornberg* who had a crew member down with appendicitis. Oct 14: Sold to Compagnia Genovese di Armamaento, Cogedar Line, Genoa for £740,000.
Completely rebuilt as drawn on page 90. R/n *Flavia*. **T** 15,465. P 1,200 One Class.
1962 Sept: Placed on the Genoa-Suez-Australia service. Dec: Bremerhaven-Southampton-Australia route.
1963 Based at Rotterdam. Australia service out via Panama back by Suez.
1968 Cruising in the Mediterranean. Winter: Caribbean.
1969 Sold to Costa Armatori S.p.A, Naples. Based at Miami. She returned annually to Italy for overhaul. Oddly the ship was not given a Costa 'C' ending name.
1982 May: Sold to Flavian Shipping S.A., one of W. Wong's Virture Shipping Enterprise (HK) Ltd. group, Panama registered. R/n *Flavian*. Oct: Laid up at Hong Kong.
1986 Sold to Lavia Shipping S.A. Panama. R/n *Lavia*. Laid up at Hong Kong.
1989 Jan 7: 0605 hrs. Fire broke out and she had to be beached. Total loss. Her owners were now Virtue Shipping Co., Hong Kong.

168 **PARTHIA (II)**
Sister to *Media* except: **B** 1948 Harland & Wolff, Belfast. **T** 13,362g, 7,393n.
1947 Feb 25: Launched. The only passenger ship which they built for Cunard.
1948 Apr 10: M/v Liverpool-New York.
1953 Denny-Brown stablisers fitted.
1960 A 13 week strike of ship repairers prevented sailings.
1961 After *Media* was strike bound the pair were put up for sale. Nov 1: Sold to the New Zealand Shipping Co, for £750,000. Rebuilt aft by Alex, Stephen & Sons, Linthouse. Cost £450,000. **T** 13,619g. **P** 350 One Class.
1962 Apr 11: R/n *Remuera,* June 1: First sailing London-Panama-Auckland-Wellington.
1965 Transferred within the P. & O. group to the Eastern & Australian S.S. Co, R/n *Aramac*. Feb 8: Inaugurated their Melbourne-Hong Kong-Japan route. There was no change in ownership.
1967 Passed to Federal S.N.Co. ownership but no other change.
1968 Into Eastern & Australian ownership.
1969 Nov 22: Arrived at Kaohsiung for demolition.

169 **CARONIA (II)** (Drawing on page 90)
B 1949 John Brown, Clydebank. **T** 34,274g, 17,921n.
D 715/217.93 oa, 666/203 x 91.5/27.89 x 53.3/16.23.
E Tw scr, 1 sgl + 1 dbl reduction geared turb; 35,000 SHP, 6 blrs, 725 psi. 22 kts. By builder.
H Steel. 5 dks. F & B 594/181.05. Prom 495/150.88 C 69,450/1,966 cu g.
P 580 1st, 350 Cabin. One class when cruising. Crew 600.
1946 Feb 13: Keel laid. Dual purpose for North Atlantic and Cruising.
1947 Oct 30: Launched from the same builder's berth as *Caronia* (I) The first large post war British built liner. Carried six 45ft/13.72 launches for shore excursion passenger work.
1949 Jan 4: M/v Southampton-New York. Green livery all her career. In service she suffered continuous minor turbine gearing trouble and work had to be done on every annual overhaul. The problem was that the 'metal creepage' in one turbine was greater than that in the other. Made a seasonal World Cruise out of New York.
1956 Oct: Air conditioning fitted. **P** 528 1st, 332 Cabin.
1958 April 14: Entering Yokohama the tugs lost their hold on her and she hit the mole demolishing the lighthouse and buckling her bow.
1962 Oct: Her winter cruise took her into Varna, Black Sea. The first Cunard liner to visit the port since the Crimean War. Calls by Cunard Mediterranean cargo ships were, of course, made from time to time.
1967 Nov 24: Laid up at Southampton. A sale to the Jugoslav Domus Turist then fell through because permission to berth her at Dubrovnik as an hotel was refused.
1968 May: Sold to Universal Line S.A. for cruising. R/n *Columbia*. July 29: Sailed Southampton-Piraeus and overhauled. R/n *Caribia*. Her owners changed to the Franchard Corporation. They reverted temporarily to *Caronia* because the original purchase price had not yet been fully discharged to Cunard. The sum was £1,250,000. By the year end she had reverted to *Caribia* and probably never had her name changed physically.
1969 Mar 11: An engine room explosion while cruising off St Thomas killed one crewman. The ship drifted for 20 hours. Mar 25 Towed into New York and laid up at Gravesend Bay, unseaworthy.
1970 In Dock at New York with debts of $5 million.
1974 Apr 27: Left New York in tow of the tug *Hamburg* for breaking up at Taiwan. In the Pacific the generator of the tug failed and the ships made for Apra Harbor, Guam. In a gale the tug had to cut *Caribia* adrift and she drove ashore on Apra breakwater where she broke into three pieces and had to be demolished as she lay.

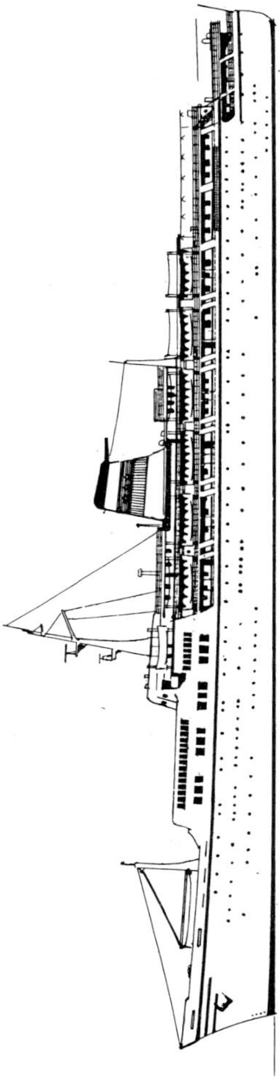

167 *Rebuilt as FLAVIA*

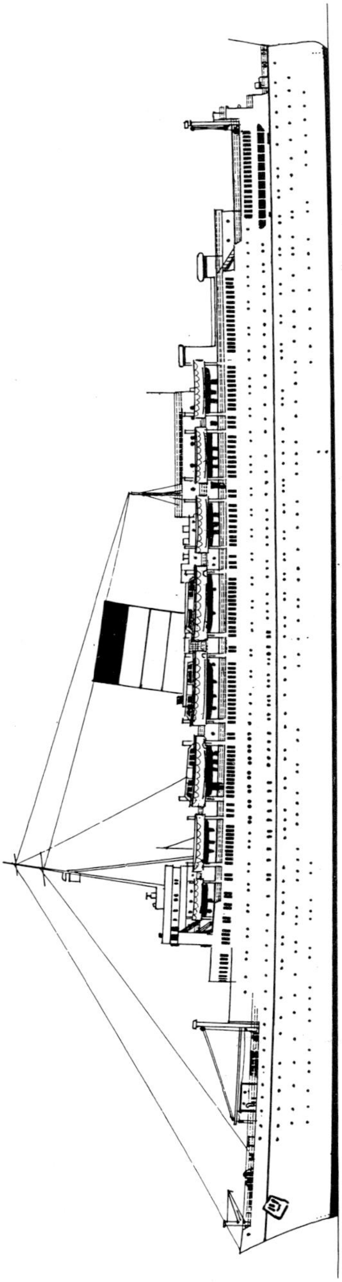

169 *CARONIA (II)*

ALSATIA (II), ANDRIA (I)

170 **ALSATIA (II)**
B 1948 J. L. Thompson & Sons, Sunderland. **T** 7,226g, 5,080n. 10,750 dwt.
D 503.4/153.42 oa, 468.8/142.88 x 64.9/19.79 x 31.9/9.73.
E Sgl scr, 3 DRG turbs, 8,800 Shp, 2 blrs, 590 psi, 16 kts. By Parson's Marine Steam Turbine Co, Newcastle.
H Steel, 1 dk + Shelter dk, F 97/29.56. P 41/12.5. C 681,916/19,310 cu b in 6 holds. **P** 12 1st (8 single + two twin cabins).
1947 Nov 30: Launched. The forward funnel was a dummy; master's quarters.
1948 Completed as *Silverplane,* Silver Line. S. & J. Thompson & Co managers, London. Used to combine two of their services into a round the world route.
1951 Purchased, with *Silverbriar,* for £1,250,000, R/n *Alsatia.* Oct 6: First Cunard sailing Liverpool-New York then London-Canada.
1963 Jan 28: Sold with her sister for £245,000, to China Union Lines, Taiwan, R/n *Union Freedom.*
1977 Jan 7: Left Singapore and broken up at Kaohsiung.

171 **ANDRIA (I)**
As *Alsatia:* **T** 7,301g, 4,002n.
1947 May 30: Launched as *Silverbriar,* Silver Line Ltd.
1948 Entered the same service as her sister.
1952 To Cunard at the end of her voyage; three months after her sister. The Canadian cargo fleet was now up to its complement of 5 ships. April 17: First company sailing London-Le Havre-New York.
1963 Feb 4: Joined China Union Lines as *Union Faith.*
1969 April 7: Collided off New Orleans with three oil barges being towed by the tug *Warren J. Doucet.* The spillage caught fire and engulfed *Union Faith* with the loss of 26, including barge crew, the ship sank off Poydras Wharf, New Orleans. Demolished as she lay.

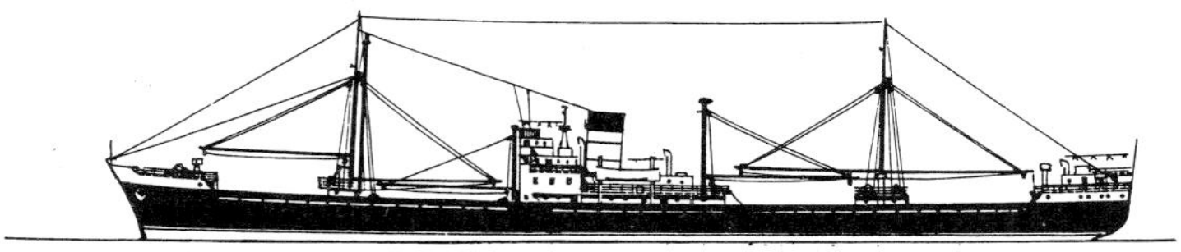

PAVIA (II), LYCIA (II), PHRYGIA (II)

172 **PAVIA (II)**
B 1953 Wm. Hamilton & Co, Port Glasgow. **T** 3,411g, 1,828n, 4,400dwt.
D 348.3/106.17 oa, 320/97.54 x 49.8/15.19 x 28.5/8.69.
E Sgl scr, oil; 4 cyl 2S.SA, Doxford type, 13 kts. By D. Rowan, Glasgow.
H Steel. 2 dks. F 32/9.75. P 29/8.84. 4 holds 12 derricks. C 210,000/5946.5cu g, 7,166/203cu ref.
1953 Mar 19: Launched. The first motorship built for the company and the first ship to be built for Cunard S.S. Co since the *Bactria* class of 1928. It reflected the name change from Cunard-White Star in Jan 1950. June 1: M/v Mediterranean service. Her bridge house was one deck lower than that of her sister ships.
1965 Aug 25: Sold to Seaswift Maritime Co, Piraeus, R/n *Toula N.* The three ships were sold to the same group but operated by different companies.
1974 Apr 1: Paid off at Singapore and broken up in Taiwan.

173 **LYCIA (II).**
As *Pavia* but **B** 1954. **T** 3,543g, 1,731n, 4,295dwt.
1954 Sept 24: M/v to Greece and Turkey with general cargo.
1964 Transferred to the Great Lakes service. Replaced by the chartered tonnage *Leabeth.*
1965 Sept 23: Sold to Diapora S.A. Piraeus, R/n *Flora N.*
1970 Became *Nea Tihi,* Compania Maritima Lounino, Piraeus.

1974 Dec: Sold to Allied Shipping Co, Bangkok. R/n *Sothon.*
1975 Renamed *Patanporn* by her owners.
1977 April: Broken up at Hong Kong by Loy Kee Shipbreakers.

174 **PHRYGIA (II)**
As *Pavia* except: **B** 1955, **T** 3,534g, 1,730n, 4,295dwt.
1955 Apr 10: M/v to the Mediterranean ending at Istanbul.
1964 Replaced by the chartered *Johanna* upon transfer to the Great Lakes service.
1965 Sept 7: Sold to Firgournes S.A. Panama. R/n *Dimitris N.*
1974 Became *Asia Developer,* Kai Fah Maritime S.A. Panama.
1976 Broken up.

SAXONIA (II)/CARMANIA (II), IVERNIA (II)/FRANCONIA (III)
CARINTHIA (III), SYLVANIA (II)

CARMANIA (II), FRANCONIA (III)

175 **SAXONIA (II)/CARMANIA (II)**
B 1954 John Brown & Co, Clydebank. **T** 22,592, 11,721n.
D 608,3/185.4 oa, 570/173.74 x 80.3/29.49 x 46.2/14.1.
E Tw scr, 2 x 2 DRG turbines, 24,500 BHP, 4 blrs, 550 psi, 20 kts. By builder.
H Steel. 9 dks total. 5 holds. C 300,000/8,495cu g + 15,000/4247cu ref.
P 125 1st, 800 tst. (One class when cruising). Crew 457.
1954 Feb 17: Launched by Lady Churchill. The first of four sisters for the Canadian service. Costing £21 million. Had no funnel stays. Denny-Brown stabilisers. Sept 2: M/v Liverpool-Quebec-Montreal. Their design was the maximum to permit going the 1,000 miles up to Montreal. Cut two days off the time.
1957 June 19: Terminus moved to Southampton.
1961 London-New York service. Winter cruising out of Port Everglades.
1962 To builders, with *Ivernia,* for conversion into dual North Atlantic and cruise services. Rebuilt aft with a Lido deck. Air conditioning installed. Given *'Caronia'* green livery. Cost £1 million each.
1963 Jan 1: Renamed *Carmania.* **P** 600. Apr 8: Resumed service Rotterdam-Southampton-Quebec-Montreal.
1964-70 Used on Mediterranean 'Fly-Cruise' sailings with Caribbean winter cruises. White hull.
1969 Jan 12: Because the Admiralty charts were wrong went aground for five days on Gardiner's Reef, San Salvador Island. Cogedar's *Flavia, ex Media* (167), carried her passengers to Miami. Repaired at Newport News. May 8: Back in service. May 11: Grazed the Soviet ship *Frunze.*
1970 Southampton became her port of registry.
1971 Laid up for sale as a result of a failure to agree manning levels with the National Union of Seamen who would not agree to British and Foreign crews. They insisted only on the higher paid British.
1972 May 14: Moved to the River Fal.
1973 Aug: Sold to Nikreis Maritime Corp, Panama, as Agents for Sovtorflot. After a three months refit by Swan, Hunter Ship repairers she was renamed *Leonid Sobinov.* Registered at Nakhodka.
1974 Feb 26: Managed by Soviet controlled C.T.C. Lines, she sailed Southampton-Australia. Based at

Sydney for U.K. voyages and cruises.
1975 Nov 24: *Leonid Sobinov* was the first liner to pass through the Suez Canal after its clearance following the 1967 war.
1979 Dec: Following the entry of Russian troops into Afghanistan she was banned from Australian ports and went to Nakhodka.
1980 In the services of the Russian Far East Shipping Co.
1989 Still in service.

176 **IVERNIA (II)/FRANCONIA (III)**
Details as *Saxonia* except: **T** 22,637g, 11,721n.
1954 Dec 14: Launched.
1955 June 16: Acceptance trials. July 1: Her maiden voyage was delayed two weeks because of a catering strike; Greenock-Quebec-Montreal. Thence from Liverpool.
1957 Apr 17: Commenced Southampton-Le Havre-Quebec-Montreal service.
1961 Apr 22: Went aground in Southampton Water en route to Le Havre. Nine tugs pulled her off five hours later.
1962 June: Her Surgeon went to and operated on a severely ill seaman aboard the Dutch *Korendyk,* (Holland America Line). Winter: At John Brown's for rebuilding similarly *Saxonia.*
1963 Jan 1: R/n *Franconia.* Green hull. Used for cruising out of New York in summer and Port Everglades in the winter.
1967 Nov: Became the last Cunard liner to terminate a scheduled sailing at Liverpool.
1968 On winter New York-Bermuda run for Furness-Burmuda Line. White hull. June 4: First sailing Rotterdam-Canada. Not a successful route.
1971 Because of unprofitability across the whole of the four Canadian service sisters she was, with them put up for sale. Oct: On her final inbound voyage aided the burning *Anatina* (Chas. Stray) and took off 8 crewmen. Laid up at Southampton.
1972 May 14: Arrived River Fal; lay alongside *Carmania.*
1973 Aug: Acquired by Russia through Nikreis Maritime and renamed after the great singer *Fedor Shalyapin.* Nov 20: Left Southampton-Australia.
1979 Dec: Banned from Australian ports with her sister.
1980 Feb: Left for Vladivostok and Far East service. Then transferred to the Black Sea for Odessa-Yalta-Novorossisk-Sotchi service.
1989 Still in service. USSR-Far Eastern Shipping Co, Vladivostok.

177 **CARINTHIA (III)**
As *Saxonia* except: **B** 1956. **T** 21,947g, 11,630.
1955 Dec 14: Launched by Princess Margaret.
1956 June 27: M/v Liverpool-Quebec-Montreal.
1960 Chartered by Canadian Government for trooping to N.A.T.O. Europe.
1967 The only one of the four not to be given a white hull. Oct 13: Made the last Cunard passenger voyage out of Liverpool to Montreal with a return to Southampton. Dec 9: Laid up at Southampton.
1968 Jan 31: Sold to Sitmar Line, Genoa. R/n *Fairland.* Remained in port for two years bearing the Sitmar funnel.
1970 Jan: To Trieste. Converted by Arsenale Triestino San Marco for the Australian route. The ship and her sister were extensively rebuilt and were unrecognisable compared with their original appearance.
1971 Nov: Renamed *Fairsea.* Entered service. **P** 925. Crew 450. Owned by Fairsea Shipping Corp. Liberian flag. Sept: Transferred to Sitmar Cruises Inc., Monrovia.
1972 July: After further conversion commenced cruises out of Fort Lauderdale or Miami.
1983 Cruised out of San Francisco.
1987 Still in service.
1988 July 29: P&O acquired Sitmar Cruises (for $210 million R/n. *Fair Princess.* Still in service.

178 **SYLVANIA (II)**
Details as *Saxonia* except: **B** 1957, **T** 22,017g, 11,679n.
1956 Nov 22: Launched.
1957 June 5: M/v Greenock-Quebec-Montreal. With the four in service sailings were weekly out of Liverpool alternating with Southampton.
1961 Replaced *Britannic* on the Liverpool-New York route.
1964 June 20: Went to aid the U.S. Coast Guard cutter *Cools Bay;* brought a seaman across for an appendectomy.
1965 Feb 10: Made the first Cunard cruise out of Liverpool since 1939.
1966 Nov 24: Made the final Cunard sailing out of Liverpool to New York.
1967 White hull. Feb. She was also experimentally fitted with a hovercraft for 'fly-cruise' excursion work. Based at Gibraltar. July 15: Went aground in the St Lawrence for four days. Nov 30: Made the

last Cunard passenger sailing Liverpool-New York. Dec: Laid up at Southampton.
1968 Jan 31: Sold with her sister to Sitmar. R/n *Fairwind,* Fairwind Shipping Corp. Monrovia. She too stayed at Southampton for two years before going to Trieste.
1970 Jan 14: At Trieste: Rebuilt, like her sister, for a New Zealand service.
1972 Transferred for cruising Fort Lauderdale-Puerto Moralos-Isla San Andres-San Blas-Cartagena-Nassau-Fort Lauderdale. T 16,667g. The services planned to Australia and New Zealand were abandoned because of immigration difficulties. Sitmar Cruises Inc, Liberia. Still the Vlasov group.
1988 R/n *Sitma Fairwind.* July 29: Acquired with the Sitmar fleet by P&O. Sept 9: R/n *Dawn Princess* for Princess Cruises Inc. Still in service.

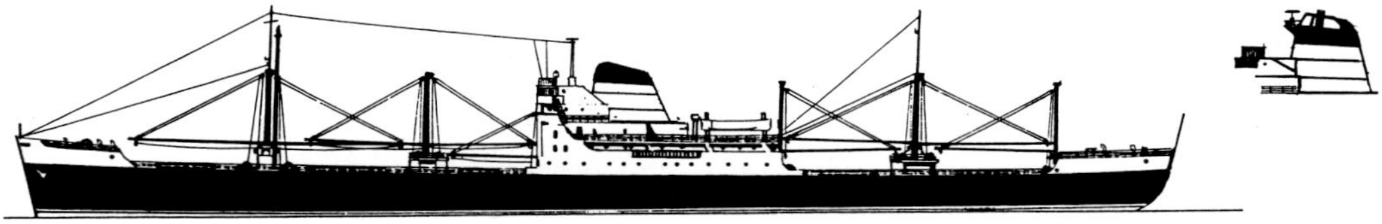

ANDANIA (III), ALAUNIA (III)

179 **ANDANIA (III)**
B 1959 Wm. Hamilton & Co, Port Glasgow. **T** 7,004g, 3,501n, 7,500dwt.
D 490.4/149.48 x 63.3/19.28 x 26.7/8.12.
E Sgl scr, 2 DRG turbs, 10,000 SHP, 2 blrs, 690 psi, 17½ kts. By D. Rowan & Co, Glasgow.
H Steel. 1 + shelter dk. F 42/12.8. B 106/32.31. P 25/7.62. C 550,000/15,574cu g + 25,000/708cu ref. Crew 65.
1959 Dec 19: Launched for Gulf of Mexico and St Lawrence services plus the Manchester Ship Canal. (As drawn).
1960 May 3: M/v to Gulf of Mexico.
1969 Transferred to Cunard Brocklebank Ltd on charter. R/n *Macharda.* Indian routes.
1971 Sold to Soja Shipping (Liberia) Inc, Panama. R/n *Humi Mahis.*
1973 became *Yngjian,* Ocean Tramping Co, Mogadishu, Somalia.
1975 Sold to the People's Republic of China. R/n *Hong Qi No. 107.* Kwangtung branch.
1987 Registered at Canton. Still listed.

180 **ALAUNIA (III)**
As *Andania* except: **B** 1960.
1960 May 12: Launched for the same duties as her sister. Her funnel differed as drawn inset. Oct 9: Maiden sailing.
1969 R/n *Malancha,* Cunard-Brocklebank Ltd on charter.
1971 Became *Humi Nastta,* same owners as her sister.
1973 Sold to Ocean Tramping Co, Mogadishu, R/n *Yungming.*
1975 Sold to China. R/n *Hong Qi No. 108.* Registered at Canton.
1987 Still in service.
1989 Still listed.

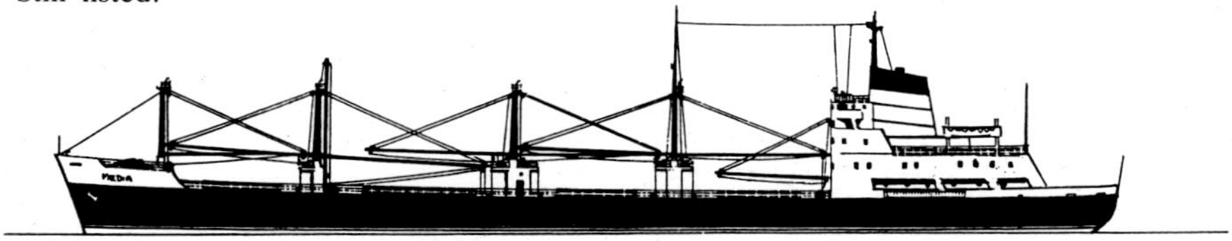

MEDIA (II), PARTHIA (III), SAXONIA (III), IVERNIA (III)

181 **MEDIA (II)**
B 1963 John Readhead & Co, South Shields **T** 5,586g, 2,658n.
D 436.8/133.12 oa, 400/121.92 x 60.2/18.36.
E Sgl scr, Sulzer diesel, 7 cyls, type 7RD68,2S.SA. 17 kts. By Hawthorn Leslie (Eng) Co, Newcastle.
H Steel. 1 + shelter dk. F 52/15.85. C 385,795/10,924cu g. Crew 45. Strengthened for ice. Part containerised.
1963 June 20: Launched. Oct 18: M/v Atlantic cargo services.
1971 Sold to the Western Australian Coastal Shipping Commission, Fremantle, R/n *Beroona.*
1979 Sold to Seaforth Investment Trust Inc. Greece. r/n *Palm Trader.*
1983 Oct 18: Damaged by engine room fire at Bandar Abbas. Condemned.
1984 Broken up.

182 **PARTHIA (III)**
Media class except: **B** Caledon S.B. & E. Co, Dundee. **E** John Brown & Co.
1963 July 18: Launched. Nov 29: M/v Liverpool to New York.
1971 Sold with her sister to the Western Australian Coastal Shipping Commission. R/n *Wambiri.* During the year she also bore the name *Staship I.*
1979 Sold to Sport Maritime Inc, Piraeus. R/n *Rice Trader.*
1984 Jan 27: Her engine failed off Socotra. Towed into Djibouti. Apr 4: Left in tow for Karachi and, Aug, scrapped at Gadani Beach.

183 **SAXONIA (III)**
As *Media* but **B** 1964.
1963 Oct 17: Launched.
1964 Feb 28: M/v to North America. As the ships arrived they opened a weekly Liverpool service on a monthly rotational basis.
1969 Sept: Left Liverpool with the steam locomotive 'Flying Scotsman' plus 4 L.N.E.R. liveried coaches for a 38 day tour of the U.S.A. (The tour failed financially and bringing back the entourage was a sorry story).
1970 Lengthened at Swan, Hunter Shiprepairers, South Shields by 80ft/24.38m. Transferred to Cunard-Brocklebank Ltd R/n *Maharonda.*
1972 Chartered to Christian Haaland. R/n *Concordia Foss* then reverted to *Maharonda* in the autumn.
1978 March: R/n *New Deer* Chung Chiao Shipping Co., Singapore.
1983 May 21: Left Hong Kong and broken up in China.

184 **IVERNIA (III)**
As *Media* except **B** 1964 Caledon S.B. & E. Co., Dundee. **E** John Brown & Co.
1964 Jan 15: Named. Jan 28: Launched. Sept: Completed.
1970 Transferred to Cunard-Brocklebank Ltd. R/n *Manipur.* Lengthened by Swan, Hunter like her sister. **T** 6,443g.
1971 Chartered to Christian Haaland, R/n *Concordia Manipur.* Reverted to *Manipur* by the year end.
1977 Sold to Mediterranean Shipping Co., Panama. R/n *Philippa.*
1980 Owned by Cia Naviera Philippa S.A. Panama. Same name.
1985 Feb 9: At Chittagong for breaking up by Rahman Shipbreakers.

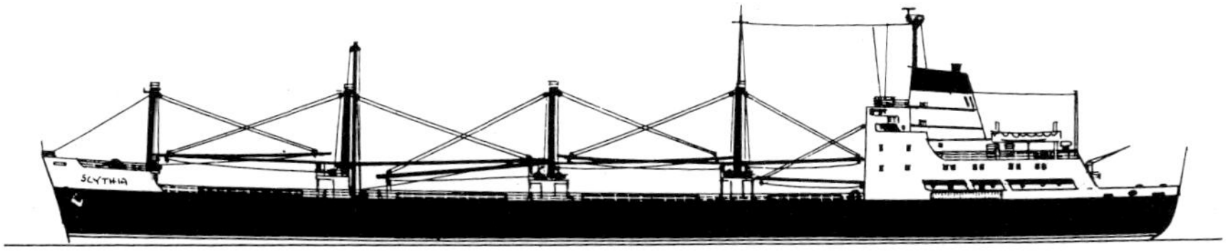

SCYTHIA (III), SAMARIA (III), SCOTIA (II)

185 **SCYTHIA (III)**
B 1964 Cammell Laird & Co., Birkenhead. **T** 5,837g, 2,829n, 7,662 dwt.
D 456.9/139.24 oa, 420/128 x 60.2/18.34.
E Sgl scr, 6 cyl Sulzer diesel, turbocharged, 8,640 BHP. 17½ kts. By Sulzer Bros, Winterthur.
H Steel. 1 + shelter dk. F 52/15.85. C 848,007/24.015cu g. Crew 45.
1964 Aug 25: Launched for North Western Line (Mersey) Ltd, a subsidiary of the builders. Long term bare boat charter to Cunard S.S.Co. Dec 4: M/v London-New York.
1969 Nov: Cunard's investment in the Atlantic Container Line rendered these semi-containerised vessels unnecessary. The charter contract was therefore purchased by Cunard so that the ship, with *Samaria* could be sold to T. & J. Harrison. R/n *Merchant.*
1979 June: Became *Sisal Trader,* Totnes Shipping Corp, Monrovia. Shortly afterwards she was sunk in cyclone 'Kamisy' off Mayotte Island, Madagascar.

186 **SAMARIA (III)**
Details as *Scythia* except: **B** 1965
1964 Oct 22: Launched. Same owners as *Scythia.*
1965 Feb 11: M/v London-New York.
1969 Nov: Sold to T. & J. Harrison, Liverpool. R/n *Scholar.*
1980 Jan: Sold to Manta Shipping Co., Liberia. Greek owned. R/n *Steel Trader.* Later Greek registered and operated by Brora Shipping Corp, Piraeus.
1989 Still in service.

187 **SCOTIA (II)**
Sister to *Scythia* except: **B** 1967. **T** 5,825g, 2,822n.
1966 Aug 17: Launched. The first Cunarder with her engine room controlled from the bridge. Equipped with special winches for low temperature working. Like all the class ice strengthened.
Owned by United Dominions Leasing Ltd. Chartered to Cunard-Brocklebank.
1967 Jan: M/v Liverpool-Montreal up the St. Lawrence Seaway kept open by icebreakers.
1970 Sold to Neptune Orient Lines, Singapore. R/n *Neptune Amber.*
1977 Became *Sri Kailash.* Himalaya Shipping Co., India.
1982 May 1: Laid up at Bombay.
1984 Sold for demolition to Akbarally & Sons, Bombay.

188 **QUEEN ELIZABETH 2**
B 1969 Upper Clyde Shipbuilders Ltd, Clydebank Division (formerly John Brown Co). **T** 65,863g, 38,244n.
D 963/293.53 obb, 887/270.39 x 105.2/32.09 x 56/17.07.Dft 32.62/9.94.
E Tw scr, 2 DRG turbs, 110,000 SHP, 3 blrs, 1,025 psi, 28½ kts. By builder. 2 Kamewa bow thrusters. Denny-Brown stabilisers.
H Steel. 13 dks in all. 10 lounges, 11 bars. Prom dk 750/229. Keel to topmast 202.3/61.57. Height of funnels 67.3/20.52.
P 564 1st, 1,979 tst. When cruising 1,400 one class. Crew 906.
1964 Dec 20: The contract was signed: The last ship built by John Brown as such.
1965 July 5: Her keel was laid; same slip as her predecessors.
1967 Sept 20: Launched by the Queen. The name Queen Elizabeth II was avoided because in Scotland she is actually Queen Elizabeth I.
1969 Apr 22: On her pre-view cruise turbine trouble put her back to the builders prior to hand over to Cunard Line Ltd.
May 2: M/v Southampton-New York. Turbine trouble put her out of service for four months. Her schedule became: Summer: North Atlantic. Winter: Cruising.
1971 Jan 9: Rescued the passengers of the French Line's burning *Antilles.*
1972 May: A bomb aboard ship hoax led to the dropping into the sea by parachute of 4 bomb disposal experts. Winter refit cost £1,800,000.
P 604 1st, 1,223 Tst; 1,740 one Class for cruising.
1974 April 1: When oil impregnated the water all three boilers failed 270 miles off Bermuda. The ship was towed into Bermuda and her 1,600 passengers taken back to New York by *Sea Venture* (Oivind Lorentzen). The papers pointed out that *Queen Mary* had had 27 boilers, *Queen Elizabeth* has 12 and asked whether there were sufficient enough for safety but the solution was to triplicate the water feed source.
1977 Sept: At Bayonne, New Jersey the Bethlehem Steel Corp installed two decks of penthouse suites abaft the bridge (as drawn). By crane they were lifted aboard completely furnished.
1980 For a year the ship had a blue waterline in place of red.
1982 May: Requisitioned for the Falklands War. Captain Peter Jackson. Converted in 8 days and carried 3,500 troops to South Georgia (of these men 39 were later killed in action). She was refuelled 3 times at sea. July: Arrived back at Southampton carrying survivors of the sunken warships *H.M.S. Coventry* and *H.M.S. Antelope.* Went to Vosper Shiprepairers for reconversion. Emerged with grey hull and Cunard funnel coloured outer casing. Sept: Suffered engine trouble off Land's End.
1983 May: Put into Genoa with engine trouble. Her winter overhaul went to Hapag-Lloyd Werke, Bremerhaven causing outcry in the U.K. But no British yard would guarantee the time limit imposed. Once again Trade Union demarcation practices damaged only its own membership. Black hull again.
1986 Oct 27: Went to Bremerhaven, Kaiser II Dock, for an £100 million 179 day conversion from steam to diesel-electric. Nine M.A.N. diesels drive 2 44-megawatt motors in an unmanned engine room. Variable pitch propellers fitted. Speed 32.2 kts. Fuel saving 250 tons daily. Her original machinery, which was lifted out by the floating crane *Hebe 2,* had covered more miles than *Queen Mary* and *Queen Elizabeth* combined.
1987 Apr 24: Handed back with a life expectancy of 20 years. Her extra earnings from the conversion economies is said to recoup the cost in five years. Had a larger black funnel uptake installed which improved her appearance. An extra set of luxury cabins added on the top deck.
1988 Used on Transatlantic positioning services followed by 'Round the World' and general cruising. Still in service.

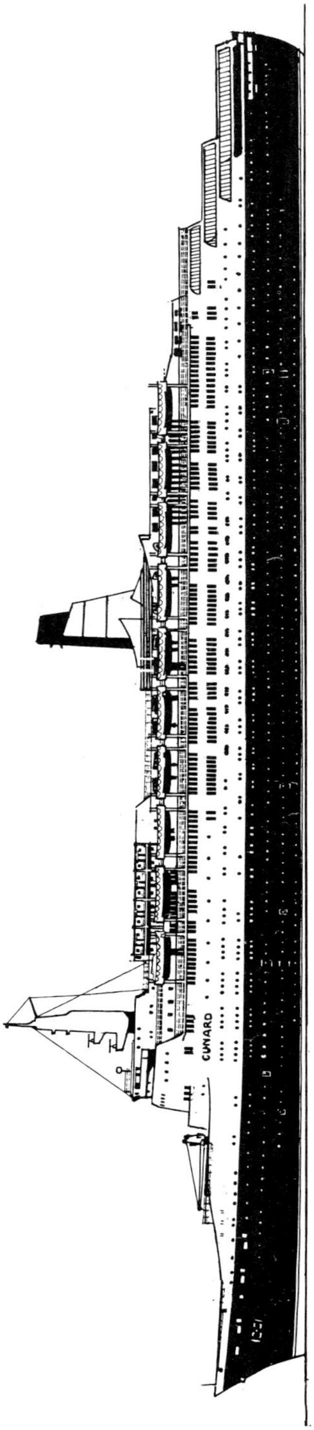

QUEEN ELIZABETH 2
(Scale 1:1600)

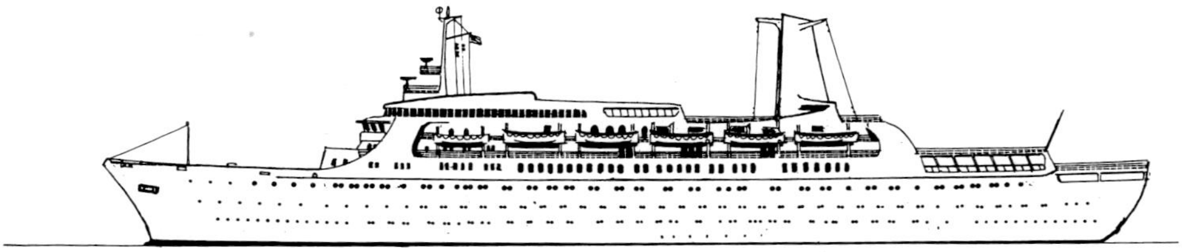

CUNARD ADVENTURER CUNARD AMBASSADOR

189 **CUNARD ADVENTURER**

B 1971 Rotterdamsche Droogdok, Rotterdam. **T** 14,151g, 8,135n.

D 483.8/147.52 obb,412.8/125.9 x 70.6/21.5 x 19/5.79.

E Tw scr, 2 x 2 diesels, 12 cyls, DRG, 26,800 SHP at 530 rpm, 21½ kts. By Stork-Werkspoor, Amsterdam. Pleuger bow-thruster. Air conditioned.

H Steel. 10 dks. in all, 7 for public use. F & B 434.9/132.6.

P 806 One class; 320 cabins plus 86 pullman berths. Crew 300

1970 Shallow draught design for Overseas National Airlines for short cruises out of San Juan, Puerto Rico. Cunard owned 50%.

1971 Feb 2 Launched. July: Taken over by Cunard and redesigned internally. Nov 20: On her delivery voyage drifted for four hours in Bay of Biscay with engine failure. Nov 22: Repaired at Lisbon. Dec: Entered service. Summer: Vancouver-Alaska. Winter Caribbean.

1976 Overhauled by builder.

1977 March: Sold to Lauritz Kloster A/S Oslo. R/n: *Sunward II.*

1980 Rebuilt. Twin funnels, greater rake.

1989 Still in service.

190 **CUNARD AMBASSADOR**

Details as 188 except: **B** P. Smit, Rotterdam.

1972 March 16: Launched for the same purposes as her sister. Oct 23: M/v Southampton-San Juan then cruising from there.

1974 Sept 12: En route from Port Everglades to New Orleans to embark passengers an engine room fire caused the ship to be abandoned 39 miles south west of Key West. 240 of her crew were taken off by the U.S. tanker *Tallulah;* 50 remained on board. Towed into Key West by the tug *Cable.*

1975 Sold, as a total constructive loss, to C. Clausen D/S A/S, Copenhagen. Towed there by the tug *Willem Barendsz* and rebuilt as a livestock carrier. R/n *Linda Clausen.* Australia-Persian Gulf service.

1976 Jan: Further modified at Hamburg to carry 32,000 sheep. June 15: Back in service. Her original appearance was not greatly altered.

1980 Dec: Sold to Lembu Shipping Corp, Panama. R/n *Procyn.*

1983 Became *Raslan,* Qatar Transport & Marine Services Co., Qatar.

1989 Still in service.

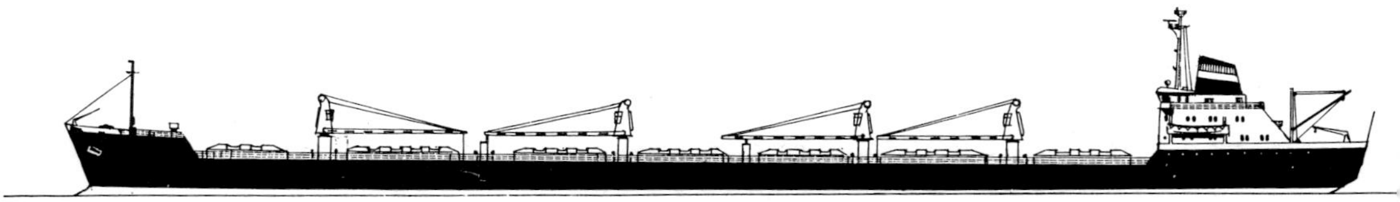

CUNARD CAMPAIGNER, CUNARD CARAVEL, CUNARD CARRONADE
CUNARD CALAMANDA, CUNARD CAVALIER, CUNARD CARRIER
CUNARD CHAMPION, CUNARD CHIEFTAIN

191 **CUNARD CAMPAIGNER**

B 1972 Astilleros Espanõles S.A, Seville. **T** 15,498g, 11,227n, 27,000dwt.

D 598.8/182.6 oa, 563.9/171.68 x 73.5/22.4 x 46.5/14.2.

E Sgl scr, oil; 6 cyl. Sulzer diesel RND68 type, 9,900 BHP, 15½ kts. By builder.

H Steel. F 52/15.9. P 100/30.5. C 1,270,551/298,773cu g. 4 x 15 ton Haggland-Hydraulic deck cranes. Crew 32.

1971 Oct 23: Launched by Mrs Nigel Broakes. Owned Cunard S.S. Co.

1972 July: Delivered for worldwide trading. Design: Eskalduna Type 27. Operated by Cunard-Brocklebank Bulkers Ltd.

1974 Dec: Sold to the Great Eastern Shipping Co, India. R/n *Jag Shanti.*

1989 Still in service.

192 **CUNARD CARAVEL**
Details as 190. All six 'Ca' were built at Seville.
1971 Dec 4: Launched. Carried the Brocklebank funnel not Cunard.
1972 Sept 19: Delivered.
1974 Dec: Sold to the Great Eastern Shipping Co, Bombay, R/n *Jag Shakti.*
1989 Still in service.

193 **CUNARD CARRONADE**
As 190 except: **B** 1972.
1972 March 17: Launched. Nov 9: Delivered.
1978 Sold to Olympic Maritime S.A. R/n *Olympic History.* Operated by Rossway Transportation Co, Piraeus (Onassis Group).
1989 Still in service.

194 **CUNARD CALAMANDA**
As 190 except: **B** 1973.
1972 May 4: Launched. **1973** Feb: Completed.
1978 R/n *Ionian Carrier.* Naftitan Maritime & Transportation Enterprises, Piraeus. Neville Corp. as managers.
1989 Still in service.

195 **CUNARD CAVALIER**
As 190 except: **B** 1973.
1973 Feb 10: Launched. Sept: Delivered.
1978 Sold to Eastside Transport Co, Monrovia. R/n *Olympic Harmony.* Owned by Olympic Maritime S.A, Monaco. Onassis Group.
1989 Still in service.

196 **CUNARD CARRIER**
As 190 except: **B** 1973.
1973 March 31: Launched. Dec: Entered service.
1978 Became *Aeneas,* Silverdale Ltd; later Caroline Maritime Pte, Singapore. Later transferred within the group to Transocean Maritime Agencies, Singapore.
1989 Still in service.

197 **CUNARD CHAMPION**
As 190 except: **B** 1973, **T** 15,448g, 11,221n.
The two ships whose second name commenced with 'ch' were built at the Bilbao yard.
1973 April 7: Launched. Aug: Completed.
1978 Sold to Eddie Litonjua Shipping Inc, Manila. R/n *El Champion.*
1985 Sold via Litonjua Chartering (Edyship) Co. Inc to Sea Dove Shipping Inc. R/n *Sea Dove,* Manila.
1989 Still in service.

198 **CUNARD CHIEFTAIN**
As 190 except: **B** 1973. **T** 15,448g, 11,221n.
1973 June 28: Launched. Nov: Completed.
1978 R/n *Chieftain.* Superblue Trading inc, Panama. Chartered for three years to Orconsult S.A. Zurich. Ore carriage Venezuela to Europe.
1981 Became *Great City,* Great City Navigation S.A, Panama. One of the 75 single ship companies owned by the Wah Kwong Shipping Agency, Hong Kong.
1989 Still in service.

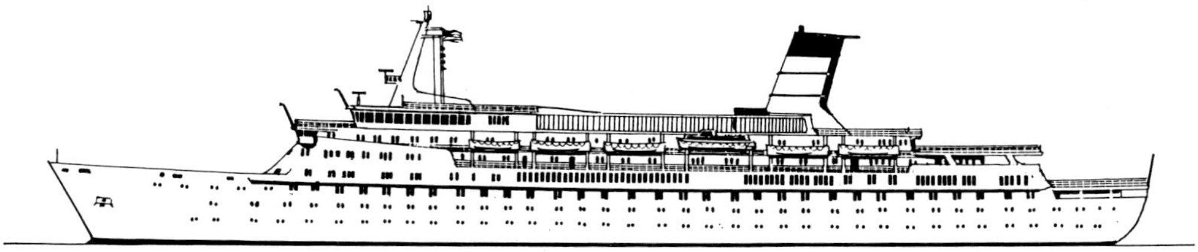

CUNARD COUNTESS, CUNARD CONQUEST/CUNARD PRINCESS

199 **CUNARD COUNTESS**
B 1975 Burmeister & Wain Skibs., Copenhagen. **T** 17,495g, 10,096n.
D 534.5/163 oa, 459.1/140 x 74.7/22.81 x 49.5/15.14.

E Tw scr, 2 x 2 B & W geared 2S. SA diesels; 7 cyls. Type 7S50HU, 21,000 BHP. 21½ kts. By Hitachi Zosen. Variable pitch propellers.
H Steel. 6 dks. Bow thruster.
P 800 One class in 373 cabins. Restaurant 431 seats.
1974 Sept 20: Launched for Cunard Cruise Ships Ltd., Replaced *Cunard Adventurer.*
1975 May 21: Left for La Spezia and fitted out by Industrie Navali Mechaniche Affini. White funnel and livery.
1976 Aug 27: M/v Barcelona-San Juan. On arrival there she was formally christened by Mrs Neil Armstrong, the wife of the Astronaut. Cruises out of San Juan-La Guaira-Grenada-Barbados-St Lucia-St Thomas-San Juan.
1980 Oct: It was planned to transfer the ship to the Bahamas flag. When the news was received at Bridgetown the crew refused to sail and the passengers were flown home. As a compromise only *Cunard Princess* was transferred. Cunard funnel given to both ships.
1982 Oct: Chartered as a troop ferry Ascension-Falkland Islands. Afterwards the winter refit was at Malta.
1983 May 4: Arrived at Malta.
1989 Still in service.

200 **CUNARD CONQUEST/CUNARD PRINCESS**
Sister to *Cunard Countess* except: **E** by builder.
1974 Dec 12: Launched as *Cunard Conquest.*
1975 Nov 6: At La Spezia for fitting out like her sister.
1977 Jan 1: Completed. March 29: Officially named *Cunard Princess* by Princess Grace of Monaco at New York. The vessel having been delayed a day by storm. April 2: Sailed to Bermuda on weekly cruises. Winter cruises are from Florida to San Juan.
1981 Jan: Transferred to Nassau, Bahamas registry.
1986 Operated trans-Panama Canal cruises from New York. A major refit was undertaken.
1989 Present fleet.

ALAUNIA (IV), ALSATIA (III), ANDANIA (IV), ANDRIA (II)

201 **ALAUNIA (IV)**
B 1973 Smith's Dock Co, Middlesbrough. **T** 4,938g, 2,636n, 7,869dwt.
D 461.5/140.7 oa x 60.3/18.04 x 38.1/11.64.
E sgl scr, oil; 9 cyl Sulzer design, 2S. SA, 14,850 BHP, 23 kts. By G. Clark & N.E.M, Wallsend.
H Steel. 4 dks. F 132/40.3. B 85/26. C 365,370/10, 342 ref.
1973 Mar 6: Launched for Island Fruit Reefers. Side doors. Entered service for Whitco Marine Services Ltd, Glasgow (A Salen subsidiary). Operated by Cardigan Bay Shipping. However the whole group of ten ships (Nos. 200-209) were controlled by the Maritime Fruit Carriers Corp., Haifa.
1974 Whitco were still the holding concern but the ship was operated by Abeyreuth Shipping Co., and others, on charter to Salen Rederei, Stockholm.
1976 Cunard purchased ten ships in three classes: 4 'Clippers', 2 'Fruits' and 4 'Flowers'. Initially as *Cardiff Clipper* but R/n *Alaunia.*
1979 Nov: Chartered with the other nine for two years to United Brands of America.
1981 July: Sold with the other 4 'A' class to the Restis Group for $6.5 million each cum charter to United Brands of America. R/n *Oceania Freezer.* Operated by Amorgos Maritime S.A.
1986 Renamed *Frosty* by Laval Maritime S.A. Greek flag.
1989 Still in service.

202 **ALSATIA (III)**
As *Alaunia* except **B** 1972. **T** 7,722g.
1972 Jan 19: Launched as *Edinburgh Clipper* for the Maritime Fruit Carriers Corp. Entered service for Chichester Shipping Lines, Glasgow.
1976 Acquired by Cunard. R/n *Alsatia.* She was actually the first of the four to be built but Cunard renamed them alphabetically.
1981 July: To Restis, R/n *America Freezer,* Alaska Maritime. Co., S.A. Piraeus. Owned by Enterprise Shipping & Trading S.A.
1986 Sold to Daiko Shipping Ltd., Piraeus. R/n *Angelmar.*
1989 Still in service.

203 **ANDANIA (IV)**
As *Alaunia* except: **B** 1972. **T** 7,742g.
1972 June 11: Launched as *Glasgow Clipper.* . Owned by Sovertur Shipping Co., Glasgow. Managed by North West Shipping Co. Same controlling interests as the others.
1976 Purchased by Cunard. R/n *Andania.*
1981 July: To the Restis group. R/n *Europa Freezer,* Acadimos Maritime S.A. Owned by Enterprise Shipping & Trading S.A. Piraeus.
1985 Became *Balmar,* Ribarosa Shipping Ltd. Greece.
1989 Still in service.

204 **ANDRIA (II)**
As *Alaunia* except: **B** 1972 Swan Hunter. **T** 7,689g.
1972 Nov 20: Launched for Island Fruit Reefers Ltd., as *Teeside Clipper.*
1973 Entered service for Victorian Maritime Enterprises and then transferred to C.I. Curtis (Dairy Farmers) Ltd., Glasgow. Managed by North West Shipping Co.
1981 July: To the Restis group. R/n *Australia Freezer,* Akropol Maritime Co. Owned by Enterprise Shipping & Trading S.A. Piraeus.
1986 R/n *Chilly,* Rubisun Marine S.A. Greek flag.
1989 Still in service.

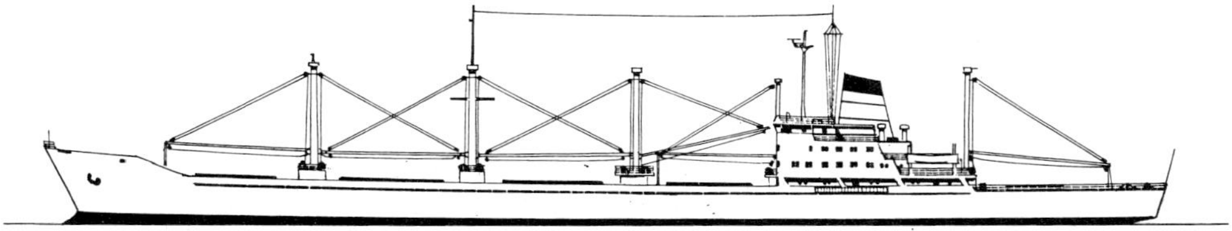

CARINTHIA (IV), CARMANIA (III)

205 **CARINTHIA (IV)**
B 1973 Nylands Verkstad, Oslo. **T** 7,330g, 3,542n, 9,551dwt.
D 511.2/155.8 oa x 70.1/21.37 x 41.6/12.7.
E Sgl scr, oil; 9 cyl B. & W. type, 17,400 BHP; 22 kts. By builder.
H Steel. 3 dks. F 50/15.24. C 481,477.5/13, 634cu ref.
1973 Jan 19: Launched for Sogar Shipping a subsidiary of the Maritime Fruit Carriers Corp., Haifa.
July: Delivered to Druidstan Ltd., Glasgow as *Cantaloup.*
1976 July: Acquired by Cunard, R/n *Carinthia.* Initially these ships had white hulls but painted grey at their first overhaul.
1984 Nov: Took part in the exercise 'Ocean Safari' whereby a mixed N.A.T.O. group of modern fast merchant ships formed into convoy and were taken into Scapa Flow down a narrow 'mine-swepted' channel cleared by the Royal Navy's Third Mine Countermeasures Squadron. The turning circle, speed, size, manoeuvrability and stopping time of each ship was measured and the Captain's logs compared. None had 'stood into danger'.
1985 May: Laid up at Vittoria Dock, Birkenhead.
Dec: Sold with ships No 206-210 for $9 million to Kappa Maritime, London for operation by Greek interests.
1986 R/n *Pegasus,* Arlen Shipping Corp., Piraeus, Chartered to Blue Star Line.
1989 Still in service.

206 **CARMANIA (III)**
As 204 except **T** 7,323g, 3,546n, 9,561dwt.
1972 March: Delivered to Chichester Shipping Lines, Glasgow as *Orange.*
1976 July: Purchased with the ten ships of Maritime Fruit Carriers, R/n *Carmania.*
1985 May: Laid up at Vittoria Dock, Birkenhead, awaiting sale.
1986 R/n *Perseus,* Garton Shipping Corp., Piraeus. Chartered to Blue Star.
1989 Still in service.

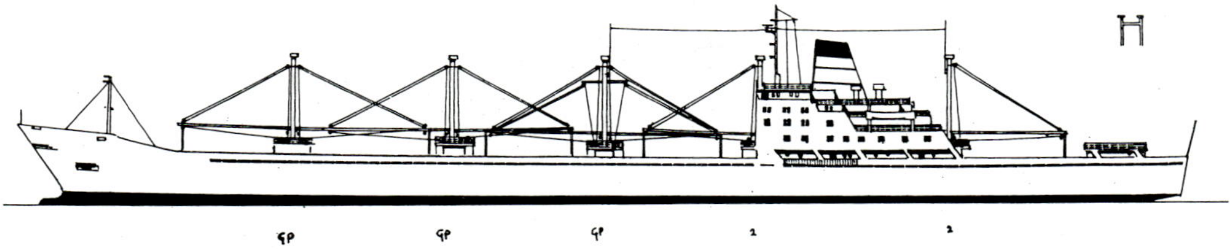

SAMARIA (IV), SAXONIA (IV), SCYTHIA (IV), SERVIA (III)

207 **SAMARIA (IV)**
B 1973 Aalborg Vaerft A/S, Aalborg. **T** 8,557g, 4,722n, 12,180dwt.
D 575.2/175.34 oa x 75/22.86 x 44.3/13.52.
E Sgl scr, oil, 9 cyl 2S.SA, 23,300 BHP, 23½ kts. By Burmeister & Wain.
H Steel. 2 dks. F 46/14.1. C 584, 142/16, 356cu g + 577, 600/16,356cu ref.
1972 Aug 31: Launched for Maritime Fruit Carriers, Glasgow. **P** 12.
1973 Feb: Delivered as *Chrysantema* to Paravon Shipping Co. & Others, Glasgow.
1976 July: Acquired. R/n *Samaria.*
1985 June: Laid up at Vittoria Dock, Birkenhead.
1986 Became *Capricorn,* Cephus Shipping Corp. Greek on charter to Blue Star.
1989 Still in service.

208 **SAXONIA (IV)**
As *Samaria* except: **T** 8,547g, 4,706n, 12,182dwt.
1971 June 2: Launched for Maritime Fruit Carriers as *Gladiola.*
1972 Feb: Delivered to Adelaide Shipping Co., Glasgow with Whitco Marine Services as managers.
1976 July: Purchased by Cunard. R/n *Saxonia.* Not all of the ten ships were taken into Cunard service at the date of purchase. Some had Salen voyage or fruit contracts commitments to fulfill. Thus *Saxonia* was not renamed until 1977. Others even made their first Cunard sailing under their old name: See *Alaunia.* Their white Salen hulls were changed progressively to grey.
1982 April: Taken over for the Falklands War as a food transport. June 28: Arrived back.
1986 Sold to Tondo Shipping Corp. R/n *Carina.* Chartered to Blue Star.
1989 Still in service.

209 **SCYTHIA (IV)**
As *Samaria* except: **T** 8,557g, 4,772n, 12,182dwt.
1972 May 23: Launched for Maritime Fruit Carriers. Nov: Delivered as *Iris Queen* to Adelaide Shipping Lines, Glasgow with Whitco as managers.
1976 July: Acquired with the other Maritime Fruit vessels. R/n *Scythia.*
1977 Disabled in the English Channel by an engine room fire, Falmouth-Casablanca. *Saxonia* stood by.
1985 Laid up at Vittoria Dock, Birkenhead.
1986 Became *Centaurus,* Toulon Shipping Corp., Piraeus. Chartered to Blue Star.
1987 Owned by Skyhope Shipping Cyprus. Same name.
1989 Feb 2: Suffered engine room fire damage while discharging at Wilmington, Del. Condemned. May 12: Left for Chittagong in tow of Russian *Neftegaz.* July 16: Arrived. Scrapped.

210 **SERVIA (III)**
Sister to *Samaria.*
1971 Oct 20: Launched for Maritime Fruit Carriers as *Orchidea.*
1972 July: Delivered to Austral Shipping Lines, Glasgow with Whitco, Salen's U.K. subsidiary, as managers.
1976 Became *Servia.* Retained her Salen colours.
1980 Cunard funnel, grey hull.
1985 July: Laid up at Vittoria Dock, Birkenhead.
1986 Became *Castor,* Iaco Shipping Corp., Piraeus.
1988 R/n *Kastora* by Gold Seal Shipping Co., Cyprus.
1989 Apr 29: Abandoned in the Caribbean on fire in the engine room.

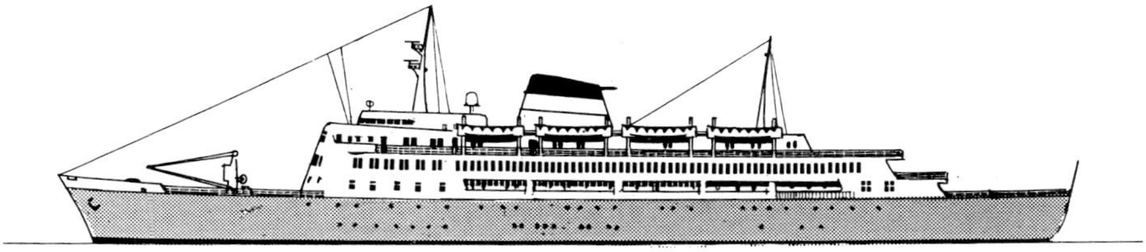

ENGLAND

211 **ENGLAND**
B 1964 Helsingor Skibsvaerft og Maskinbyggeri A/S, Helsingor (Elsinore).
T 8,116g, 3,998n. **D** 459.4/140.04 oa x 63.4/19.33 x 29.85/9.1. Dft 18/5.5.
E Tw scr, oil; 2 x 10 cyl B. & W. type, 14,000 BHP, 21 kts. By builder. Variable pitch propellers and bow thruster.
H Steel. 3 dks. C 44,779/1,268cu g + 38,140/1, 080cu ref. 2 holds.
P 668 berthed and 182 deck, pullman seats, 100 cars.
1964 Built for D.F.D.S (Forenede Dampskibs = United Shipping Co).
Esbjerg-Newcastle and Copenhagen-Oslo services.
1974 Harwich-Esbjerg service.
1982 Acquired by Cunard. Refitted in Denmark with extra fuel and water tanks.
1983 Sept 29: Left London for Port Stanley. Chartered for 18 months by a consortium made up of the airport constructors Laing, Mowlem and Arc for a service Cape Town-East Cove, Falklands carrying their Mount Pleasant airport workforce. At East Cove, where there was no suitable jetty, her base ship was Cenargo's *Providence.*
1985 July 3: Laid up at Vittoria Dock, Birkenhead.
1986 Dec 23: Left for Jeddah as *America XIII* to become an accommodation ship.

212 **SAGAFJORD** (Drawing page 104)
B 1965 Soc. des Forges de la Mediterranee, La Seyne. **T** 24,002g, 13,340n.
D 619,8/188.91 oa 549.9/167.61 x 80.3/24.47 x 55.4/16.88. Dft 27.1/8.26.
E Tw scr, oil; 2 x 9 cyl Sulzer slow running direct coupled 9RD68 type, 27,000 SHP, 20 kts. By builder, Le Havre.
H Steel, 6 dks in all, 2 holds. Bow thruster. Ice strengthened.
P 85 1st, 704 Tst. 462 One Class when cruising. Crew 350.
1964 June 13: Launched for Norske Amerikalinje A/S, Oslo (N.A.L.). The hull dimensions were fixed by the Oslo drydock in which the ships were to have their annual overhaul.
1965 May: Completed, Sept 18: Delivered after a machinery adjustment.
Oct 2: M/v Oslo-New York. The builder lost so much money on the ship that they went into liquidation in the following year. Mainly cruising.
1980 K.S. Norwegian American Cruises was formed, 90% held by the owners with 10% held by Leif Hoegh. *Sagafjord* and *Vistafjord* were transferred.
1981 Leif Hoegh acquired the 90% held by the original owners.
1983 Trafalgar House acquired Norwegian American Cruises. To Cunard; same name. Norwegian deck crews retained and the catering staff remained under contract. Given Cunard funnel. Employed mainly of Pacific cruising.
1986 Winter: Relieved *Queen Elizabeth 2* during her conversion to diesel.
1989 Still in service. Cruising out of Los Angeles.

213 **VISTAFJORD** (Drawing page 104)
B 1973 Swan Hunter Shipbuilders Ltd., Wallsend. T 24,292g, 12,771n.
D 626.9/191.09 oa, 550.1 x 82.18/25.05 x 55/16.77. Dft 27/8.23.
E Tw scr, oil; 2 x 9 cyl Sulzer type 9RD68, 24,00 BHP, 20 kts. By G. Clark & N. E. M. Ltd., Wallsend. Bow thruster. Variable pitch screws. Ice strengthened.
H Steel. 7 dks in all (600 tons more aluminium).
P 830 reduced to 550 for cruising. Dining room for 620. Crew 390.
1972 May 15: Launched for Norske Amerikalinje A/S, Oslo. Very similar in hull and machinery to *Sagafjord*. All fittings on both vessels are 'non-combustable'.
1973 Apr 6: Trials, four months ahead of schedule, May 22: M/v Oslo-New York. Used for cruising. To deal with American clientele her catering staff were supplied by Global Catering Co., Bermuda.
1980-83 Same history as *Sagafjord.*
1986 Winter: Carried out extended cruises for *Queen Elizabeth 2.*
1989 Still in service. Cruising USA and Europe.

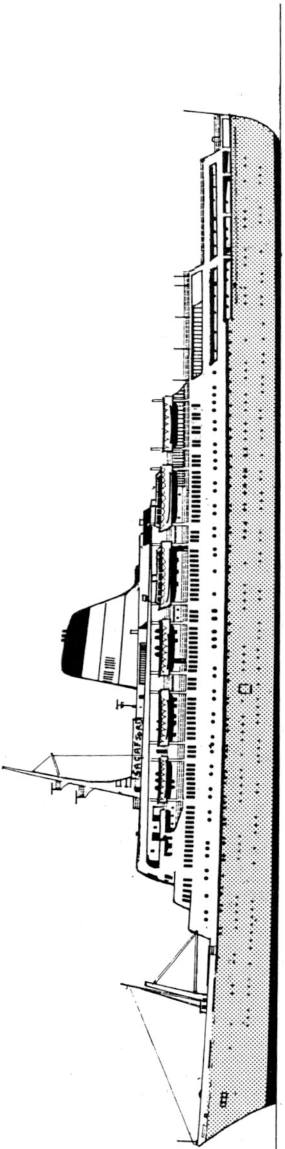

212 *SAGAFJORD*

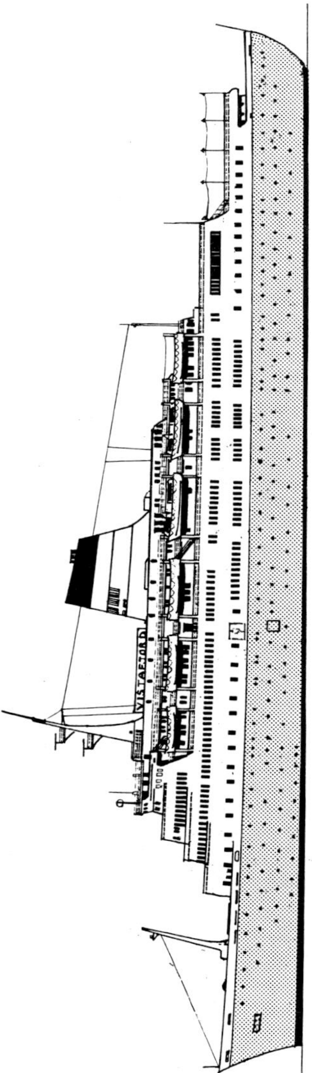

213 *VISTAFJORD*

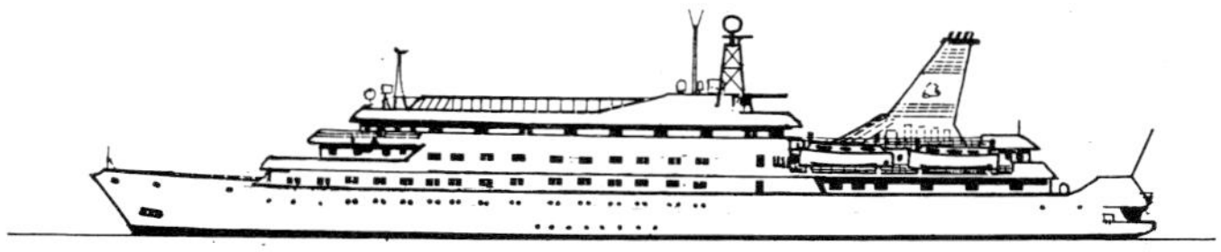

SEA GODDESS I, SEA GODDESS II

214 **SEA GODDESS I**
B 1984 Wartsila A/B O/Y Helsinki. **T** 4,253g, 1,277n.
D 344.5/105 oa, x 47.9/14.6 x 13.45/4.1.
E Tw scr, oil; 2 x Wartsila-Vasa 12V22HF, 2 x 12 cyls, 4,800BHP, 17.5 kts.
H Steel. 2 + pt 3 dks. Pool and sea access platform aft. Shallow draught for access to secluded ports and anchorages.
P 120 de luxe. 61 cabins. Dining saloon 130 seats. Crew 71: Norwegian officers and deck with U.S/European catering and cabin staff.
1983 July 11: Launched un-named.
1984 Named at Monte Carlo at the end of her delivery voyage. Owned by Norske Cruises, marketed as Sea Goddess Cruises. Managed by Wilhelm Wilhelmsen. Founded by Helge Naarstad with 820 shareholders to cater for the luxury market. A seven day cruise costing from £2,250-£2,750 and directed at the wealthy American market. No bar bills and no gratuities.
1985 based in the Caribbean.
1986 The debt to Wartsila of $50,000 million taken over by Midland Bank and then both ships chartered to Cunard Cruises Ltd for twelve years with an option to purchase.
1989 In service. Cruising Mediterranean.

215 **SEA GODDESS II**
As 214 except that the hull was subcontracted to F. W. Hollming O/Y Rauma.
1984 Dec 11: Launched.
1985 Apr 17: Delivered. Named at Monte Carlo by Princess Caroline. Her cabins are given as 58 with 116 passengers and 77 crew. Based Mediterranean and Red Sea.
1986 Taken over by Cunard with her sister. July: Based Tilbury for cruises Isle of Wight, Guernsey, Torquay, St Malo, Amsterdam.
1989 In service. Cruising Mediterranean.

WARTIME MANAGED SHIPS

Cunard-White Star had a number of ships placed under their control during the period 1940-1947. Of these only two Liberty ships, *Vardulia* (161) and *Vandalia* (162) were taken into service.

Others were:

After the fall of France they first took *Pasteur,* Compagnis Sud-Atlantique and then two French Line passenger ships: The massive *Ile de France* and the Caribbean route *Cuba.*

From the United States initially came three World War I standard ships: Two 'Hog Islanders' *Empire Barracuda,* ex-*Black Heron* and *Empire Hawk,* ex-*Black Hawk,* both of which became war losses and the flush decker *Empire Porpoise,* ex-*Invincible* which survived to become *Chrysanthemum.* These three were followed by two C1-S-AY1 standard ships *Empire Battleaxe,* ex-*Cape Berkeley* and *Empire Broadwsord,* ex *Cape Marshall.* The former went to the Royal Navy as a Landing Ship (Large) while the latter was lost by torpedo.

The captured 1939 built Norddeutscher Lloyd *Hannover* was managed under her new name *Empire Audacity* but was taken over and converted into an Escort Carrier and was sunk in the North Atlantic.

Cunard managed five other 'Sam's in addition to the two that they purchased. They were *Sambre, Samholt, Samouse* (officially pronounced Sam-ooze but to the Company always called Sam-mouse), *Samson* and *Samsurf.*

The final group of wartime standard ships were the 'Forts' and 'Parks' which came under their management right at the end of the war on behalf of the Canadian Government with the need to open up trade to Canada pending the arrival of Cunard ordered tonnage. By 1950 these had gone into other ownership. They were *Ford Cadotte, Fort Miami, Fort Musquarro, Fort Spokane, Fort Ticonderoga, Hillcrest Park* and *Sibley Park.* These wore a Cunard funnel over a grey wartime hull.

It should be added that after her near destruction at Suez *Georgic* was Government owned and came under Cunard-White Star management for the remainder of her career.

CHARTERED SHIPS WHICH WERE GIVEN CUNARD NAMES

With the opening of the St Lawrence Seaway Cunard commenced services to Chicago and other Great Lakes ports using chartered tonnage. Four ships were renamed:

VERIA ex-*Auguste Schulte,* Schulte & Bruns, Hamburg. **B** 1951 **T** 770g. Chartered 1960. Reverted to her original name in 1961.

CARIA ex-*Wiedenborstel,* Ahrenkiel & Bene, Hamburg. **B** 1953 **T** 1,380g. Also chartered for a year in 1960.

NORDIA ex-*Nordic.* **B** 1961. **T** 4,560g. Not strictly a Cunard name but she was launched as Nordic and completed on charter as *Nordia.* Like the remainder of these ships she bore Cunard colours and flew their houseflag but had a grey hull. Her owners were F. H. Andersson, Stockholm.

1963 Reverted to Red. A/B Nordic.

MARONIA ex-*Marion.* **B** 1961 for Ake Hogberg, Stockholm. Chartered for two seasons. **1963** reverted to *Marion.*

These ships are included for record purposes. Where ships were chartered without change of name they are not included even though some of them, like *Johanna,* Arenkiel & Bene, were given Cunard funnels, a common enough charter practice (to aid agent and shore staff identification) and even bore the legend 'Cunard Great Lakes' on their hulls.

WHITE STAR SHIPS CONTRIBUTED TO THE 1934 MERGER

The ten ships of the White Star Line:

Adriatic, Albertic, Britannic, Calgaric, Doric, Georgic, Homeric, Laurentic, Majestic and *Olympic* are not included in this volume which is essentially about Cunard vessels. They occur in the White Star work where, equally, the Cunard ships which formed the joint fleet are omitted.